Guitar Fingerboard Harmony

By Ed McGuire

Guitarists have been asking for years for a thorough and complete harmony text applicable, especially, to the unique needs of the guitar. This text will undoubtedly meet that need. It is the finest text I have ever seen dealing with chord formations, voicings, progressions, harmony, and most important of all, the practical usage of chord formations in ensemble. Ed McGuire is both an outstanding scholar and a truly great guitarist. This book will be an extremely valuable asset to any guitarist regardless of style. It is with great pleasure that I present "GUITAR FINGERBOARD HARMONY"

Mel Bay

Visit us at www.melbay.com — E-mail us at email@melbay.com

Ed McGuire

Ed McGuire has been closely associated with the guitar, as a performer/teacher, for more than thirty years. His credits include work with many top figures in the entertainment world, recording and TV work, and many years "on the road" with bands, including his own.

Formal studies include the New York Conservatory of Modern Music, the Pennsylvania State University, an independent study certificate in "Arranging and Composition" from Berklee, plus private studies in guitar, keyboard, and composition, He soent three years of private study with William (Billy) Bauer, poll-winning jazz guitarist during the 1950's. He took some classical guitar instruction from Aaron Shearer, head of guitar studies at Peabody Conservatory. In addition to all of his formal music training, he holds a degree in Psychology* and is a Registered Music Therapist with the National Association for Music Therapy. He has worked in the Pennsylvania Mental Health system for twenty years, and for the past five years has been developing a program of guitar studies at Mount Aloysius Junior College in Cresson, Pennsylvania. He is presently heading up the guitar program at this school.

For many years now he has limited his public appearances to concerts and jazz workshops. He has focused his teaching on the formal academic level and to appearances at music seminars with students from the school program.

His approach to the guitar places emphasis on a combination of physical and conceptual processes and he urges students to develop their individual musicianship, including keyboard, sight singing, sight reading, arranging, and improvisational skills.

His musical interests are varied and he has developed college level courses in the area of recreational music skills for nonmusicians. These classes are well attended by school teachers and workers from the field of mental health and its allied professions. He is a member of the National Therapeutic Recreation Society and holds a Master Therapeutic Recreation Specialist's registration from this organization.

He does a great deal of writing in the music field and has written many critical reviews for newspapers and other media. He is presently working on a follow-up to this text, which will be a "Harmony Workbook for Guitar" and which will incorporate a functional approach to the concepts presented in this book.

**He earned his Psychology Degree from Mansfield State College, Mansfield, PA.*

"Ed McGuire is an accomplished guitarist and teacher. He is also a good old boy, as they say down in the country. A thorough musician and a superb soloist and accompanist, his command of chordal "comping" and his chordal solos are evidence of the depth of his understanding of voice leading and harmonic flow."

"His Approach to guitar not only demonstrates his own fine musicianship but his devotion and almost reverence for that master guitarist George Van Eps."

"This book will enhance the guitarist's grasp of voicings, voice leading, and chord progressions, whether a beginning or advanced player. I recommend it highly."

Tommy Newsome

"Ed is a fine musician and guitarist whose years of playing and teaching experience make this book a must for the serious student or profesional guitarist. He examines chords as related entities rather than an isolated stack of tones and develops good usage through tonal cycles and voice leading processes."

George Shearing

PREFACE

A good chord method should, figuratively speaking, "Try to light a candle rather than fill a bucket". The following pages do not represent a complete dictionary of chords. I have tried to approach the problem from a musical standpoint, rather than a complete series of chord possibilities from any given root tone. Diagrams are used to speed the learning process — The notated forms are the important factors — I strongly suggest, if you are a beginning student, that you work through this book aided by a qualified teacher. It will provide a most valuable supplement to a regular course of instruction. A good teacher will be able to expand on the material and provide you with musical examples so you may put the knowledge to practical use. The order of presentation may be changed to answer the needs of individual students — I suggest that it be introduced as soon as the student begins scale studies. The difficult fingerings will be most frustrating if the hand is not fully developed, so these should be delayed. Learning chord formations is an easy matter. Learning chordal content and understanding tonal functions requires a great deal of study. However this approach will make much more sense. It will make you a much better player. Study the following material slowly and thoroughly for best results. I sincerely hope, as you work through the book, that I have been able to light a few candles in your mind.

Ed McGuire

ACTUAL PITCH OF THE GUITAR

An important thing to remember when playing chords on the guitar is that it is actually a transposing instrument. Music for the guitar is written an octave higher than it sounds. So, actually, when you play the low "E" ⑥ string written like this :

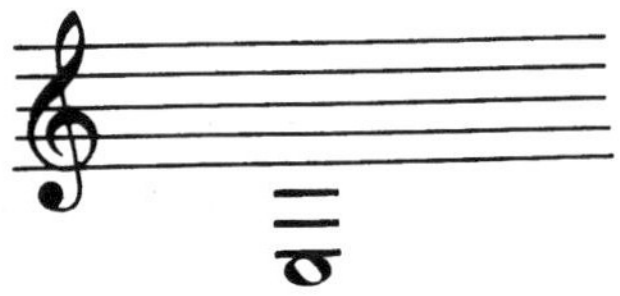

The note which is sounding is 

This means inversions must be handled with care and open spaces should be between low notes—

Open E major chord written: 

is actually "sounding" 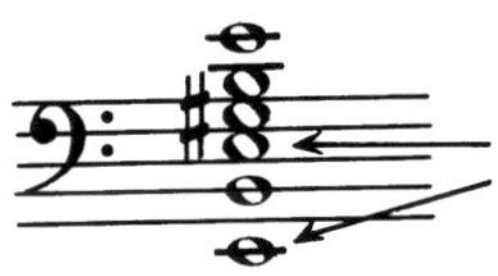 Note open spaces.

This is probably one of the best sounding chords on the guitar, when the instrument is properly tuned.

FINGERBOARD HARMONY

Learning chord formations is a relatively easy matter. Understanding the theory and structure of these forms is more complicated. This entails more work at the start. However, the results are much more fruitful. With a theoretical understanding of the building of chords, including the functions of the tones, it becomes possible for the student to build any chord he may encounter. (regardless of the complexity of the particular chord)

Our system of harmony is based of intervals of thirds – tones combined with each other, three steps apart. Chords may be defined as any combination of three, or more, tones which are sounded at the same time.

For example, this combination would be called a chord

This combination would not be called a chord

For better understanding, we will begin our study with a knowledge of triads, which are three note chords— there are four basic triads: they are ① Major ② Minor ③ Augmented ④ Diminished. The tones in the triads are drawn from the scale which would be indicated by the name of the triad.

For example: C major-tones from C scale
F minor-tones from F scale
G aug.-tones from G scale
D dim.-tones from D scale

It then becomes obvious that we must know the 12 major scales as a pre-requisite for a study of triadic harmony

We will start our study by building the four basic triads using the "C" scale as our source of material. The "Root", or the tone naming the triads will be (in this instance), "C".

FIRST : Write out the scale

SECOND : Use Numbers to indicate the various tones

Using this as a source, we can now begin to build our four basic triads using the following formula.

① Major triad = 1 – 3 – 5 tones from scale.
② Minor triad = 1 – ♭3 – 5 tones from scale.
③ Augmented triad = 1 – 3 – ♯5 tones from scale.
④ Diminished triad = 1 – ♭3 – ♭5 tones from scale.

Now let's notate each of these triads!

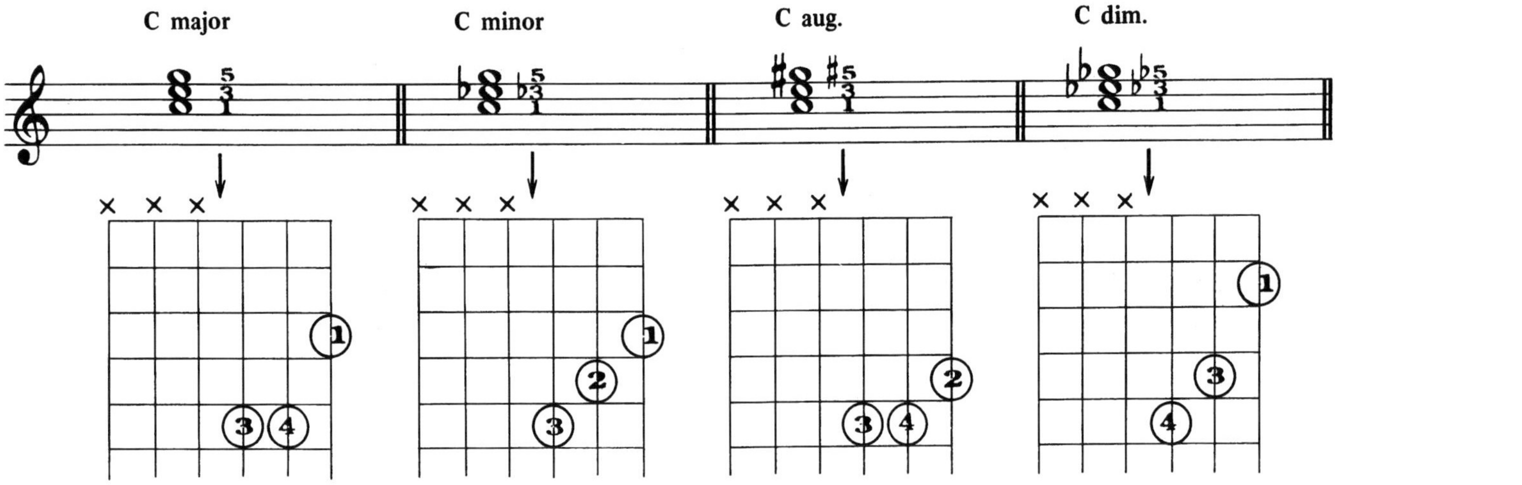

The diagrams indicate where these four triads can be played. Play then and listen to how they sound—in time, you should be able to recognize the different triads by sound alone.

Memorize the formula for each of the four triads.

Now, let's build the four basic triads using the "G" scale as our source of tones.

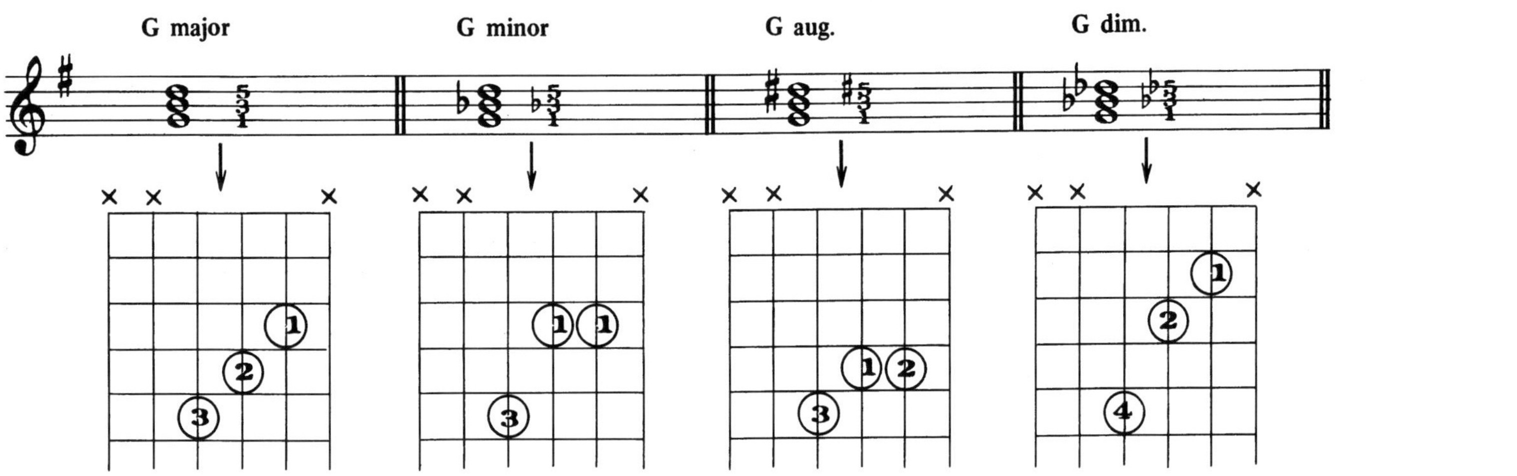

The chordal tones will always be used in the correct sequence – for ex: never spell G aug (G – B – E♭) – Though D♯ and E♭ sound the same, E♭ is incorrect when spelling this chord – a good way to remember this is as follows: if the root tone is on a line, the other two tones will be on lines. Same applies if the root tone starts on a space.

The scale tone in each triad will remain the same – use ♯ ; ♭ ; or ♮ signs to lower or raise individual tones to conform with the formula.

For example___ D♭ major would be D♭ – F – A♭ , 1st, 3rd, and 5th tones from the D♭ scale. Therefore D♭ minor would be D♭ – F♭ – A♭,and not D♭ – E – A♭ – <u>This would be incorrect.</u>

Keep the following principles in mind___

1. Use a "♯" to raise a natural tone.
2. Use a "♭" to lower a natural tone.
3. Take away the "♭" (via ♮) to raise a flatted tone.
4. Use a double "♭" (♭♭) to lower a flatted tone.
5. Use a double "♯" (*) to raise a sharped tone.
6. Take away the "♯" (via ♮) to lower a sharped tone.

Examples

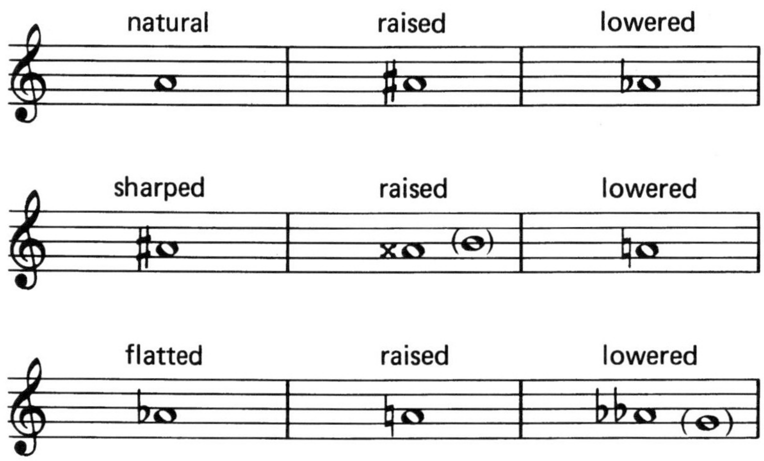

These principles become more obvious when you build triads in keys with high ♯'s or ♭'s in the key signature.

Example :

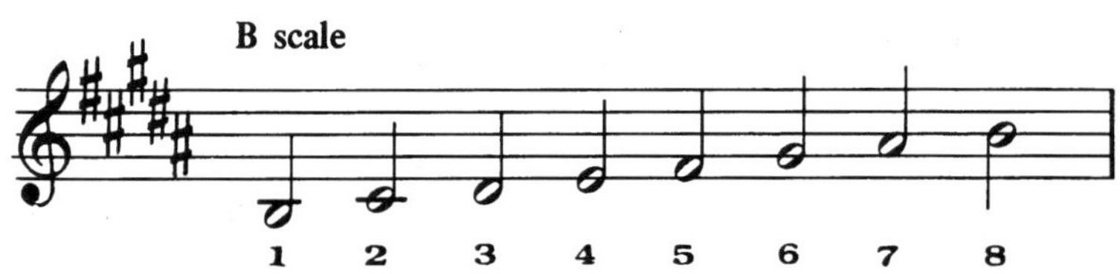

B major would be : B – D♯ – F♯
B minor would be: B – D♮ – F♯
B aug. would be: B – D♯ – F*
B dim would be: B – D♮ – F♮

Another example:

D♭ major would be : D♭ – F – A♭
D♭ minor would be: : D♭ – F♭ – A♭
D♭ aug. would be : D♭ – F – A♮
D♭ dim. would be : D♭ – F♭ – A♭♭

Re-read all this material and then build the four basic triads in all of the twelve keys. As you build the chords, try to play them on your guitar. Almost all of them will be available within the first seven frets – if necessary, use a diagram of 1st 7 frets to make locating the tones easier.

DIAGRAM FIRST SEVEN FRETS

Using ♯s'

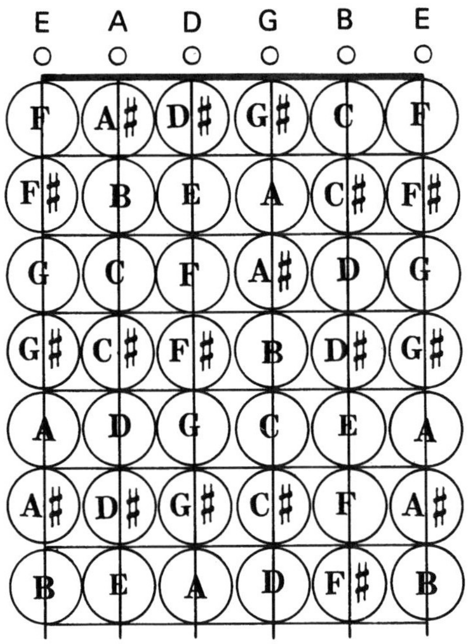

Using ♭s'

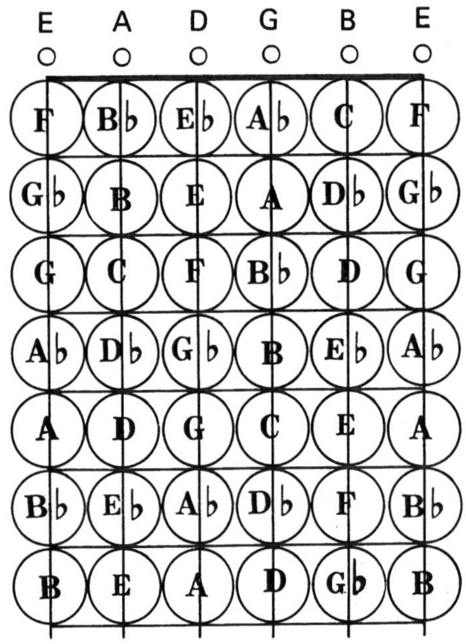

Remember there are only two natural half steps in our method of notation. They are between

B and C — E and F —

These tones may be indicated other ways when spelling chords.

Example

Keep this principle in mind.

Now try building the various triads. Notice that you must use available tones on three consecutive strings. Thus, you could not build a triad starting on the (2) string – below are some examples:

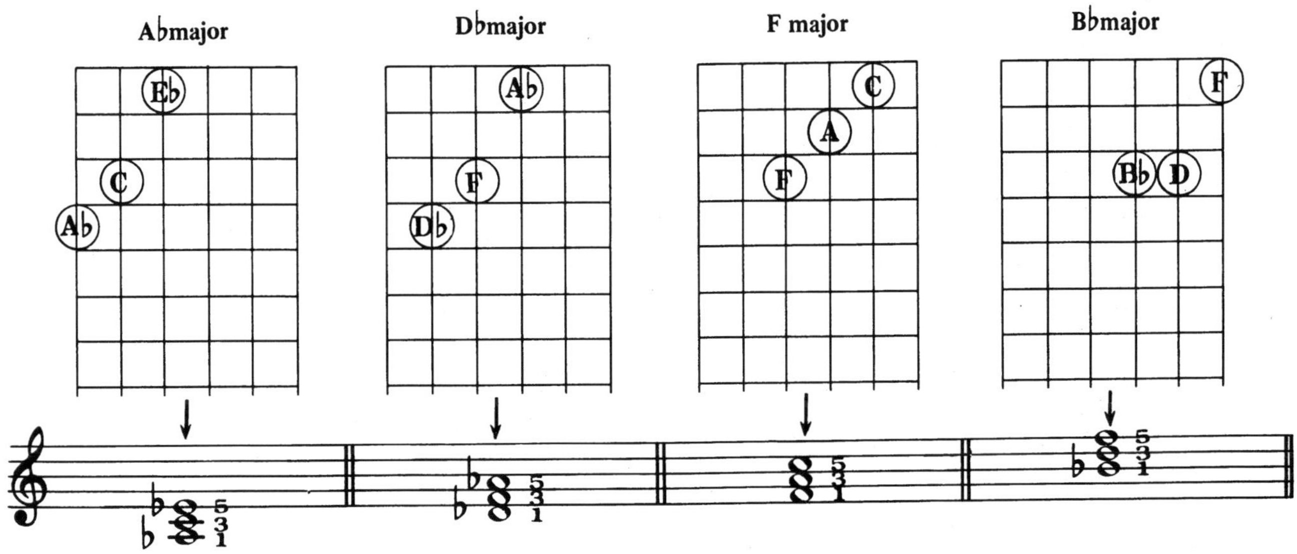

This would represent the lowest possibilities of triads which could also be made minor, augmented, diminished. You can play other triads (lower by ½ step) in each instance indicated above – however, you could not form the diminished triads in these open positions___

For example:

G dim

is not possible

Try it, and see why.

C dim

is not possible in open pos.

You would have to move to 8th fret & play C on ⑥ string.

Now begin to practice the various forms of the triads – using the major chord as a starting point___ The diminished triads starting on the low E ⑥ and A ⑤ strings will involve quite a stretch. (5 frets, to be exact) finger these using 1 – 2 – 4.

For example:

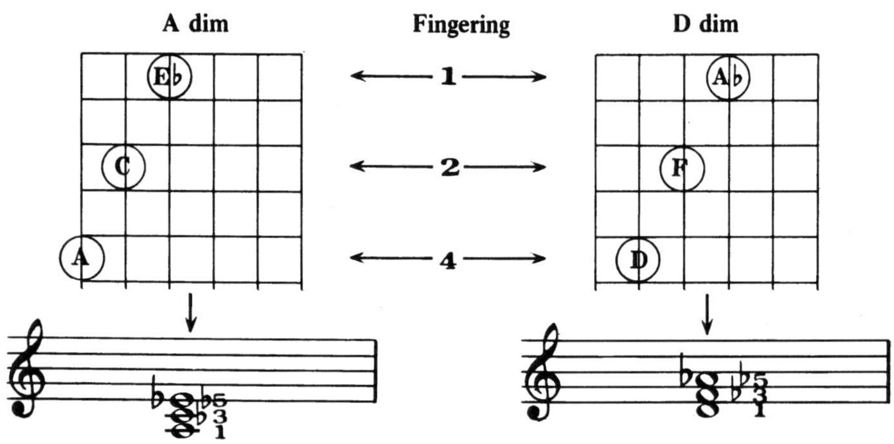

The other strings will conform to "position" fingering.

For example:

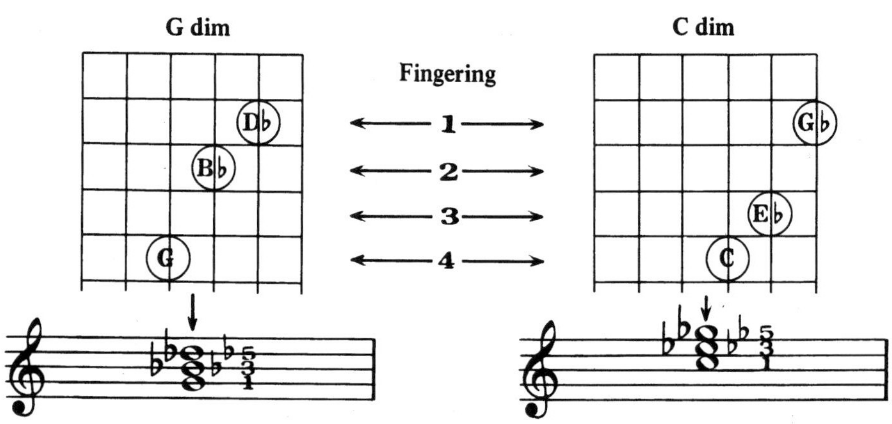

Up to this point, we have been building triads in root position— ie: Name of chord is the low tone, and the 3rd and 5th tones appear about in consecutive order.

For example

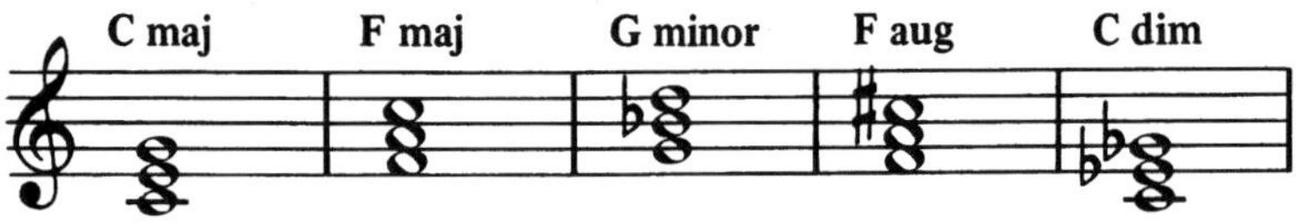

All in root position

The triads are also "closed" – ie: the three tones are as close as possible to each other. More on this, later

There are two additional positions for each triad. They are: 1st inversion and 2nd inversion—

Example

Root position

1st inversion

2nd inversion

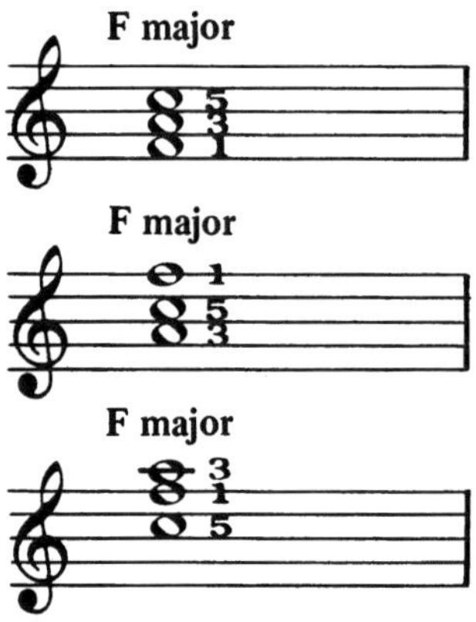

Root tone is the low note of the chord.

3rd tone is the low note of the chord.

5th tone is the low note of the chord.

[Notice that the inversions do not conform to the "line – line – line" and "space – space – space" formula.—]

Formula for minor, augmented, and diminished will still apply. Alter the appropriate tones, regardless of their position in the triad—

Example

F minor
1st inv.

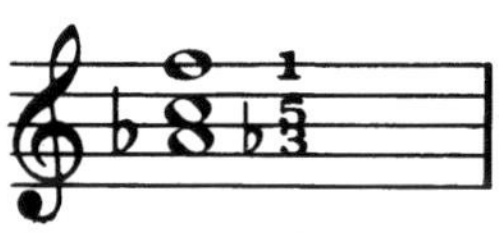

F aug
2nd inv

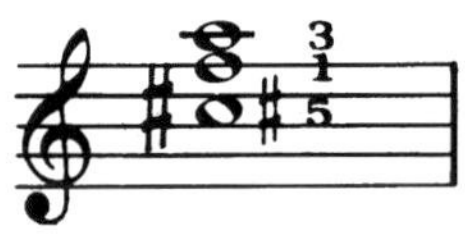

etc.

Now let's look at the inversions in relation to the guitar fingerboard—

In "open" position

C major

Try these – Be careful to play only what is indicated →

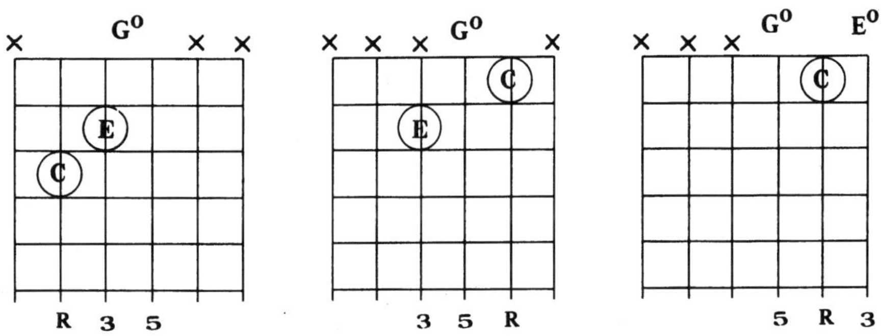

In "2nd" position

D major

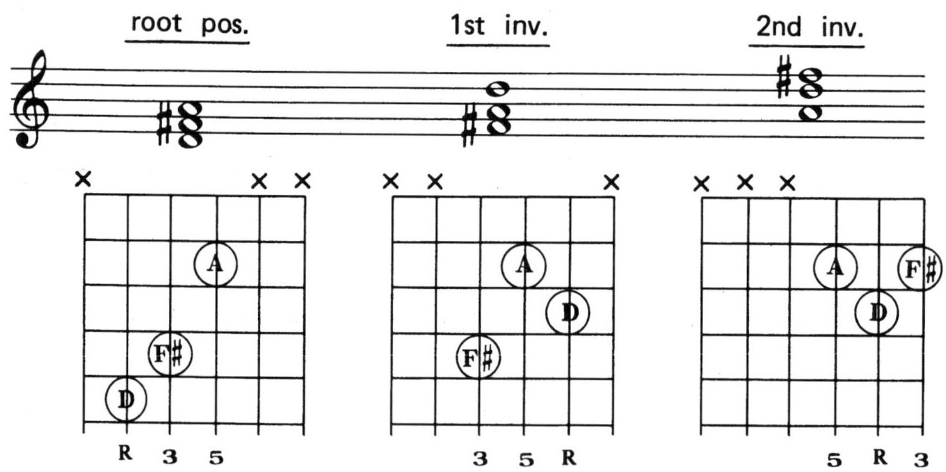

Inversions make chordal movements sound much more interesting, and add a professional touch to your playing – if handled properly__

– **Learn them well** –

In "2nd" position

A major

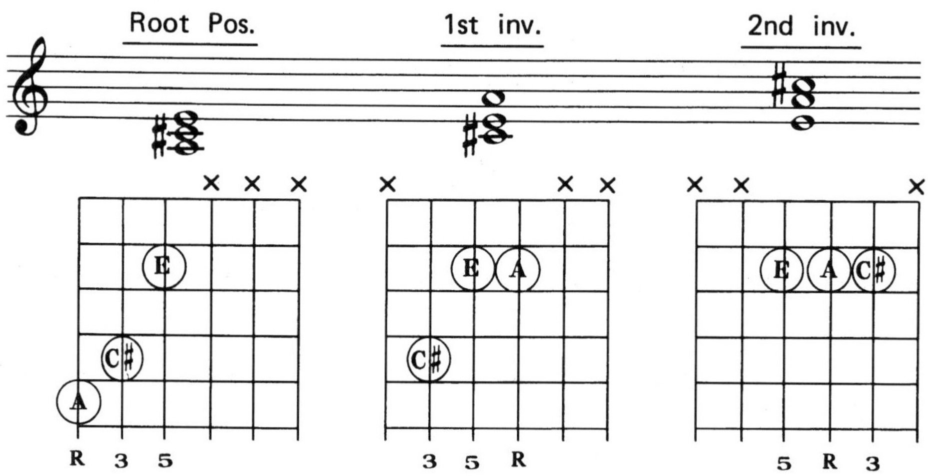

Now take each of the 2nd position forms and transform them to minor, augmented, diminished.

If we use the form starting on string (4) we must move up the fingerboard for 2nd inversion.

F major

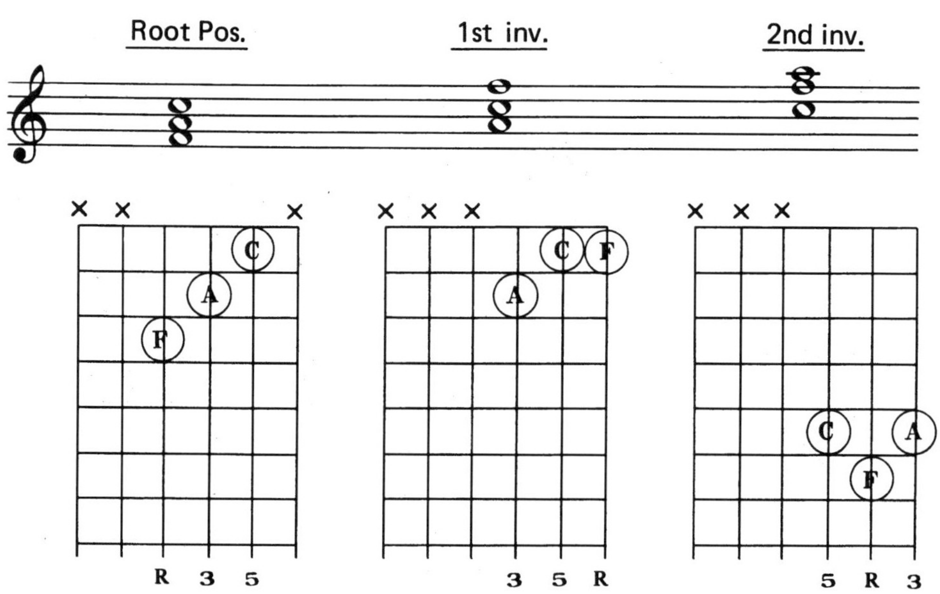

To provide a complete dictionary of all four basic triads, plus their respective three positions would take a substantial volume. With the material provided here, you have enough "starting material" to work them out yourself. Make a complete diagram of the guitar neck, and explore all of the possibilities which are available. Just being able to play each of the four basic triads, in three positions, in all twelve keys, will provide you with 144 chords. [there are more – just look!]

Tones in the triads may be doubled, giving you more than a three note chord. However, they will still contain only three different tones.

For example

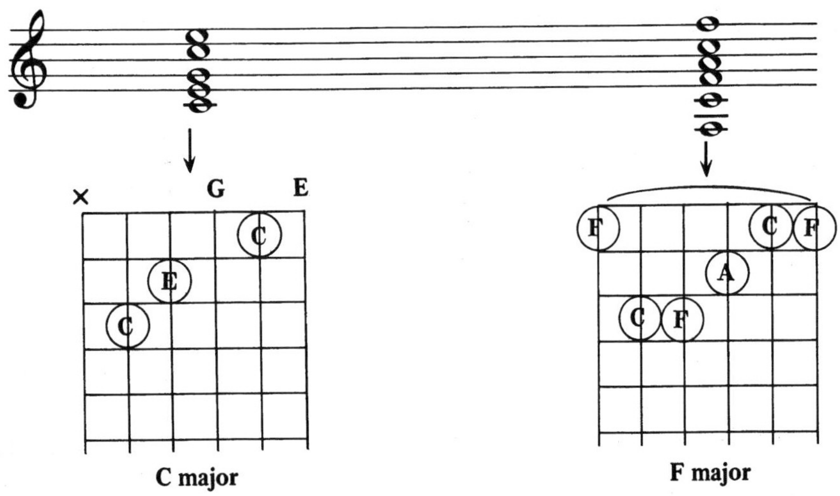

The F major utilized the 1st finger barre and conforms to the harmonic overtone series.

The C major has two 3rds (E) (not so good according to traditional harmony) – however, very good sound on the guitar.

Origin of the barre chord

If we are going to move "open position" chords, using open strings, up the fingerboard — We have to use our first finger across all of the strings at any given fret to replace the nut, where the strings cross on their way to the tuning pegs.

For example:

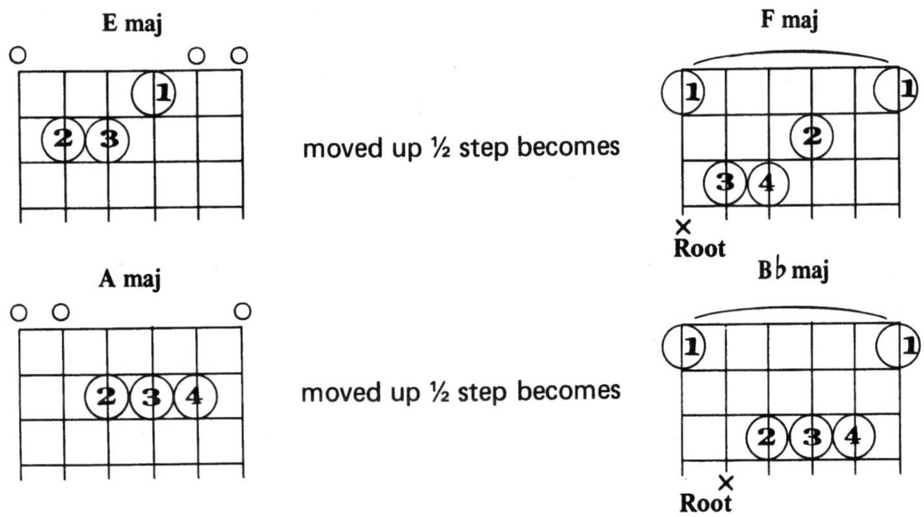

So, we can move any open position chord up the fingerboard using this process.

Try moving some other open position chords in this manner. Some of them will be most difficult to finger and very impractical. You'll discover these when you try using barre to move them.

6 String Forms, involving the BARRE

(still containing only three different tones) except the two 7th forms

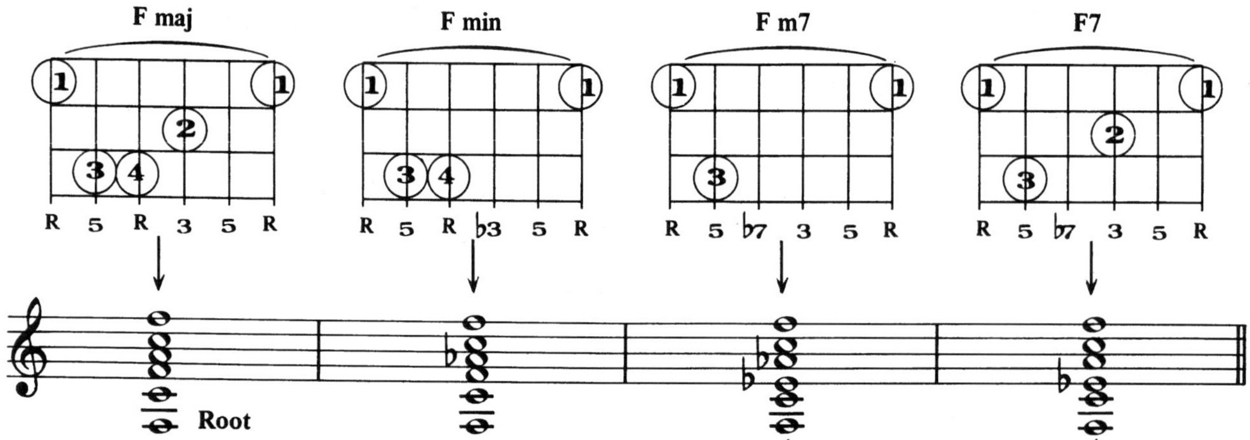

These are the basic barre forms. Move up the finger board and be able to name, and play them – in any position.

These two forms have ♭7 tone added – actually four tone chords. Move about 7ths in next section.

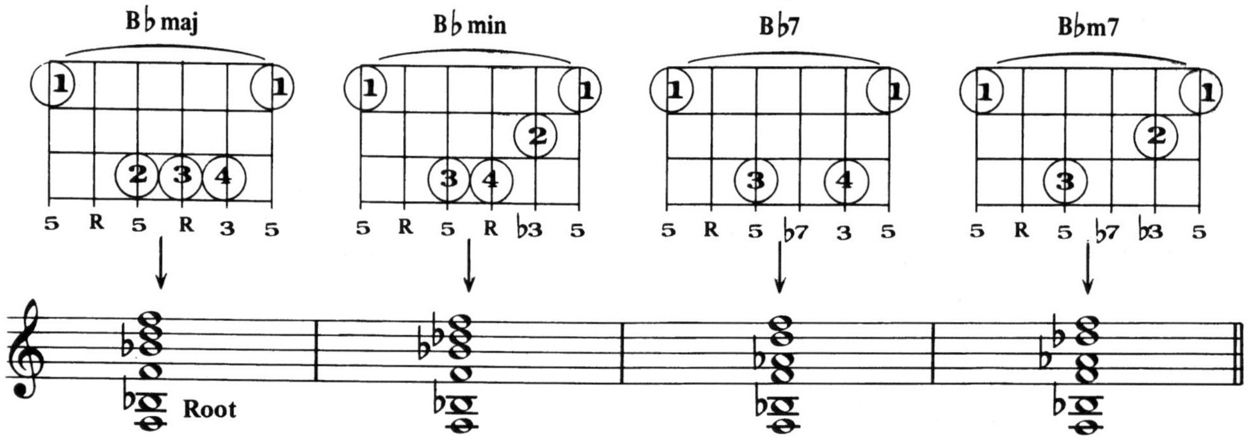

Triads in open position (tenths)

Remember, the previous triads were in "closed position". The tones followed each other in natural succession, one after the other. When we open the triad, it presents a different picture. There are, now, open spaces between the tones. (Note barre forms)

Example

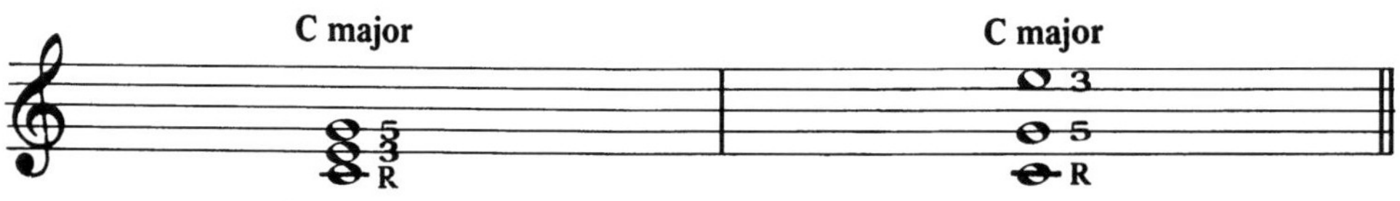

Root position "closed"

Root position "open"

The middle tone jumps an octave higher – the same principle applies to the inversions—

Example

C major — C major

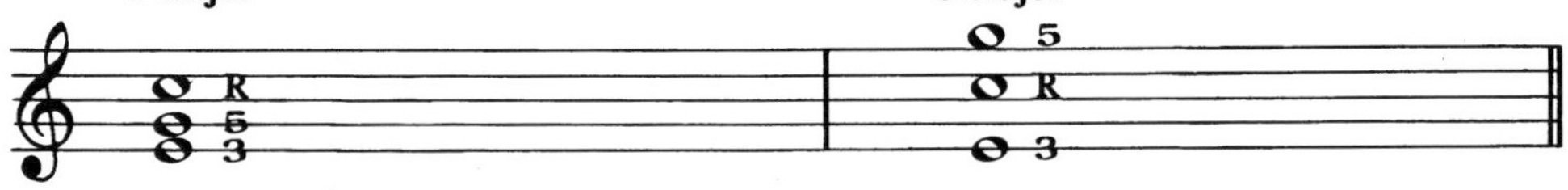

1st inversion "closed" — 1st inversion "open"

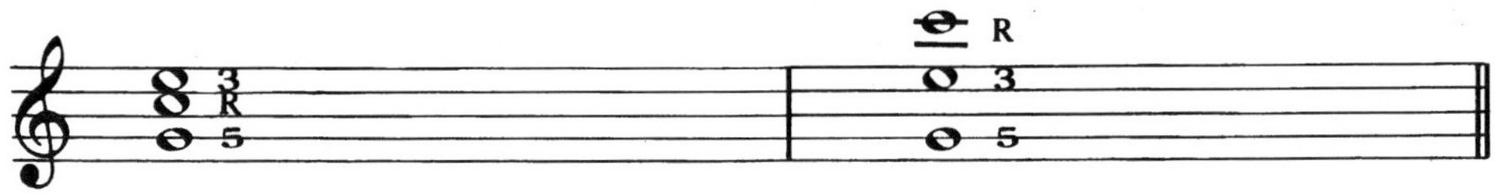

2nd inversion "closed" — 2nd inversion "open"

Minor, augmented, and diminished forms of the triad will "open-up" in the same manner — just alter the appropriate tones.

These forms, applied to the fingerboard, provide a much fuller "sound" than the closed position triads. Let's apply them to the fingerboard—

Here are the three positions of the G major triad — root position, 1st and 2nd inversions.

G major

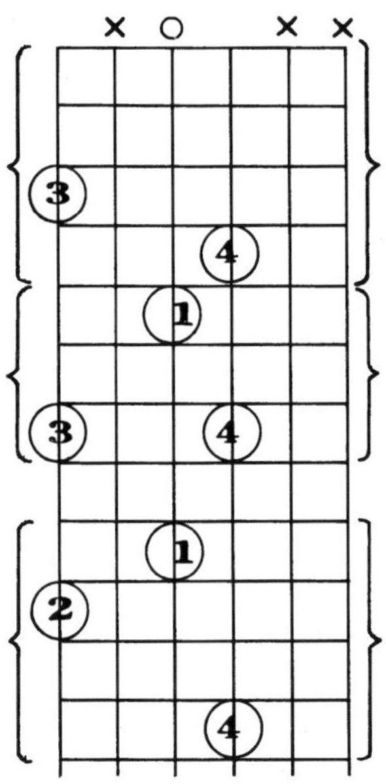

Root position

1st inversion

2nd inversion

These are the three major forms using strings ⑥ ④ & ③ — They are available using other string combinations. Use your diagram of the neck to find them. They are abundant — these three forms may be transformed into minor and augmented by altering appropriate tones.

> Forget the diminished at present. We will use a single form to represent this chord.

When you move root position form up one fret, use first finger to play E♭ on 4th string—

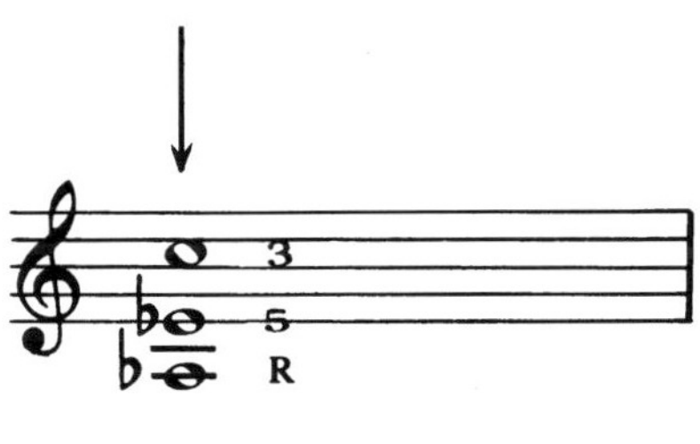

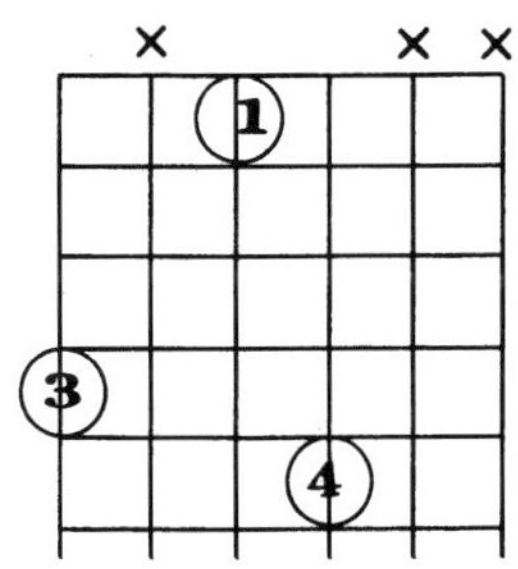

A♭ major (root position)

Fingering for various forms will remain fairly constant—There may be some deviations later—

Root Position

All root position forms using this string series will alter in exactly the same manner.

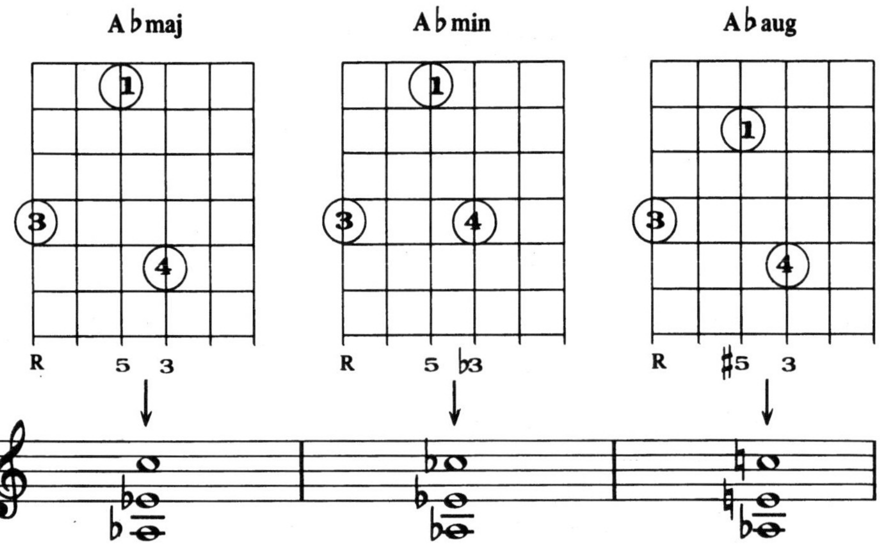

1st inversion

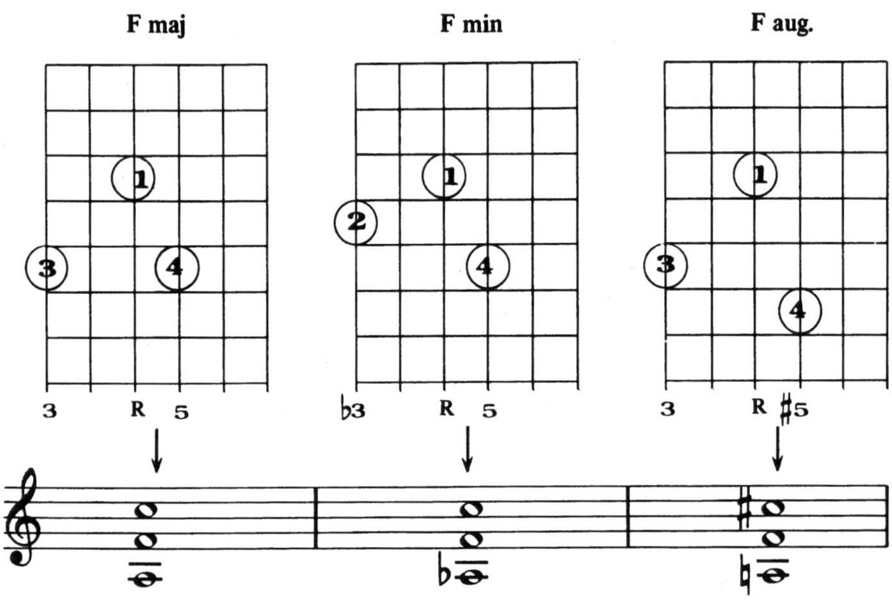

2nd inversion

Note similarity between A♭ aug and C aug.

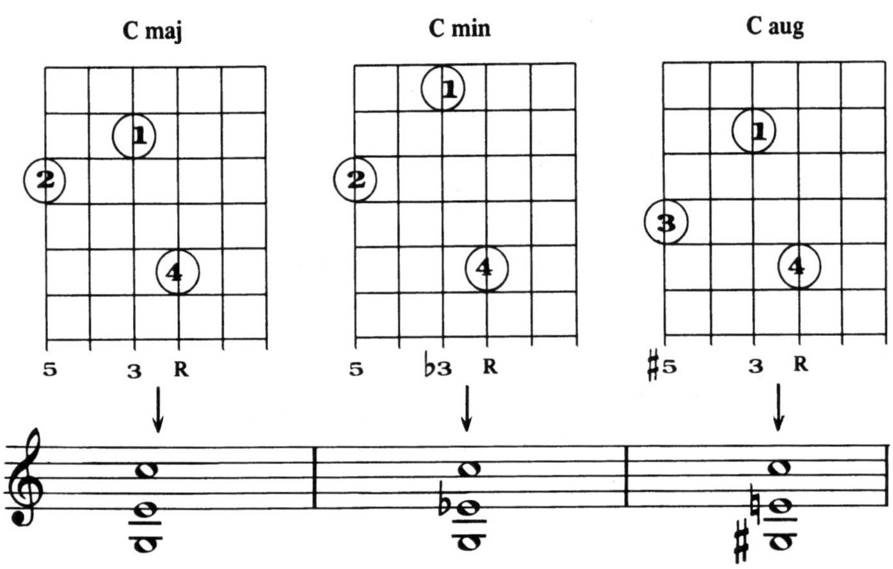

This covers all possibilities except diminished. We will use the same form for all diminished, keeping in mind how it repeats itself every 3rd time.

Dimnished form. [Incomplete]

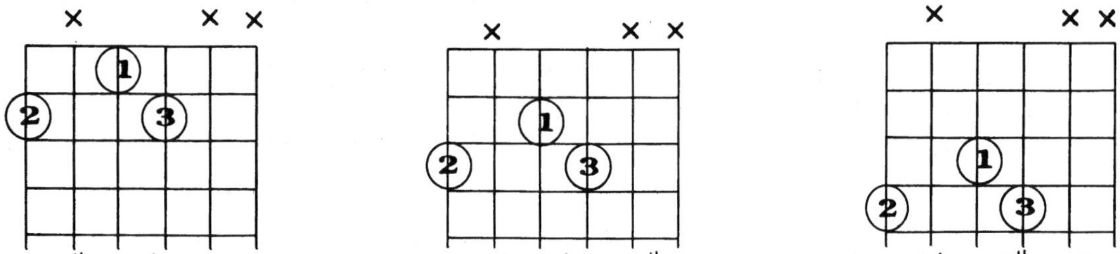

F♯ – G♭ – A   G – B♭ – A♯   A♭ – G♯ – B
D♯ – E♭ – C   E – D♭ – C♯   F – D

This gives you all availables – remember, if we move to 5th fret we repeat the one we played on the 2nd fret_<u>This is most important!</u>

Two forms will cover 7ths using this string series.

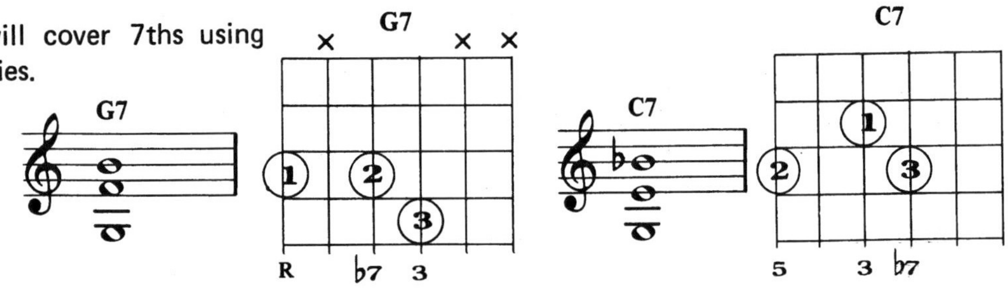

same form as dimin.

Explore the other open forms using different string combinations_

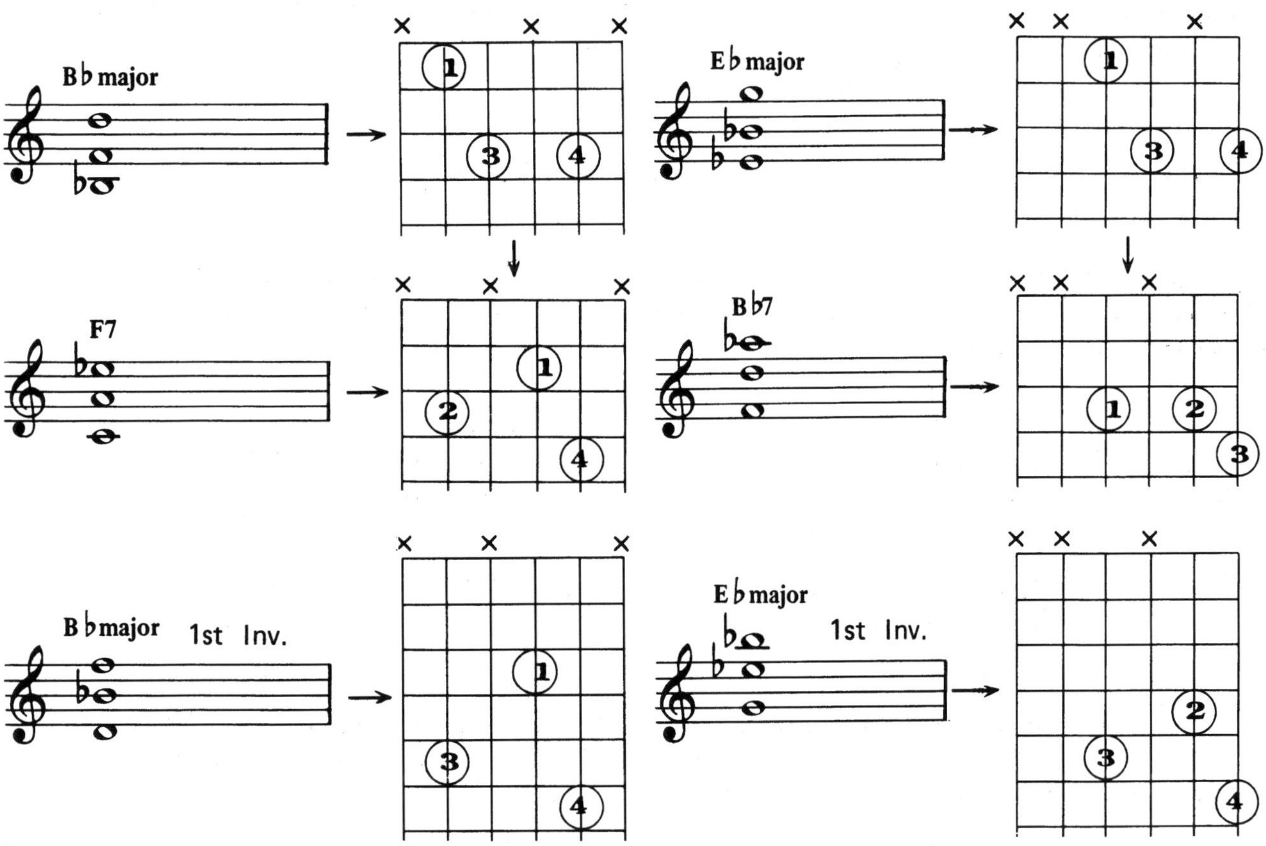

These forms are available in abundance. Remember the lower forms of these open triads will provide the best sounds_

The following Etude will demonstrate a few of the "movement" possibilities of these open triads. It isn't too hard to play — listen to the chords moving from one to the other—

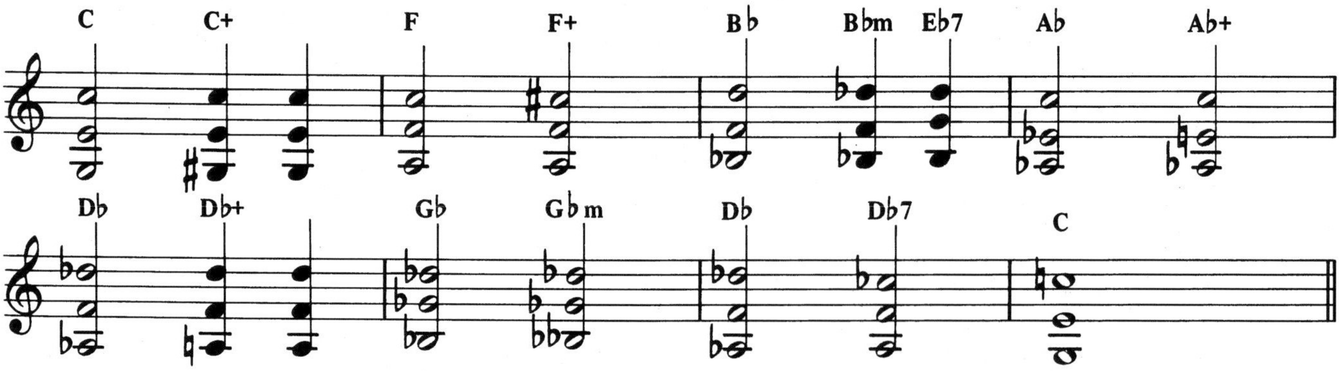

Try writing some of your own. The possibilities are endless—

Kind of interesting movement leading from C to D♭.

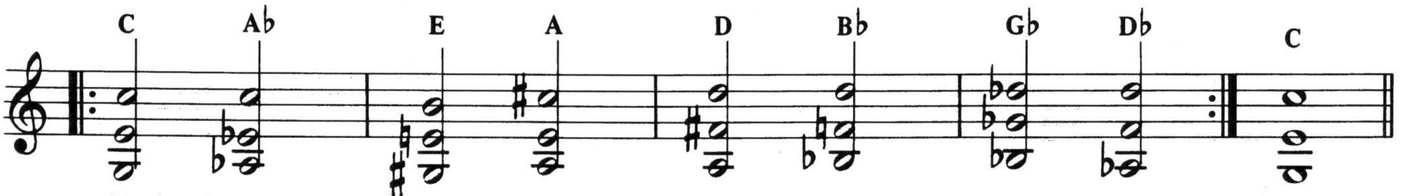

— Notice how smoothly they move —

SEVENTH CHORDS

Up to this point we have been discussing triads, or chords containing three different tones. If you remember, we stated that our system of harmony was primarily based on intervals of 3rds. If we add another 3rd on top on the triad we have a 7th chord.

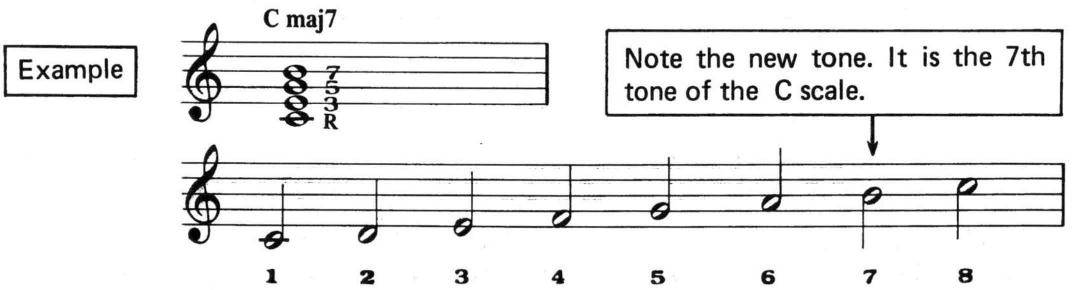

This is the major seventh, or the natural scale 7th of the particular scale. It can be found quickly by thinking back ½ step from the root, to the next alphabetical scale degree. There are three kinds of 7th intervals used to build 7th chords. They are:

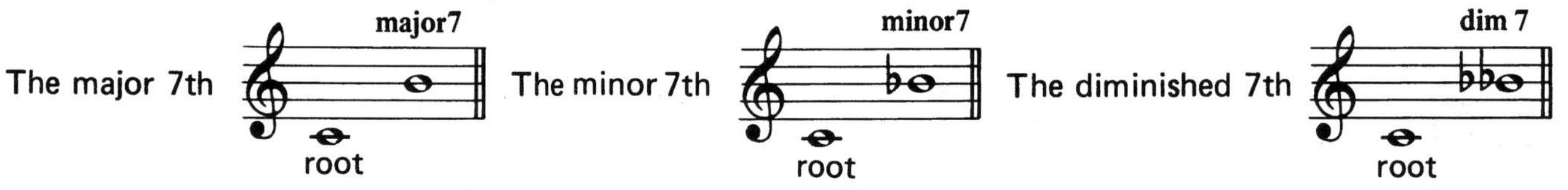

We are now ready to begin adding these intervals to the basic triads we have already learned – (if you haven't, don't move ahead)

There are four basic seventh chords. They are:

(1) major 7th (2) minor 7th (3) Dominant 7th, and (4) Diminished 7th.

Through an alteration process of the other tones in the 7th chord, we will expand our vocabulary to many more than four, as we proceed with our study of the sevenths.

Three of these appear naturally if we harmonize the major scale, building a 7th chord on each tone.

Example

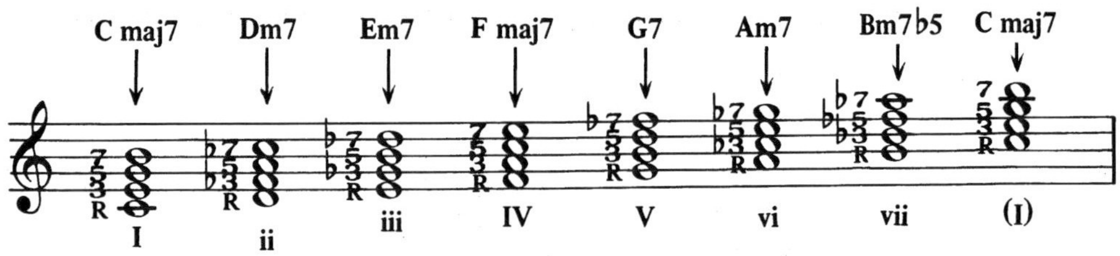

Major 7th chords appear on I and IV tones: minor 7th chords appear on ii, iii, & vi tones; dominant 7th chord appears on V tone –The chord appearing on vii tone involves one of the alteration processes we talked about. We will discuss this, as we move along.

The 7th scale degree should always be indicated by its correct alphabetical name in relation to its Root. For example, don't do this:

Theoretically the "A♮" in relation to the "C" root is the 6th tone of the scale, not the 7th—

Try to name the three different 7th intervals from different root tones—

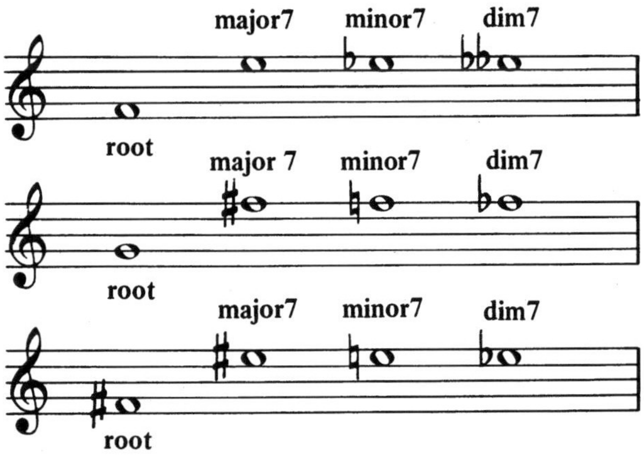

Work through all 12 tones of the chromatic scale, using them as root tones. Name the 3 kinds of 7th intervals for each root.

Work with this concept until you understand it perfectly. It will be most important when we begin to build seventh chords. Go back to the material on the four basic triads and review. Make sure you know 100%. It will pay dividends you never imagined.

The diminished 7th chord would appear on the 7th degree of the harmonized harmonic minor scale.

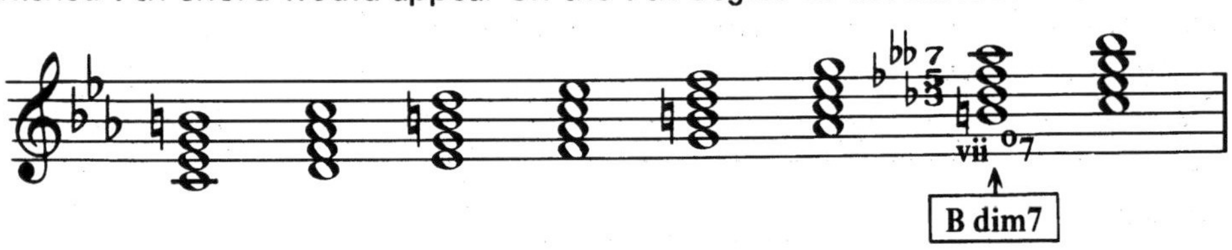

The harmonized minor scale presents many interesting harmonic combinations__ We will discuss this more fully farther along in this book. Now, let's build our four basic seventh chords, using our triads as a foundation and adding our various 7th intervals__

1. Major seventh = 1 – 3 – 5 – 7 (add the natural scale 7th to the major triad)
2. Minor seventh = 1 –♭3 – 5 –♭7(add the lowered natural scale 7th to the minor triad)
3. Dominant seventh = 1 – 3 – 5 –♭7(add the lowered natural scale 7th to the major triad)
4. Diminished seventh = 1 – ♭3 – ♭5 – ♭♭7 (add the doubly lowered natural scale 7th to the diminished triad)

Memorize the numerical formulas. They may be applied to any given root tone.__

These four represent the basic chords. It's fairly obvious that there are other possibilities.

For Example The major 7th could have the 5th tone altered in either direction.
The minor 7th could have the 5th tone altered. Also the 7th tone.
The dominant 7th could have the 5th tone altered.

Here are some of the possibilities:

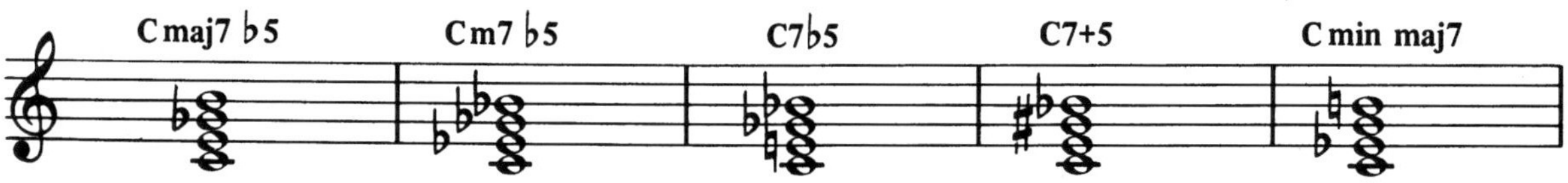

As you can see, there are many possibilities__ Some alterations will not sound as good as others. Experiment with the different alterations and combinations. Let your ear be the final judge. Some combinations will sound like other chords.__

Example Add D root to C maj7 ♭5 and you get a beautiful D13 chord.

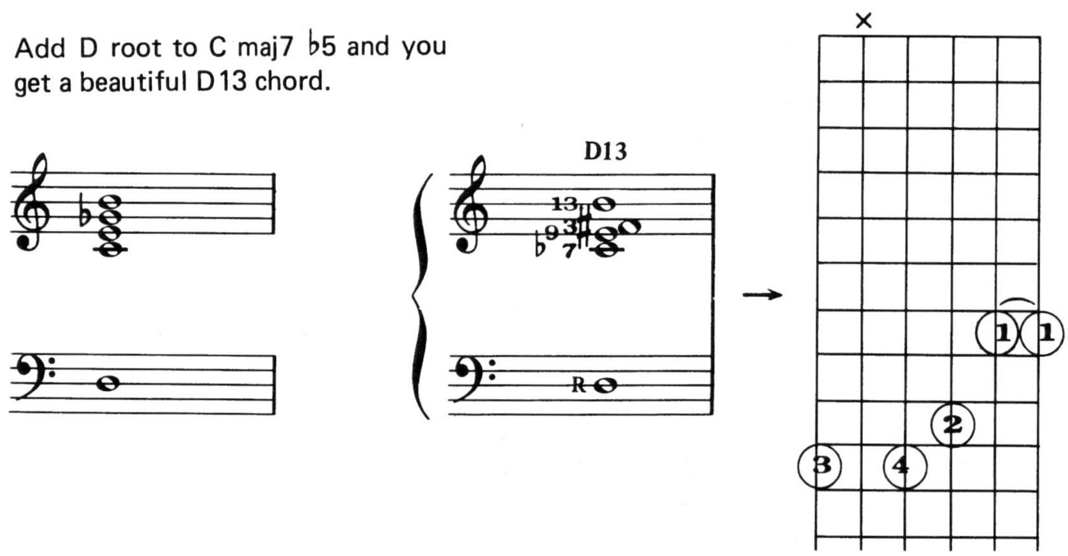

These possibilities (and there are many) will be discussed in a later section "chords performing a variety of functions."

Now let's begin to apply our knowledge to the guitar finger board – We'll start with a "G" root in a position which will make the four basic 7th chords reasonably easy to finger. (Ordinarily, closed position 7th chords involve difficult finger stretches – with some exceptions which we'll discuss later on)

Example

The four basic 7th chords built on "G" root in closed position-

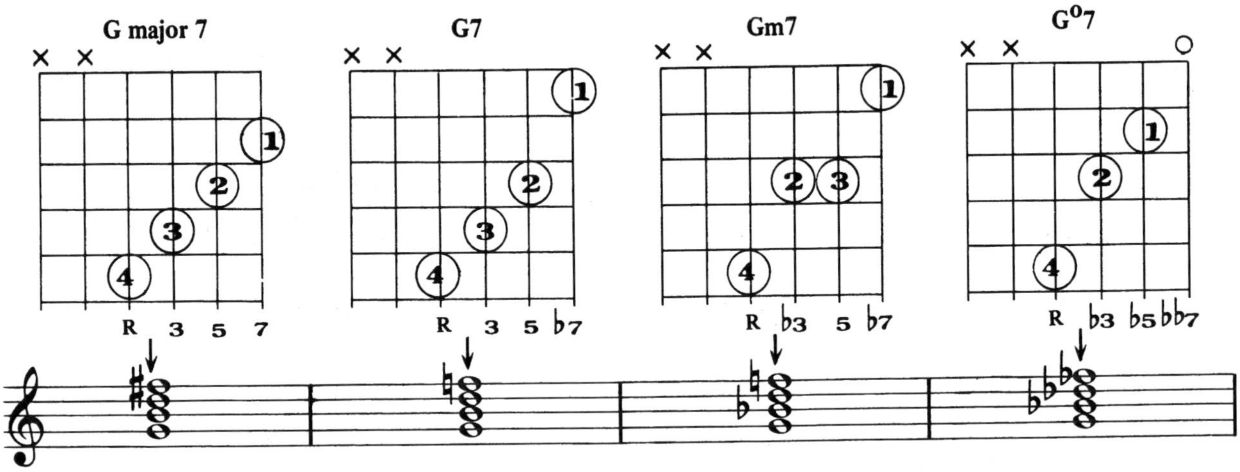

Practice these. Play them! Listen to them! The dim.7 will be hard to finger as you move up the finger board. It's possible, though.—

closed position

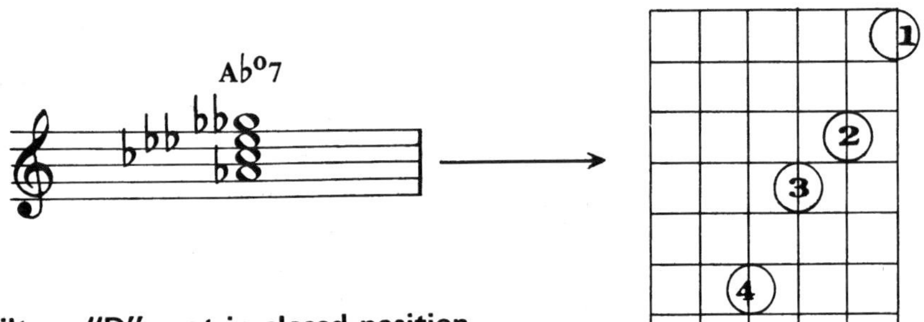

The four basic 7th chords built on "D" root in closed position

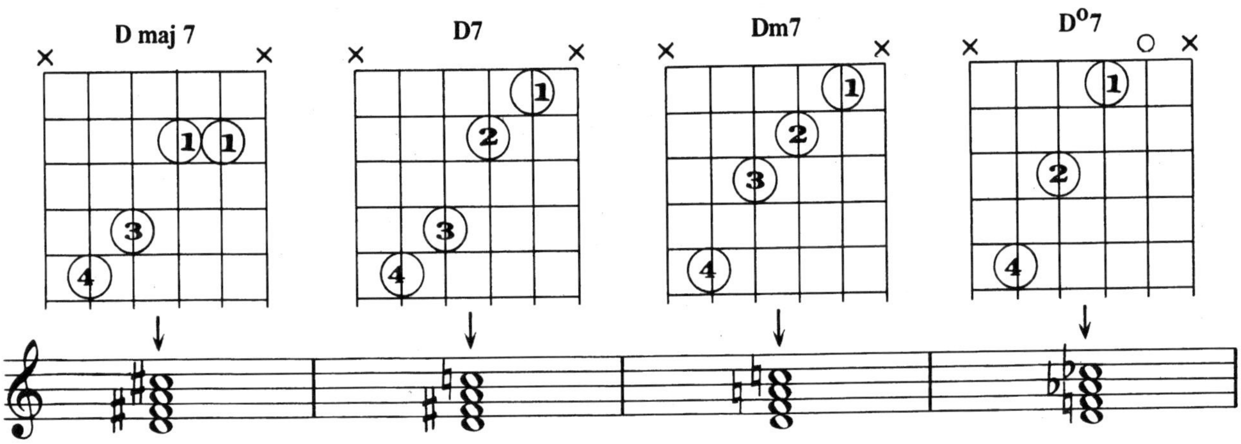

These are difficult to finger. The difficulty is greatly increased as we move up the fingerboard.

Try playing E♭ °7

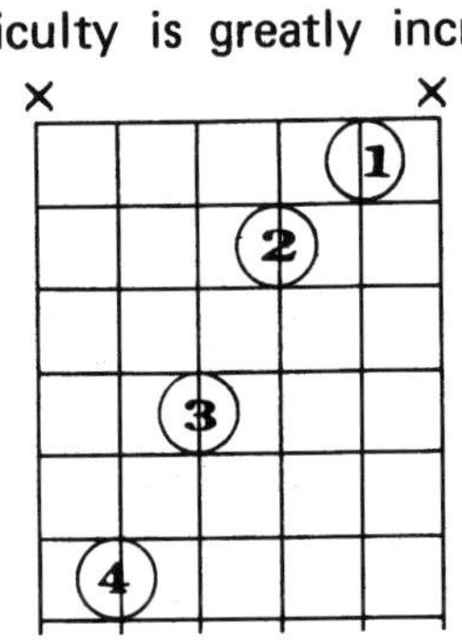

You've got some kind of hand if you can play this one.

I think it's obvious that our best chords on the guitar will be "opened" up. The tones will be rearranged so that the fingering problems are greatly diminished.

Let's back up to the G major 7th and see what we can do with a tonal rearrangement.

Let's use an open "G" triad in root position to begin.

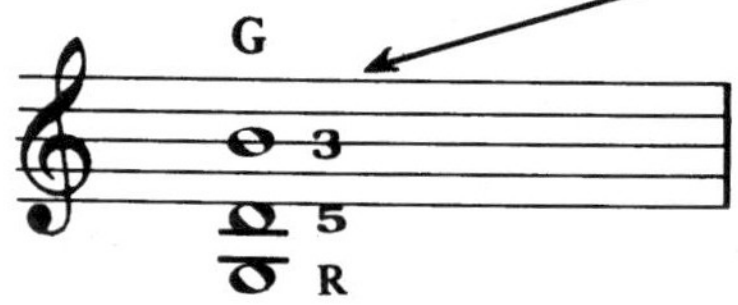

→ Now add the major 7th to this.

We now have a good sounding, practical, open position G major 7th which looks like this:

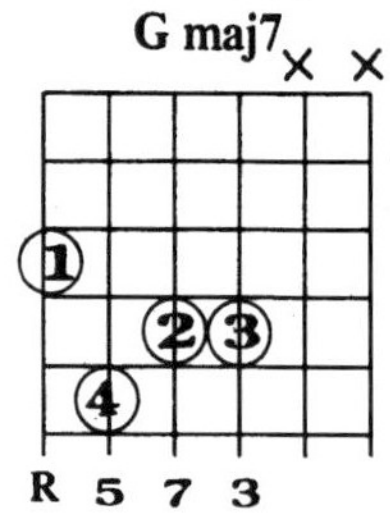

This form can be transformed into the other 3 basic 7th structures.

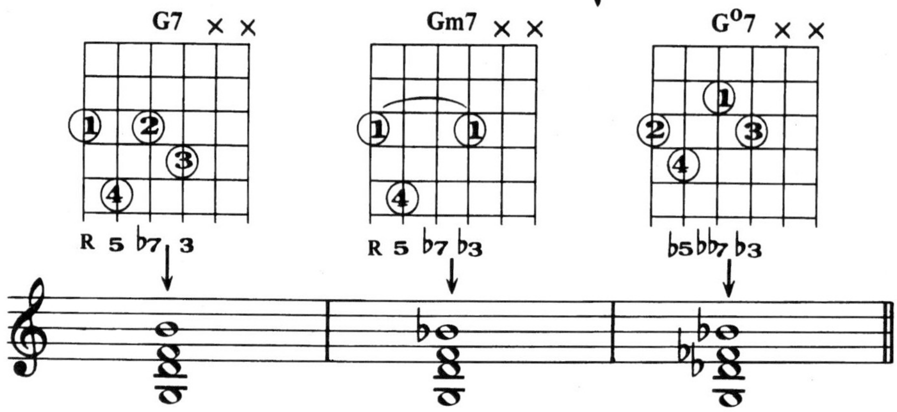

Another very practical voicing, in this position, may be obtained by raising the 5th tone of the previous maj. 7th by an octave.

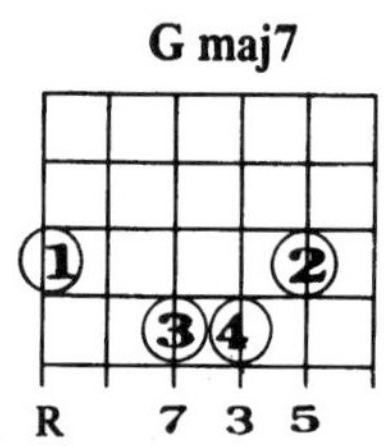

This is excellent voicing for this particular chord – good for all purposes.

The other three transformations are possible:

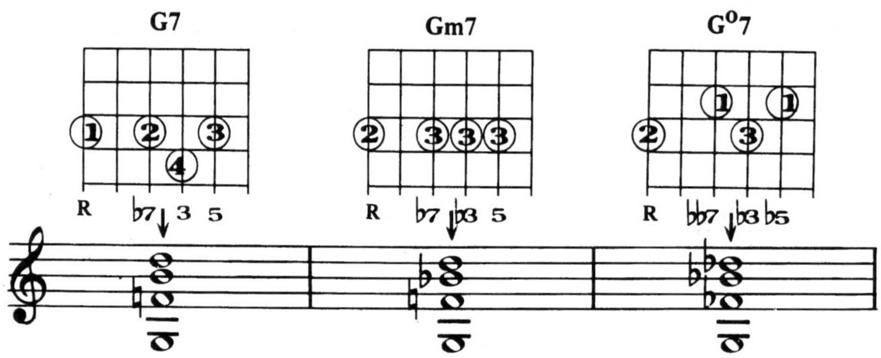

All alterations are easily available : G7+5, G7 ♭5, Gm7 ♭5, Gm maj7, G°7 sus E♭ , G13 etc We'll discuss all of these further along. You may experiment with some of the alterations if you like. Usage will be discussed fully later!

G maj7 form in 1st inversion

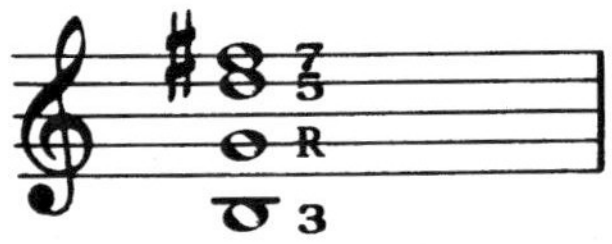

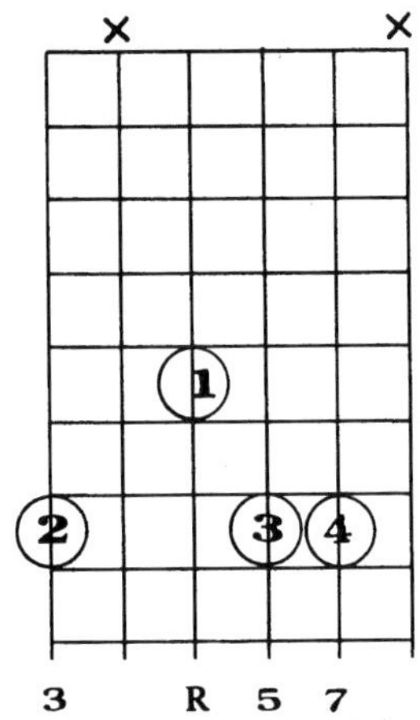

Very good voicing in this register

Transformations all possible

OR →

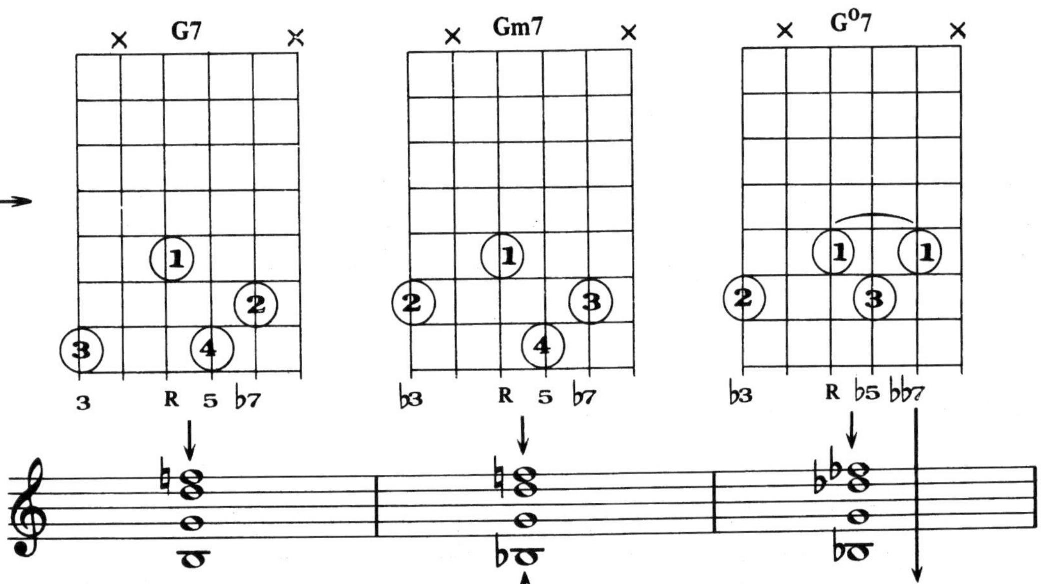

Also good Bb6 chord

Remember what we said about the dim. chord repeating itself. This is the same as the previous G we learned – this time 3rd is low tone.

G maj7 form in 2nd inversion

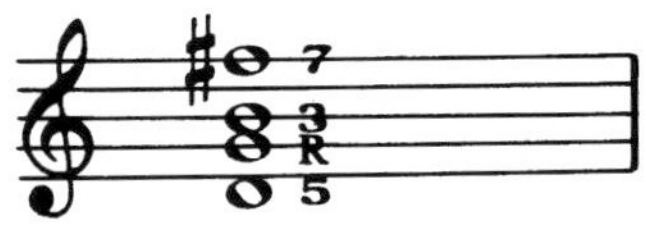

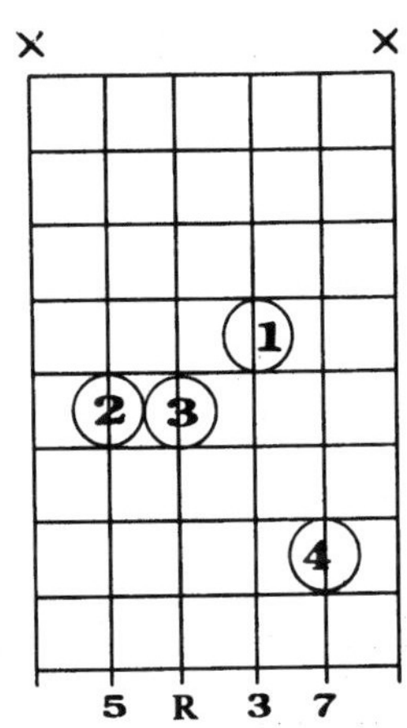

Good sound on inside four string – good for "comping" using fingers –

Transformations all possible

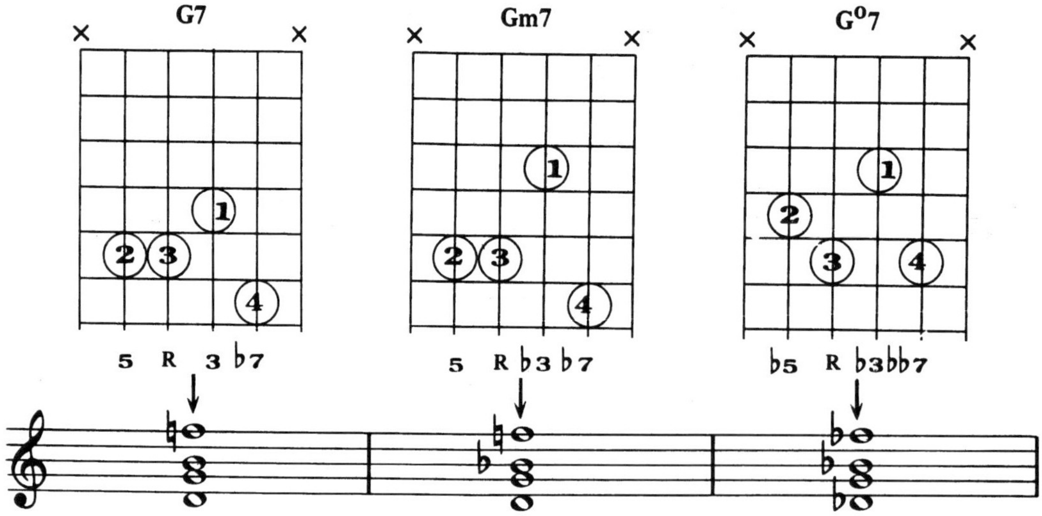

Another voicing for G maj7

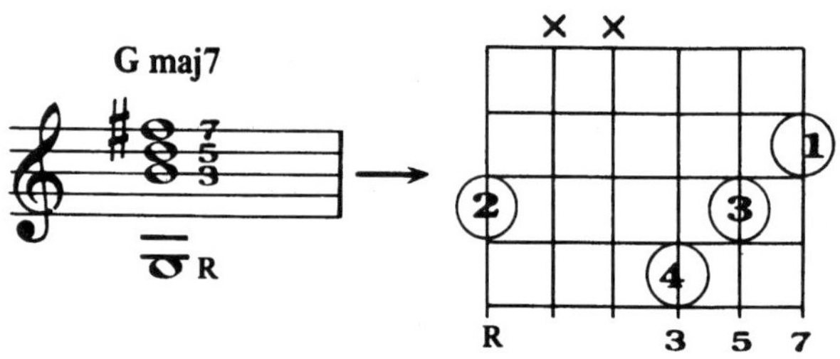

Make sure strings (5) and (4) are not included. Deaden them with finger 2.

The other three transformations are possible:

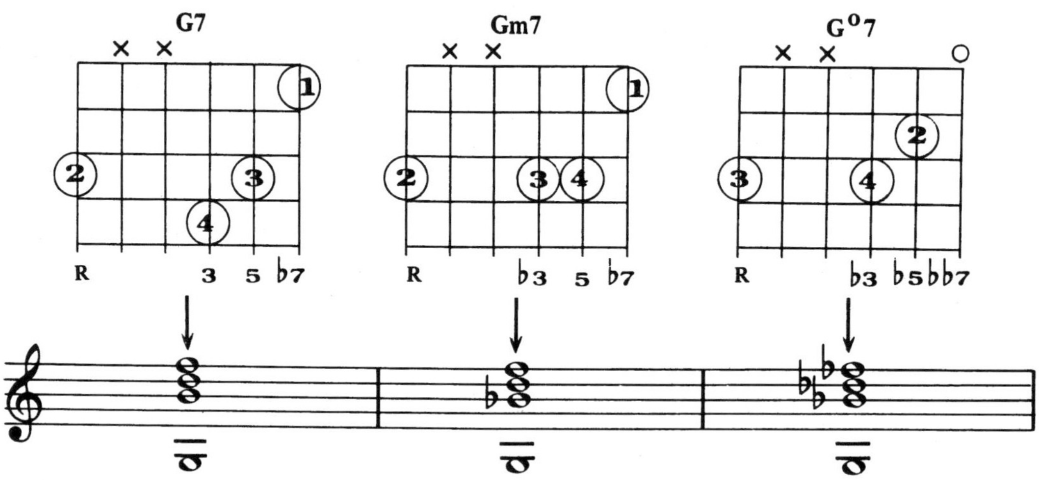

one fret up to A♭°7 requires using 1st finger on ♭♭7. →

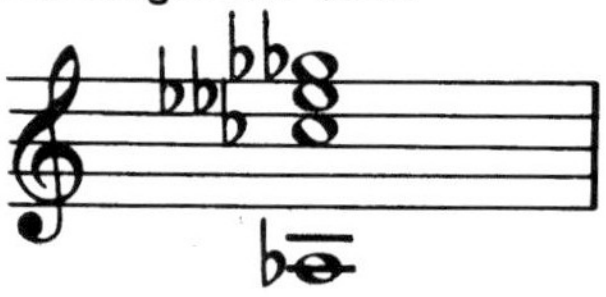

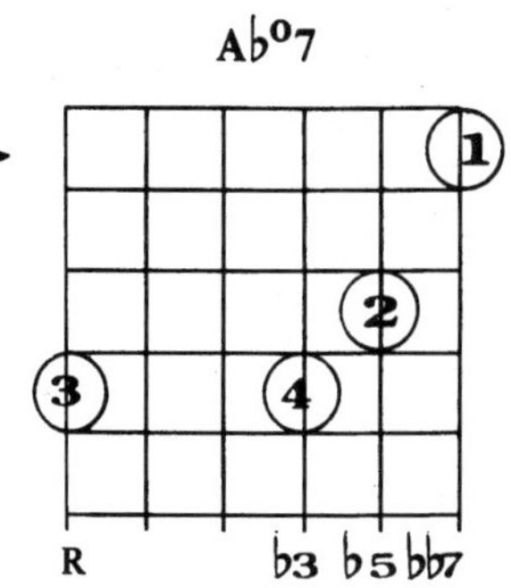

These forms are good for slower accompaniment patterns. Good as appeggios.

You may combine the tones and use a six-string major 7th in this position, with the root on top and bottom. Makes for unusual sound—

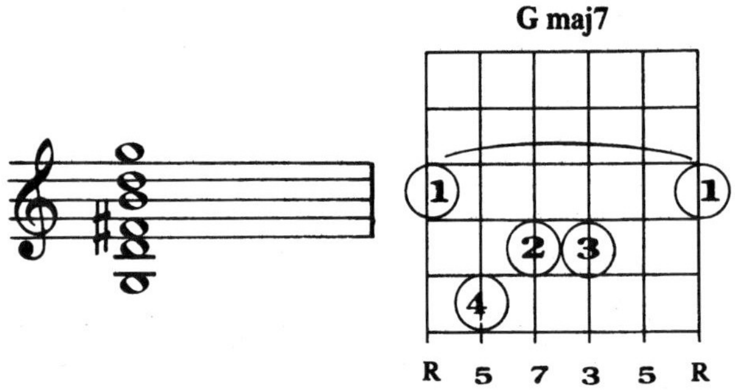

1st finger used as barre across the 3rd fret. (Use this voicing with care)

Transformation impossible

Here's a form that's really opened up –

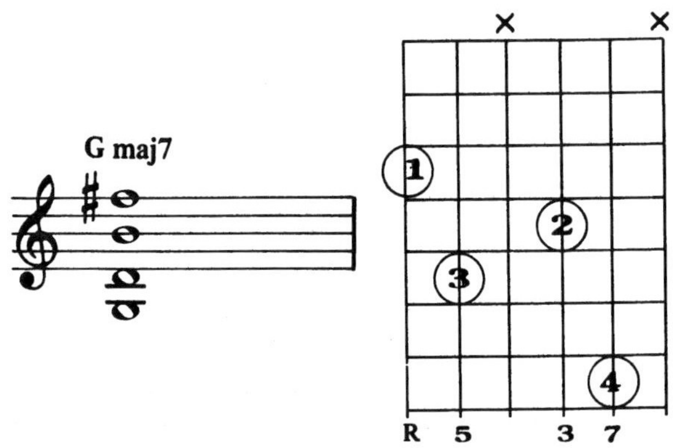

Be sure strings (4) & (1) are deadened—

Transformations possible

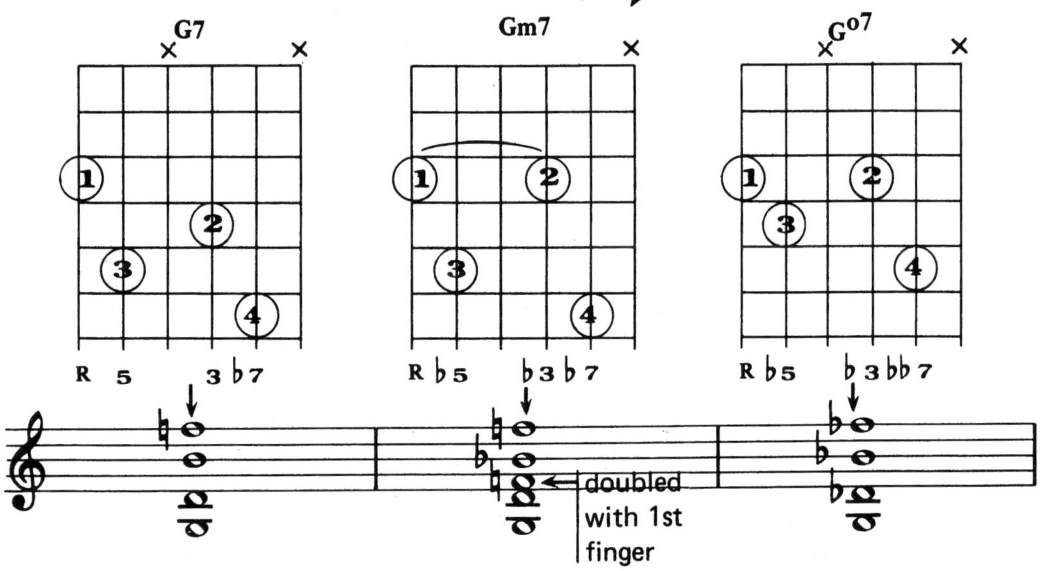

Using "C" root with same tonal arrangement as the first G maj7 (R – 5 – 7 – 3)

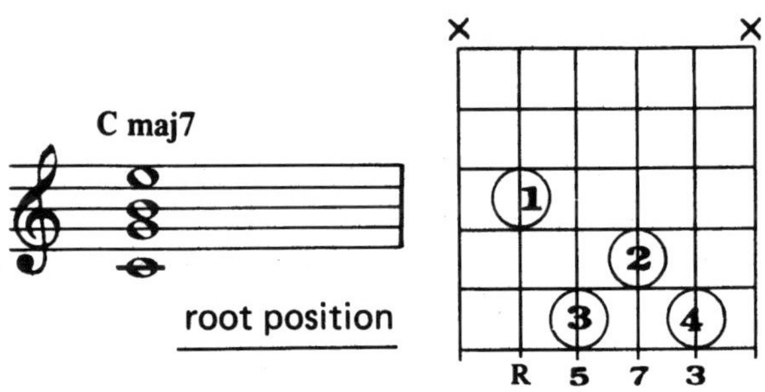

Good, inside combination – ideal for comping with fingers – barre 1st finger for use as full rhythm chord—

Transformations all possible

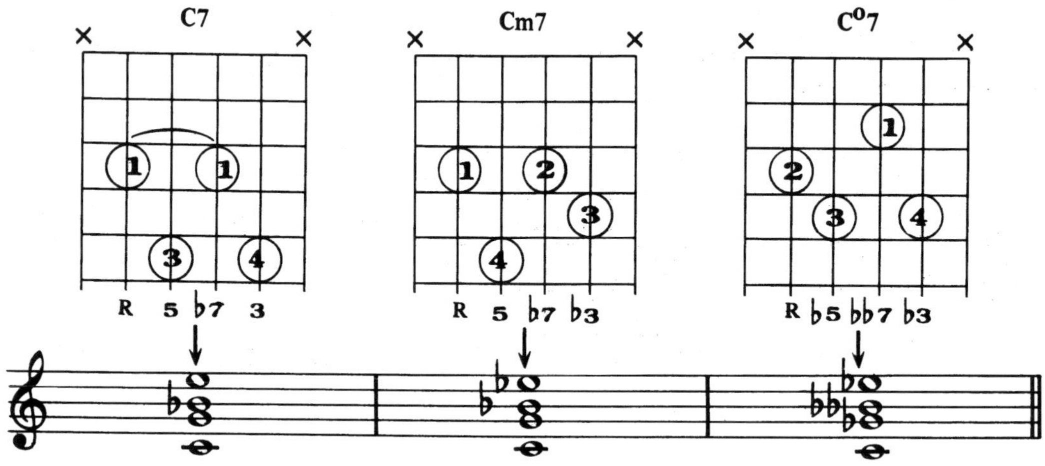

Make sure you understand, <u>and know,</u> the notated examples of all these chords. Remember that learning where to put the fingers in the easy part.

Know each tone's function in every chord you play.

Here's a good 1st inversion voicing of C maj7

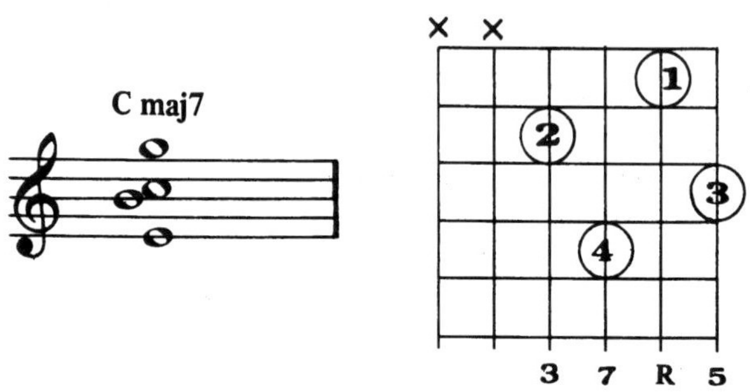

The minor 2nd interval in the middle of this chord gives it a most unusual sound – good for "comping," ballad accomp – etc – Not a good rhythm chord.

Transformations all possible

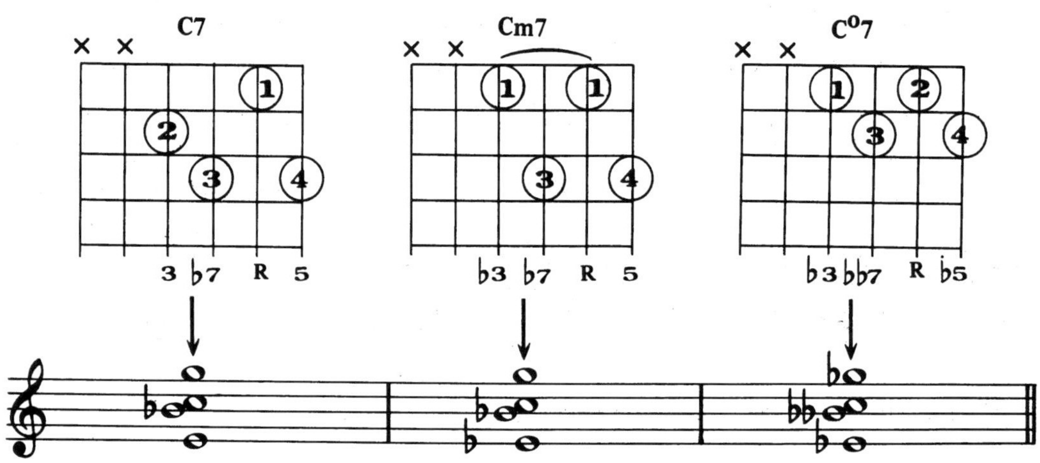

All of these chords move freely up the guitar fingerboard. The names of the chord roots will change with each move. You should be able to "spell" any of these formations, regardless of your position on the fingerboard. Remember, always name the chordal tones in relation to the major scale suggested by the root – for example, don't spell above C°7 (D♯ – A – C – F♯).

Let's look at some other voicings, in the same position — this time using "C" root —

note 5th tone in bass — 2nd inversion

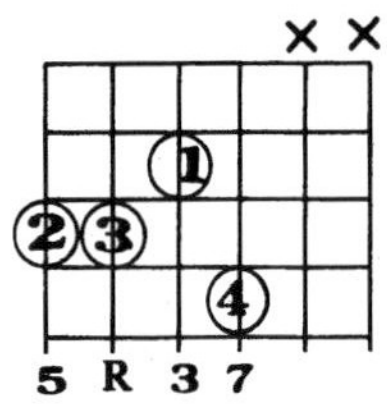

This transforms nicely to the other basic forms.

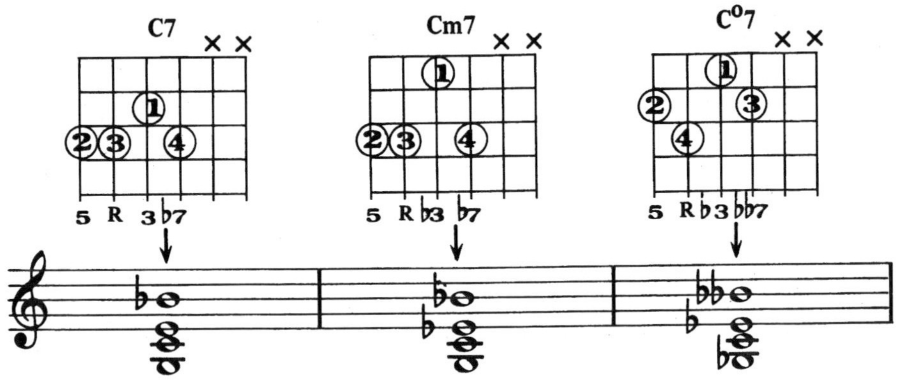

These are nice, mellow sounding, chords in this particular register—

Remember! Everything written here actually sounds an octave lower—

C major7th (another 1st inversion form)

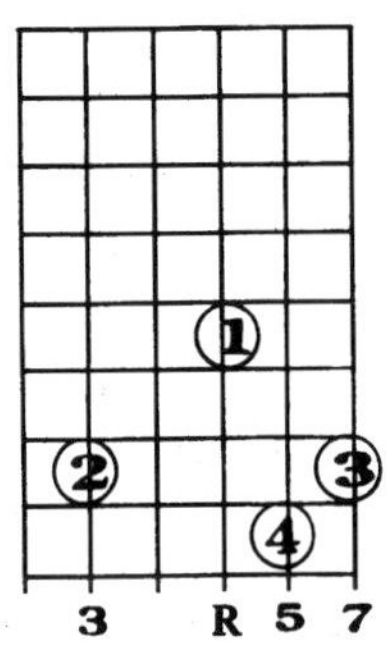

Very good form with 3rd tone in the bass.

All transformations possible

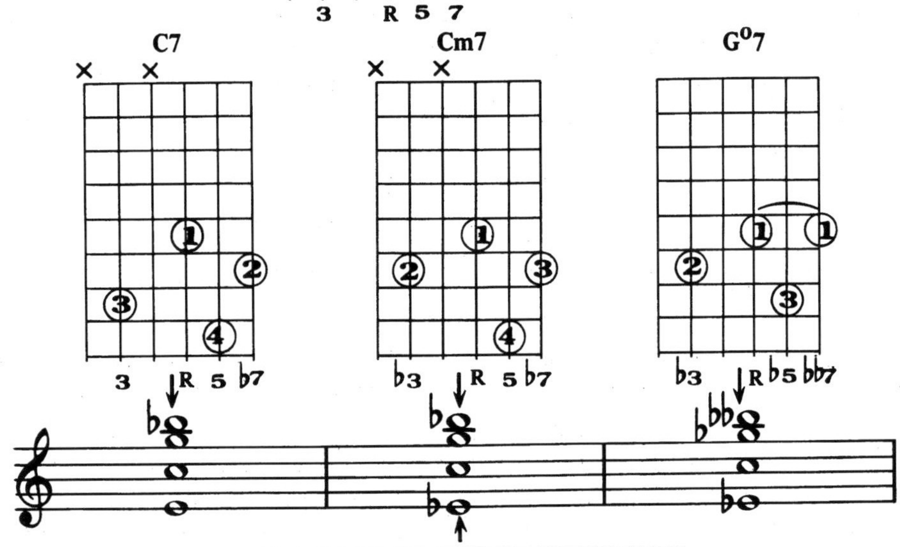

May also be used as A♭maj7/9 (minus root) 2nd inversion

We've looked at the major 7th in several positions up to this point. Now let's see what the same chord looks like on the top four strings.

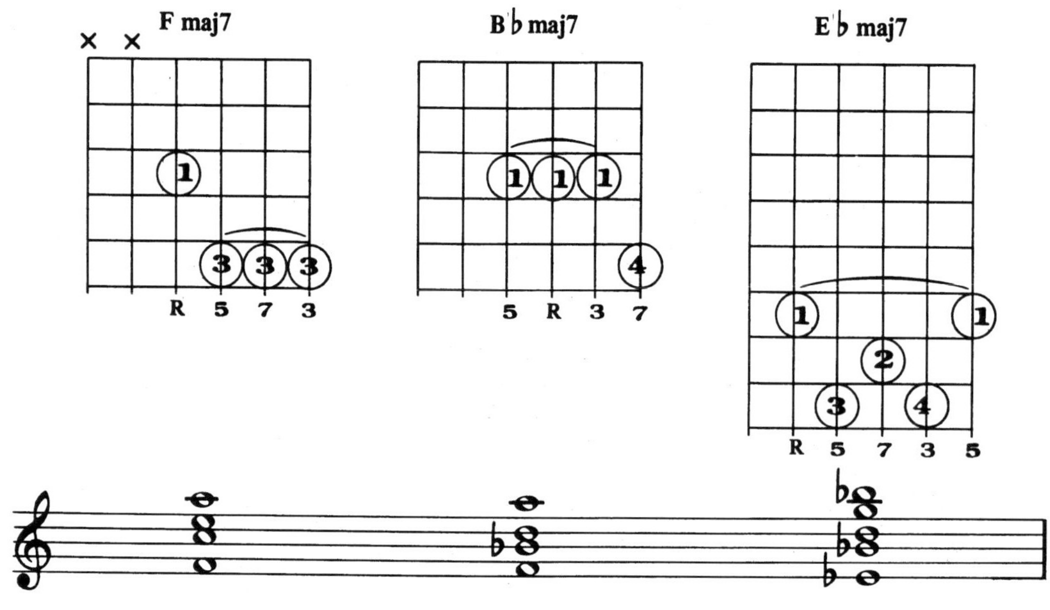

All transformations are possible. You can form each of the other basic 7th chords by making the necessary alterations, which you should know by now! The E♭ maj7 is a chord we've already had; this time we've added the 5th on top of this chord. Remember, all these chords may move to any fret on the fingerboard, new chord name will be determined by root—

We've also had another maj7 on top four strings.

Remember:

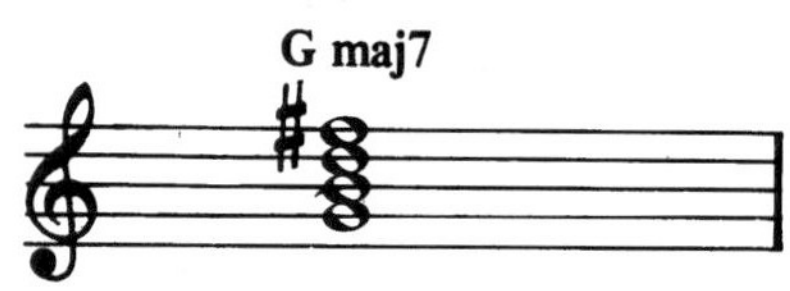

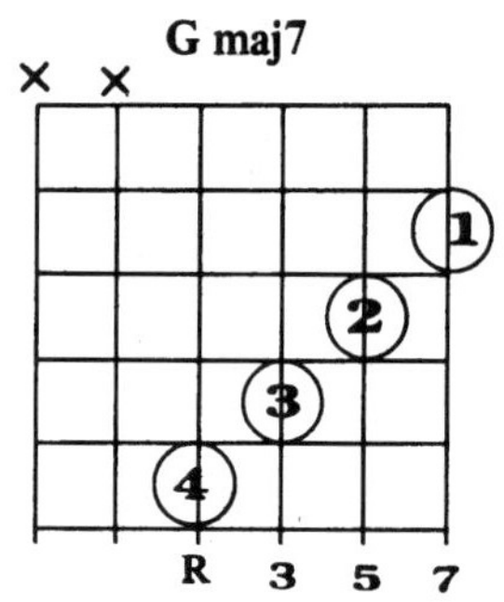

Along with our discussion of 7th chords, we now have a new inversion. (Remember, the triads may appear in three positions – root position, 1st inversion, and 2nd inversion. With the added 7th tone, we now have a new position: 3rd inversion, with the 7th tone as the lowest note in the chord—This is a good position, but one which requires careful handling—

Example:

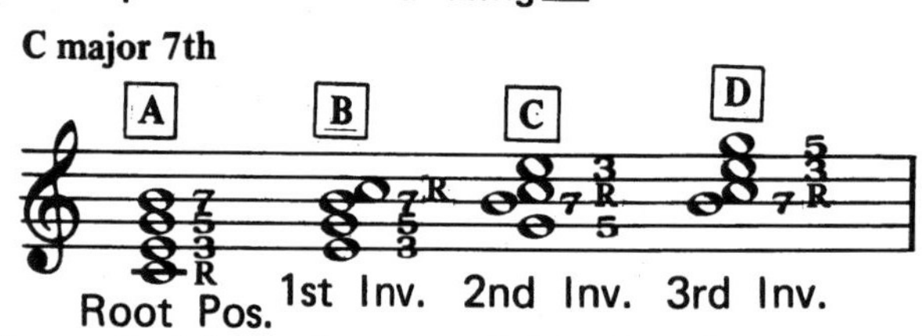

Except B, these are good closed voicings for orchestral arranging.

These are the theoretical inversions possible, with the 7th chord in closed position. It becomes obvious that B, 1st inversion, would be a most impractical sound. The minor second between B and C notes needs another tone above to soften this dissonance, and provide some support. Each of the other tonal arrangements are good – however, impractical in most instances as a guitar voicing. Remember, we said that "open voicing" was the most practical way to translate a chord from "paper to the guitar."—There are some good sounding (but hard to finger) closed position chords available—we will talk about them in a later section of this book—

All four chords in about example would work well if the 7th tone were lowered – C7, Cm7, C°7.

Remember, the minor 2nd interval()needs support above to make it practical for use as a chord — It is possible (but hard to finger) on the guitar —

F maj7 (1st Inversion) **B♭maj7** (1st Inversion) **D maj7** (2nd Inversion)

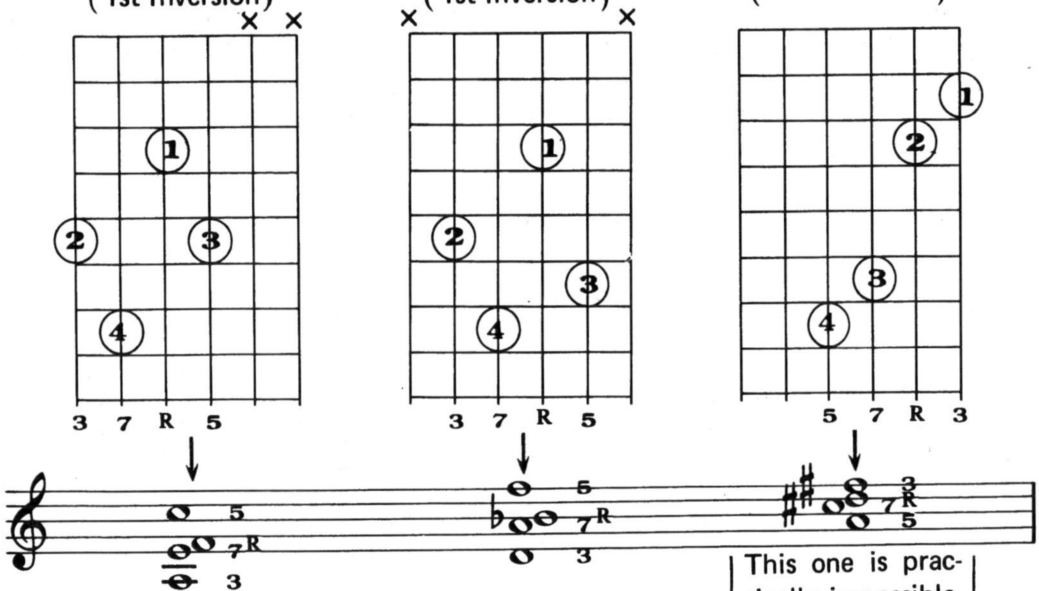

This one is practically impossible.

There are others available. See if you can find some more (using fingerboard diagram if this is necessary) some of the transformations are also possible — Try them — remember to lower the appropriate chordal tones, regardless of their position in a particular chord.

The major 7th chord with the root as the top note is possible on the guitar. (Refer back to the six string G maj7 form we discussed earlier)

There are some other possibilities available:

Example:

G maj7 **D maj7**

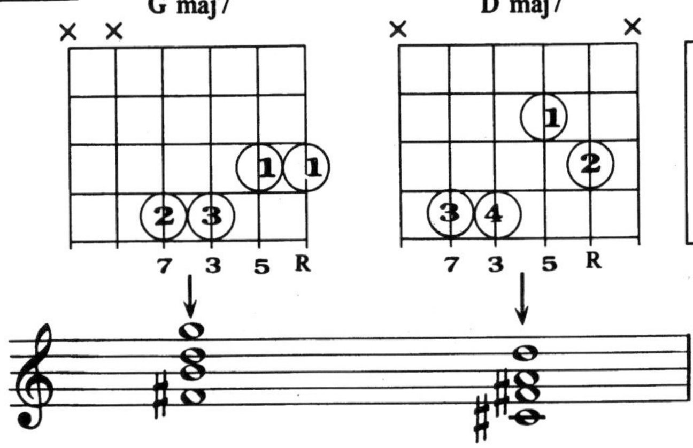

These chords might be used for special effects. They would be 3rd inv., since the 7th tone is the lowest note in the chord — handle with extreme care!

The D major 7th form has the major 7th tone (C♯) in an extremely low reqister. If we think back to the harmonic overtone series", picture where the root would appear: 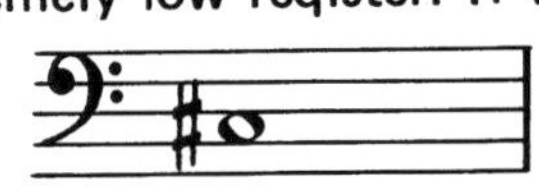 **major 7th**

Always keep in mind that written guitar music is sounding one octave lower than written; especially important when we play low triads, or chords with notes other than root, 5th, or 3rd as the lowest tone.

Previously, we mentioned that certain alterations can be made on the basic 7th chords. If you have been experimenting, as suggested, you've probably discovered some of them by now. Remember that any tone may be raised or lowered. Each change means you must now call the chord by a new name. Some alterations will not produce an effective sound__In most cases, your ear will note this immediately__ (Discuss these with your teacher). For purposes of example, we will make alterations on a few of the basic forms which were presented. To encompass all of them would make this presentation much larger than intended__ This is a good assignment for you to do__ Alter all of the chords which were presented__ Do this on paper, away from the guitar__ "Finger" them this way also__Then try them on the guitar so you can double check your fingerings__

For examples we will use two basic forms:

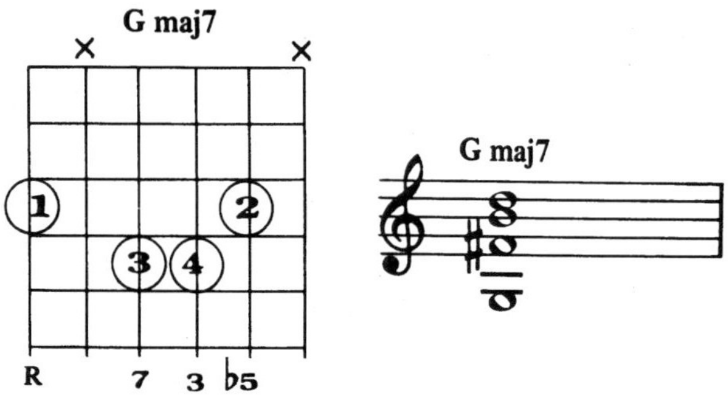

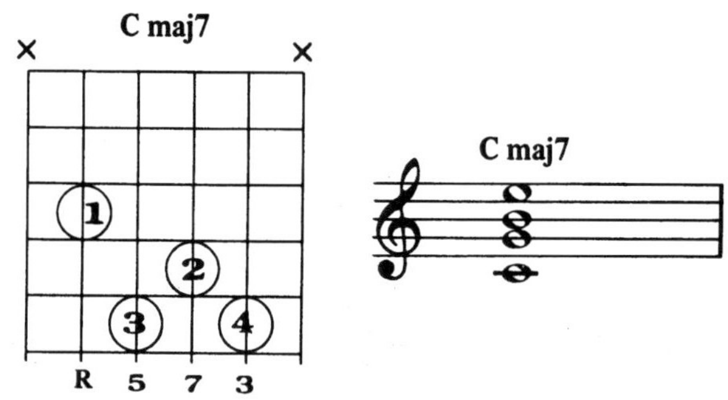

[Remember, these alterations are possible on almost every one of the chords presented so far.]

Let's begin with the G major 7th form —

(1) Lower 5th tone

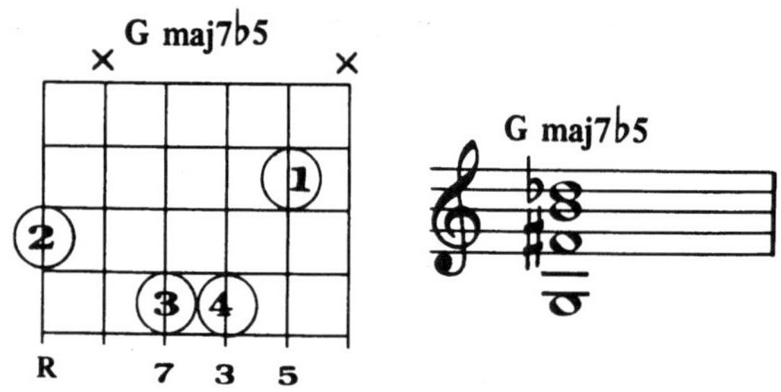

This voicing gives tonic major 7th a most interesting flavor__(Do not use, if chord 5th happens to be melody note of song.)

(2) Raise 5th tone

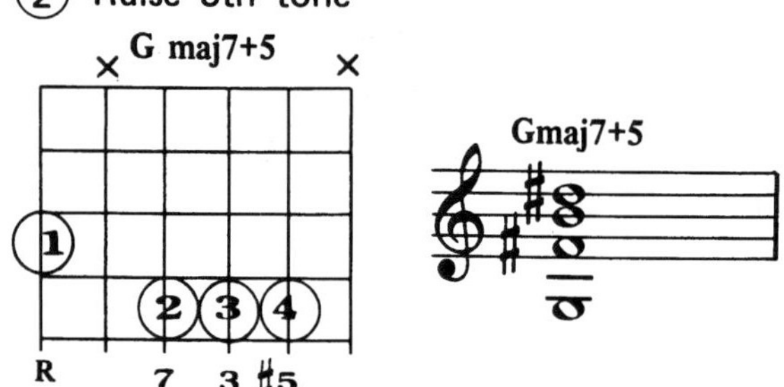

This voicing is most unusal and strange when used in this context. It is possible, though your ear should be the final judge in this case.

(3) Lower 5th tone of Dom 7th

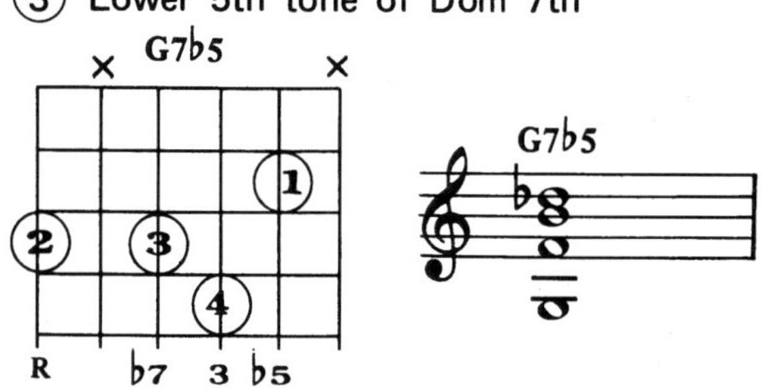

Very good, contemporary (though overworked) sound. Use on dominant 7th for unusual flavor — (Avoid this one if 5th tone happens to be in melody of song.)

④ Raise 5th tone of Dom. 7th

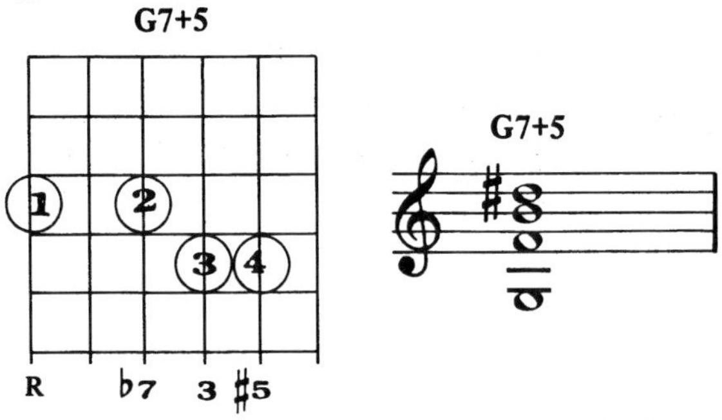

Very good alteration of dom. 7th. wants to resolve to C maj7 or Am7, in most cases – (Do not use if chord 5th is melody of song)

[The 13th chord will be discussed, along with the added 6th chord, at a later point.]

⑤ Add major 7th to minor form

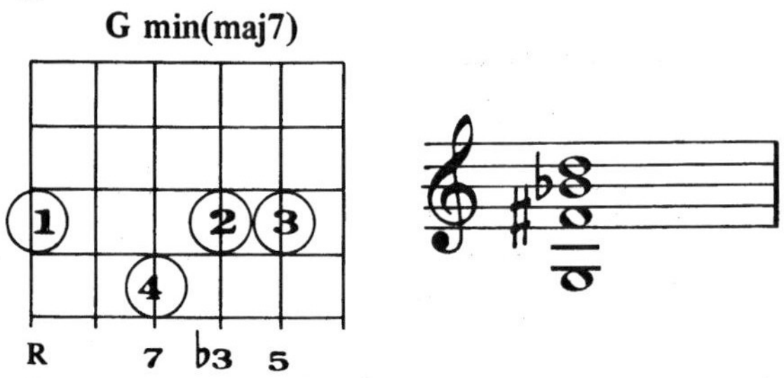

Good alteration of minor chord— Use with care— This is "high-tension chord – (Sounds bad with G melody note;

⑥ Lower 5th tone of min7th

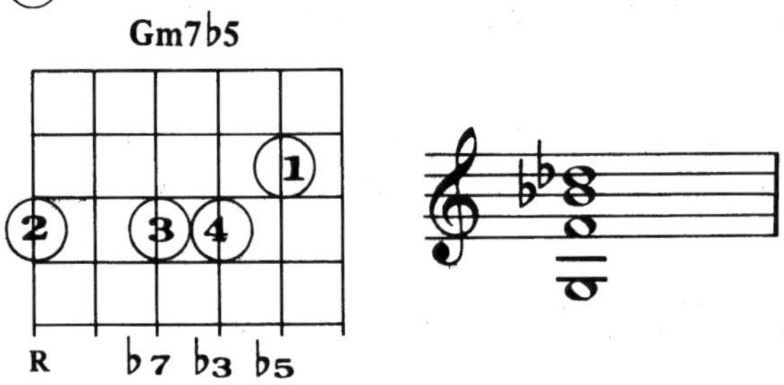

Excellent, and most usable alteration of m7 — Wants to resolve to dom7 built on C root, (good always, except with chord 5th (D) in melody)

⑦ Raise 5th tone of minor

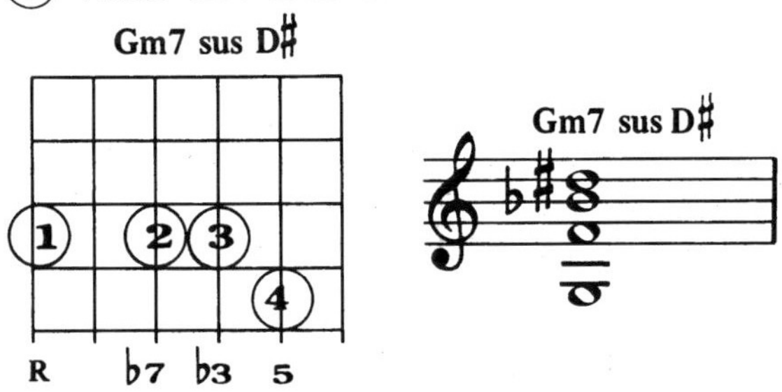

Good for very rare use, and then with extreme care – sounds more like 1st inv' of Eb major triad with suspension.

[minor 11th chord will be discussed later.]

Here are five additional alterations, or positions—These will be discussed fully in a later section—

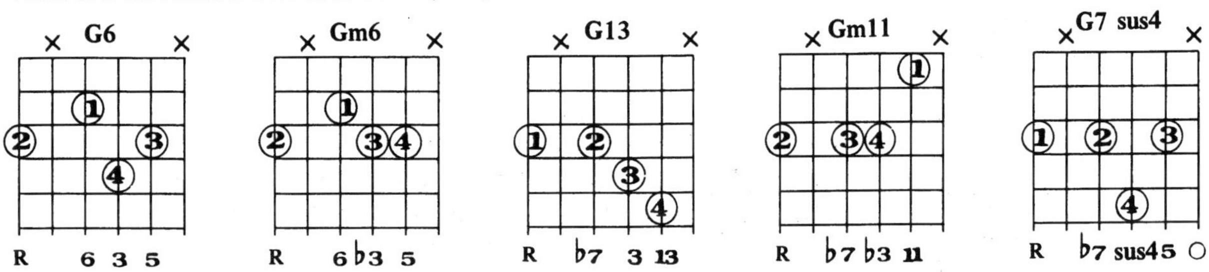

These forms are presented at this point so they are available for you to use— You will find these included in guitar parts of most band arrangements – consider the additional tones as scale tones and they are easy to analyze.

(8) Dim 7 with added suspension.

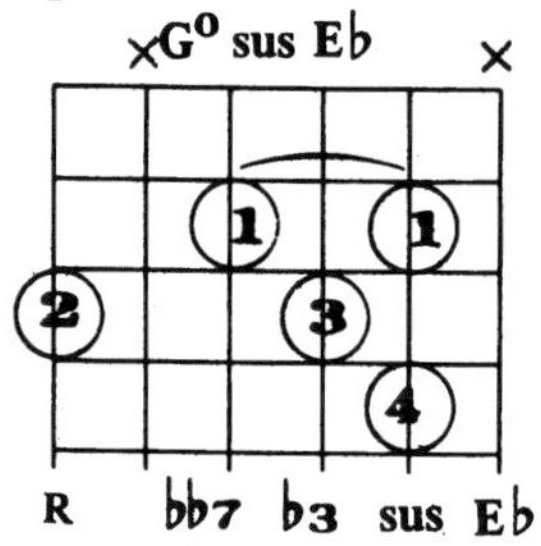

Usually resolves as indicated—

Very good additional tone to dim7 used as passing tone between two chords—

Other forms for the diminished seventh chord

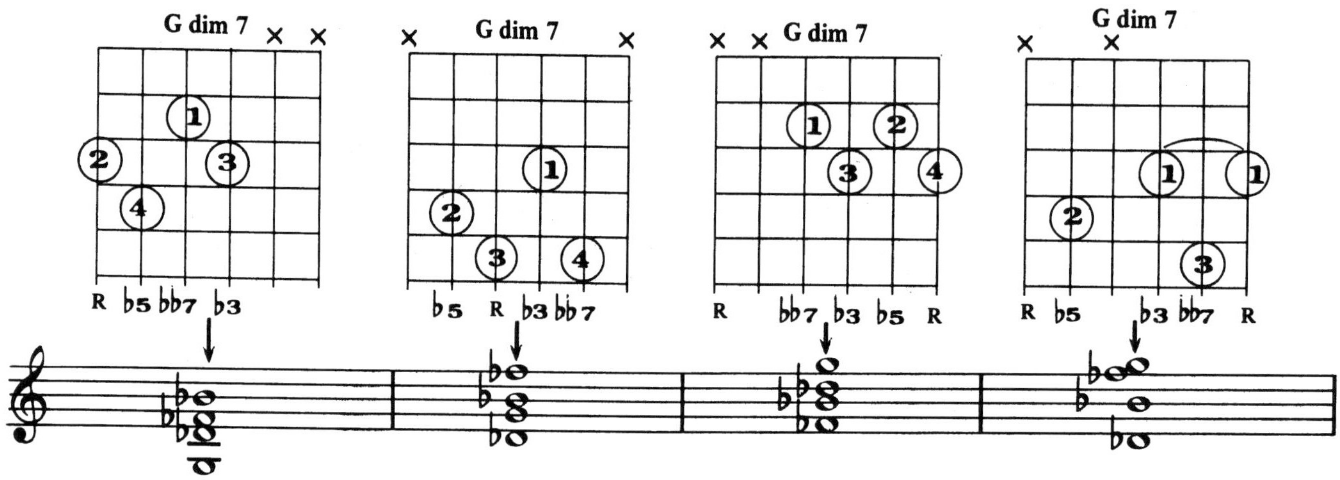

Remember : The diminished chord may be called by any of the notes it contains— Due to perfect minor 3rd construction of chord – the dim7 contains 3 minor 3rd intervals— Thus, it will repeat itself every three frets—.

USING THE C MAJ 7 FORM

(1) Flat the 5th tone

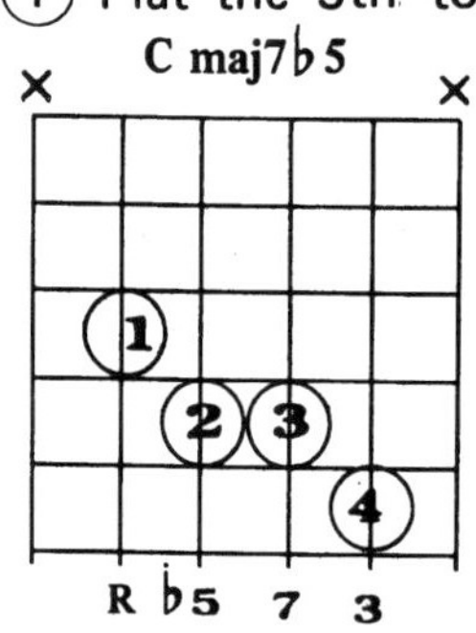

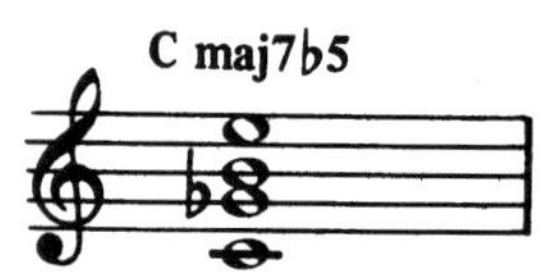

Good "ending" chord for unusual effect. Make sure piano, or other chord instrument, plays b5 along with you—

(Also good substitute chord for D13 —"Try it")

(2) Raise the 5th tone

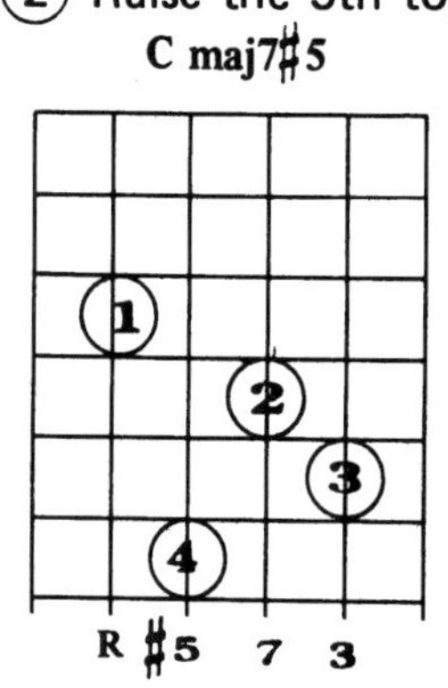

This chord appears as III chord in harmonized harmonic minor scale— In this instance, the scale would be A minor.

(Good chord for special effect.)

(3) Lower 5th tone of dom 7th

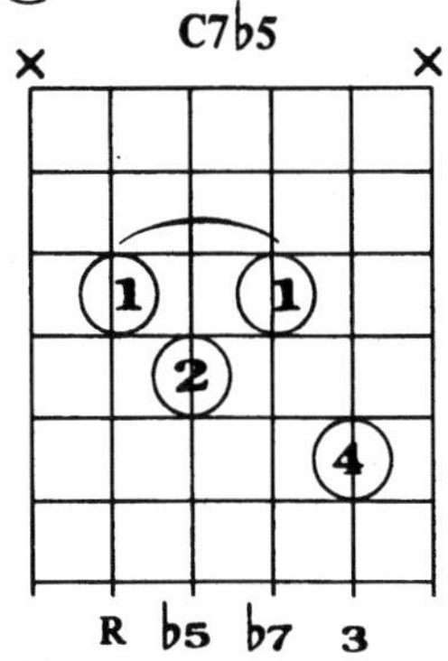

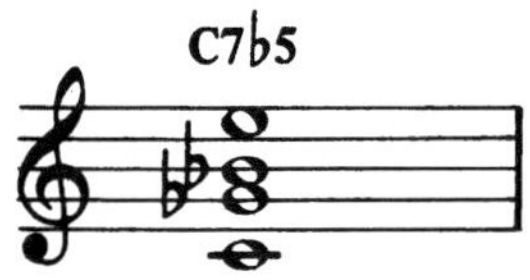

A good resolution chord through circle of 5ths to some form of F chord – (Also analyze as G♭7♭5)

(4) Raise 5th tone of dom. 7th

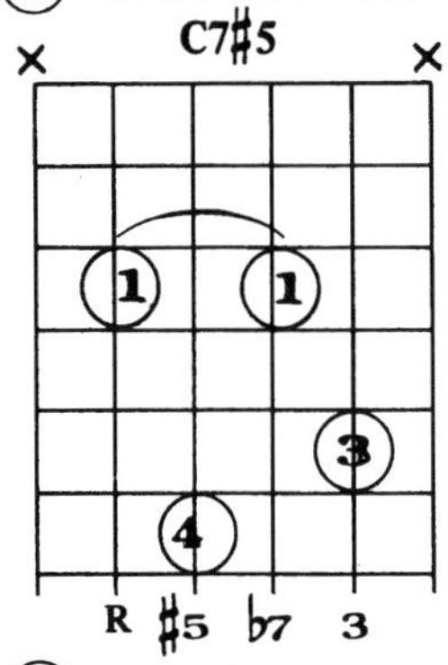

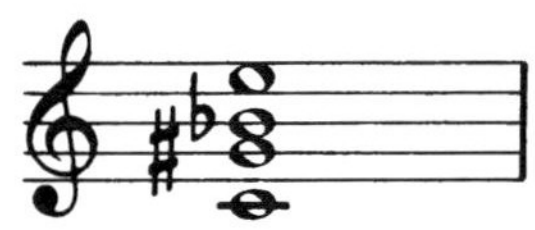

Resolve to F chord or A minor chord in most cases. Theoretically, two inner tones want to resolve to "A".

(5) Add maj7th to minor form

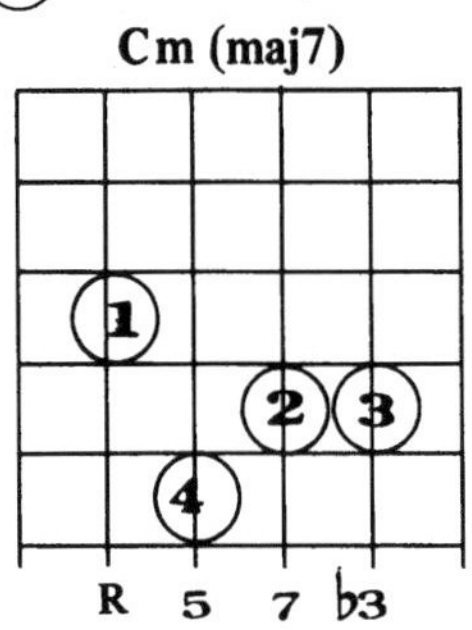

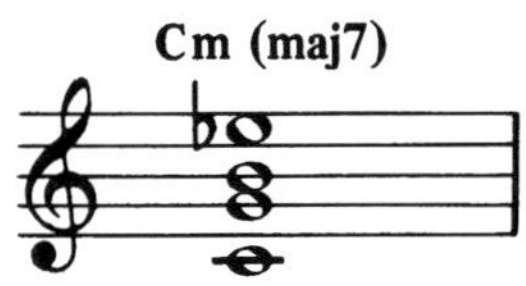

Good addition to the minor triad. Do not use if chord root happens to be in melody of song –

(6) Lower 5th tone of minor 7th

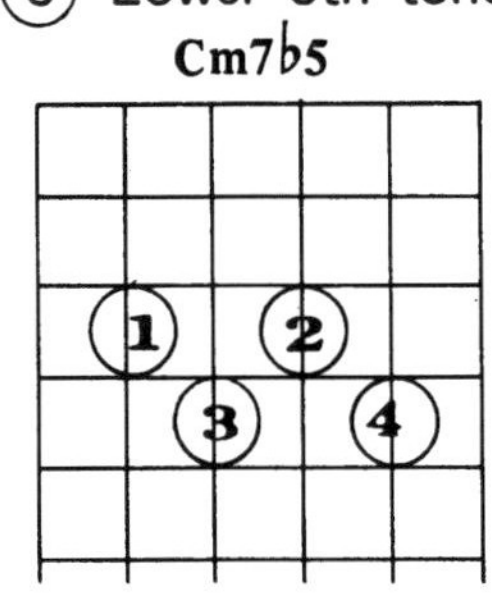

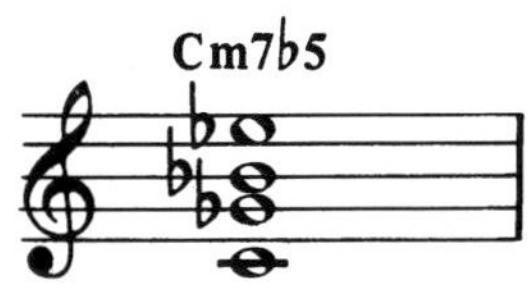

Excellent resolution through C5 to next dom7. (In this case, F7) Notice it is also A♭9, without root, and E♭m6 chord__

(7) Raise the 5th tone of minor7th

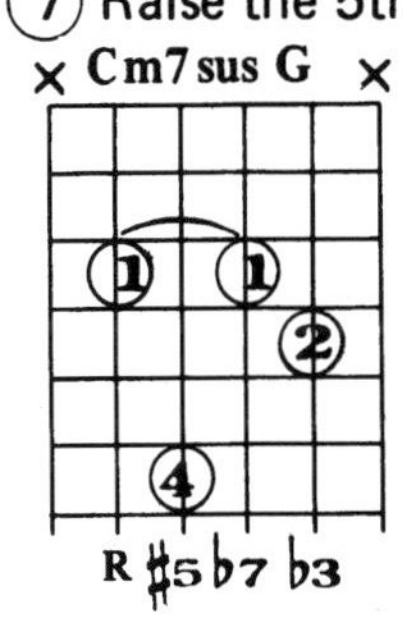

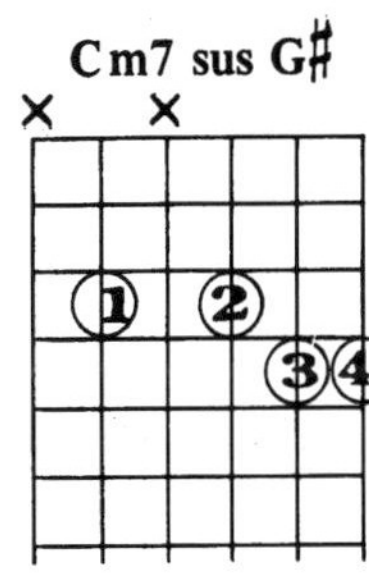

easier to play

Here are five additional alterations using the "C" form. More discussion later on high extensions.

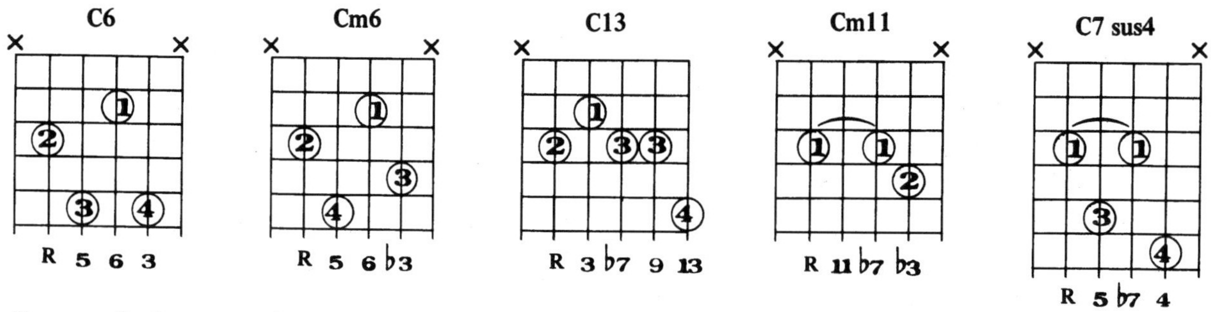

Some of these are hard to finger at first, but will "come along" with practice. They are all worth learning. There are many good uses for these forms.

4th tone and 11th tone are the same note. (an octave apart)

(8) The diminished 7th.

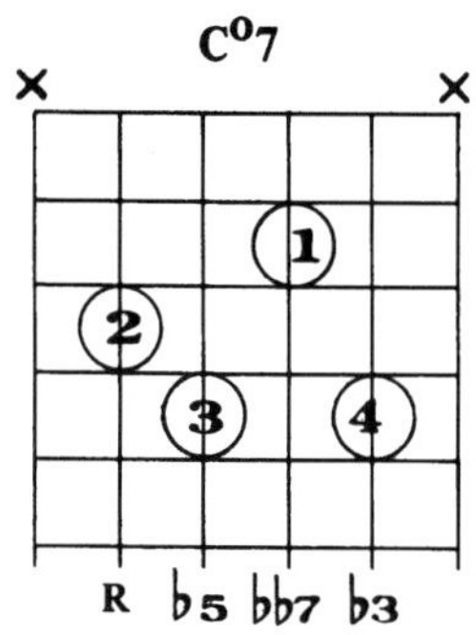

Good chord to use as passing tone between two other close chords— Root can be any note in the chord.

Other forms of the diminished seventh chord

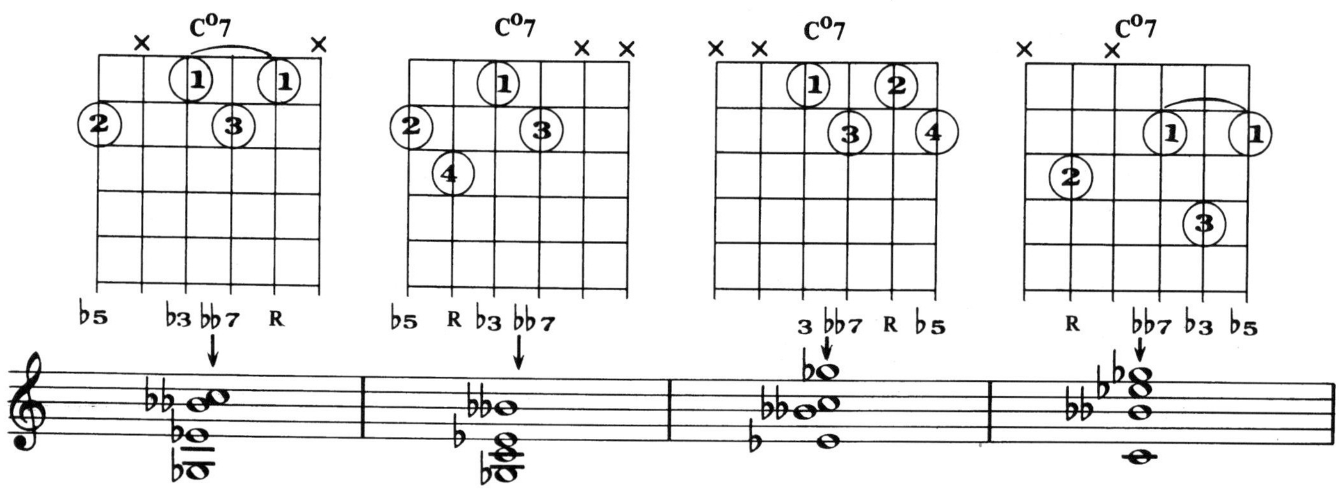

Remember how these repeat themselves every 3rd fret.— Also chord may be called by any of its member tones —.

The Added 6th Chord[to the tonic major and minor triads]

The 6th tone of the scale may be added to either tonic major or minor chords as another interesting, though overworked, color tone— The added 6th does not appear in our regular series of 3rds, until the 2nd octave—It then functions as a 13th chord — (See section on 9ths — 11ths — 13ths).

Example

Added to G triad, gives us G6 chord.

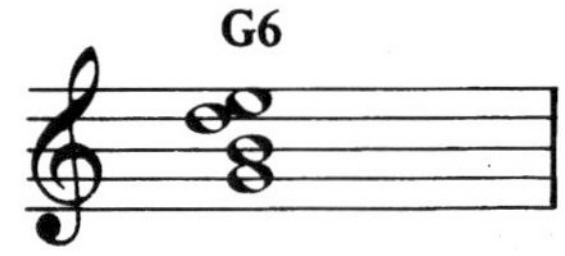

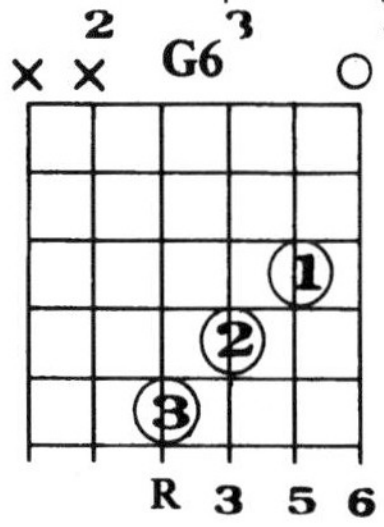

The close interval, of a major 2nd, between the top two notes (D – E) is not disturbing__Needs no support above__

It functions well as an addition to the minor triad__

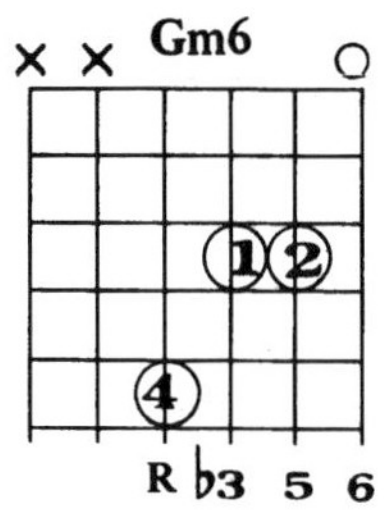

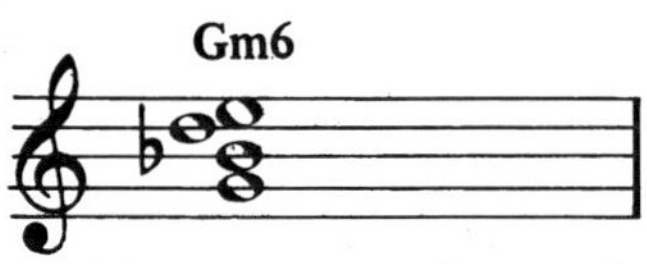

This gives a more resolved feeling to the tonic minor triad.

Also sounds like a 2nd inversion dominant 9th chord built on "C" root, (a 5th below root of m6) also sounds like a 1st inversion m7♭5 chord built on "E" root, (a minor 3rd below root of m6).

Much more on this valuable substitution later.

Good, practical forms of added 6th chord__ (lower 3rd 1/2 step for m6 chord)

Using "C" roots

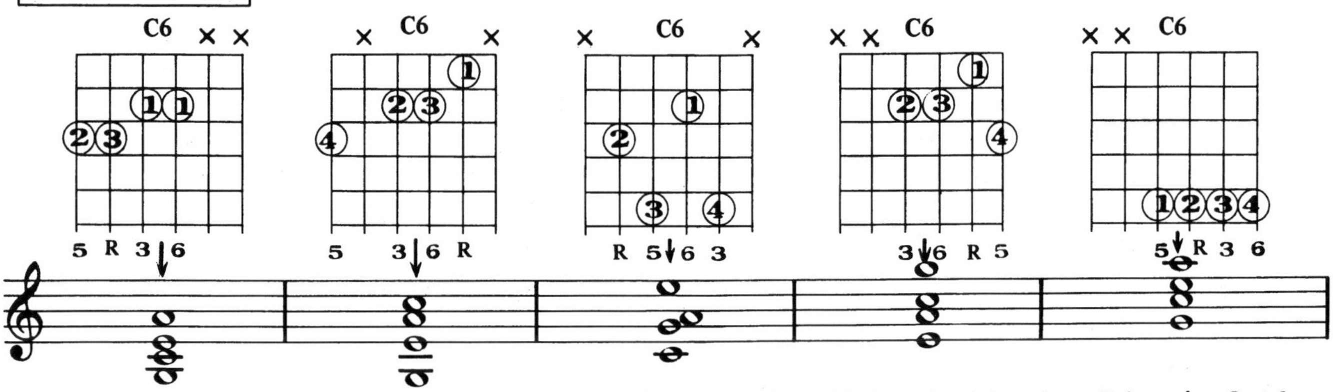

Third chord in this series takes some work. Root may be added to last chord on 5th string 3rd fret. (lower 3rd ½ step for m6 chord)

Using "G" root

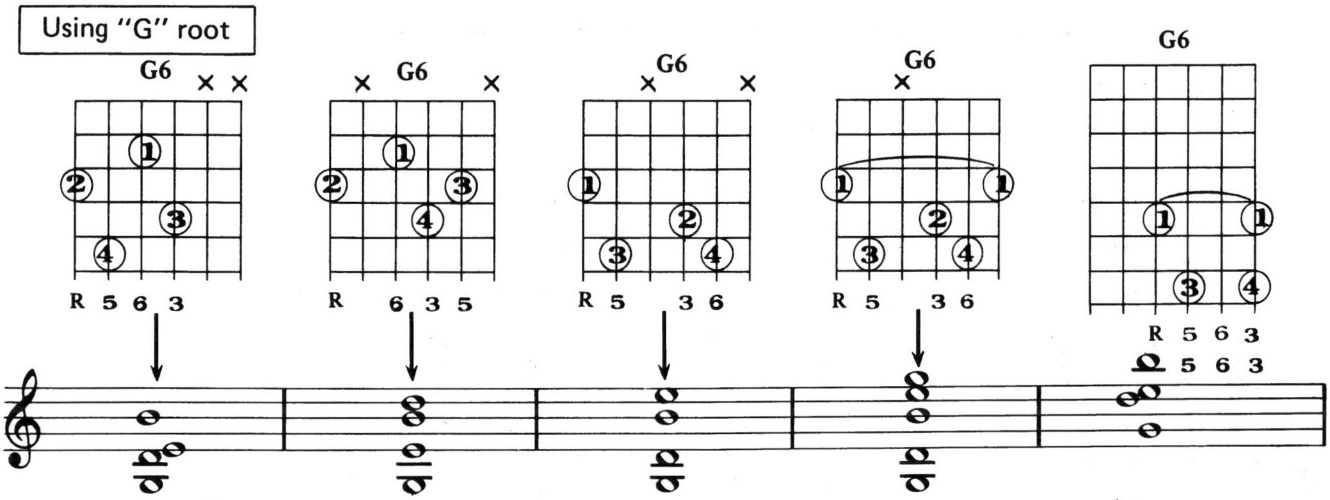

Make sure ④ string does not sound in 3rd and 4th chord of this series – (this note is ♭7 in chord)

6th Chords in closed position available using each series of four strings

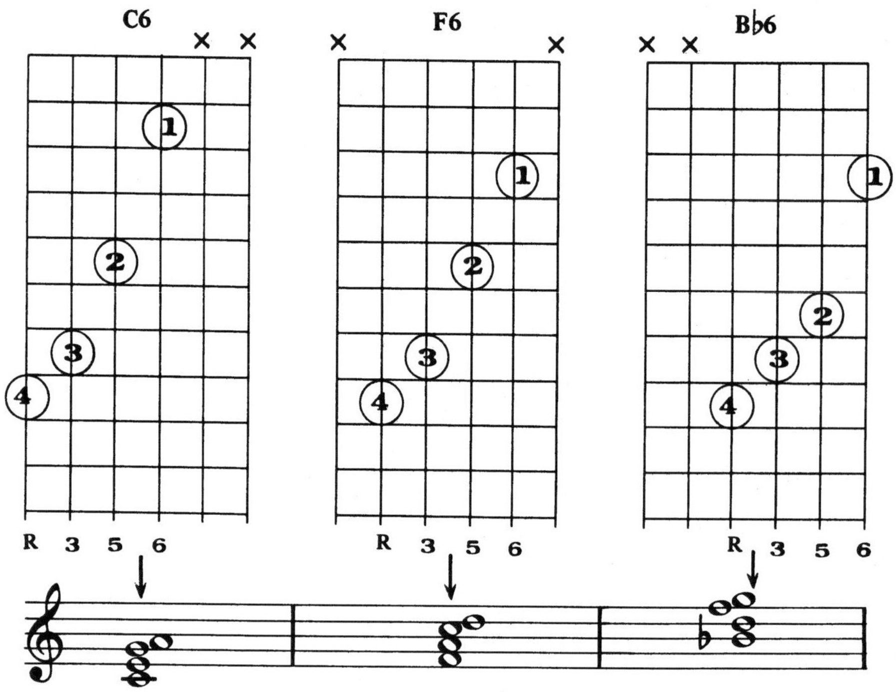

The form on the low four strings is possible, though extremely difficult. The other two forms become easier to play. All of the difficult forms are presented for "what they're worth". They do provide unusual guitar sounds, especially for chord melody playing.

Here's another, smaller, G6 form.

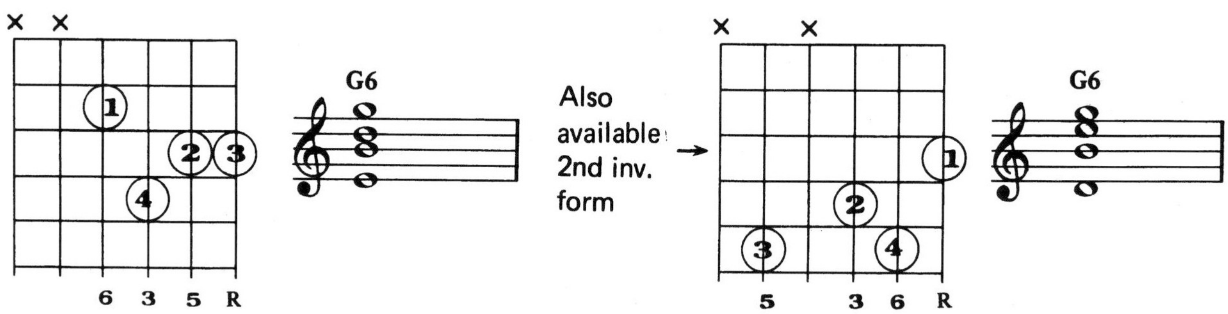

Notice the exact duplication between I6 and vi m7. We will discuss this in detail farther along in the book —

Use of added 6th, with 7 and ♭7 in a rather common progression of chords

Using "C" roots

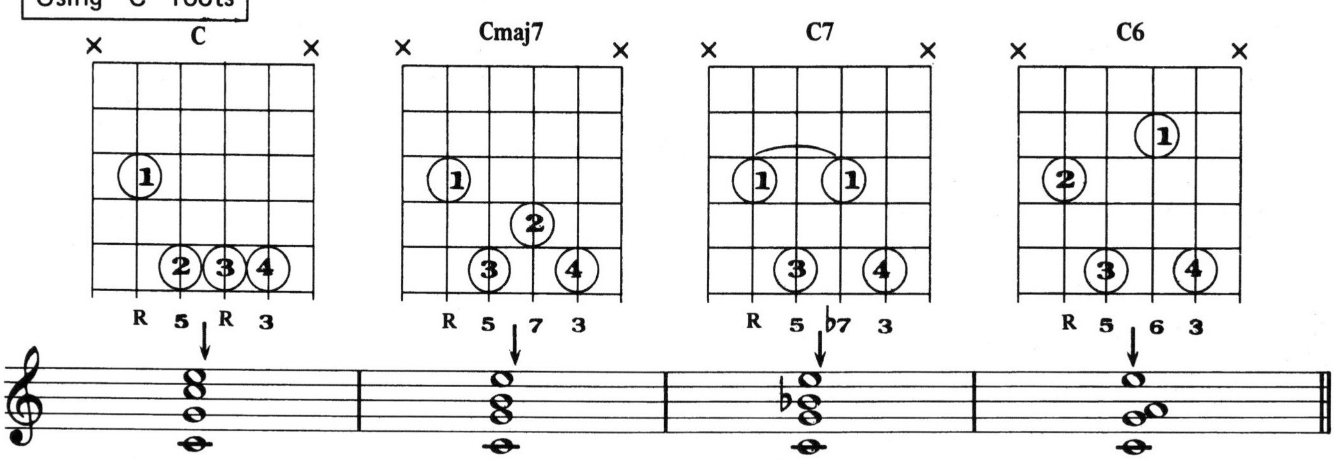

Notice the descending chromatic line in the second voice implies a melody—This provides interesting color if you have a succession of tonic chords—This device works well on both major and minor tonic Chords – Analyze melody of song before using this pattern in order to avoid conflicts with melody of song—

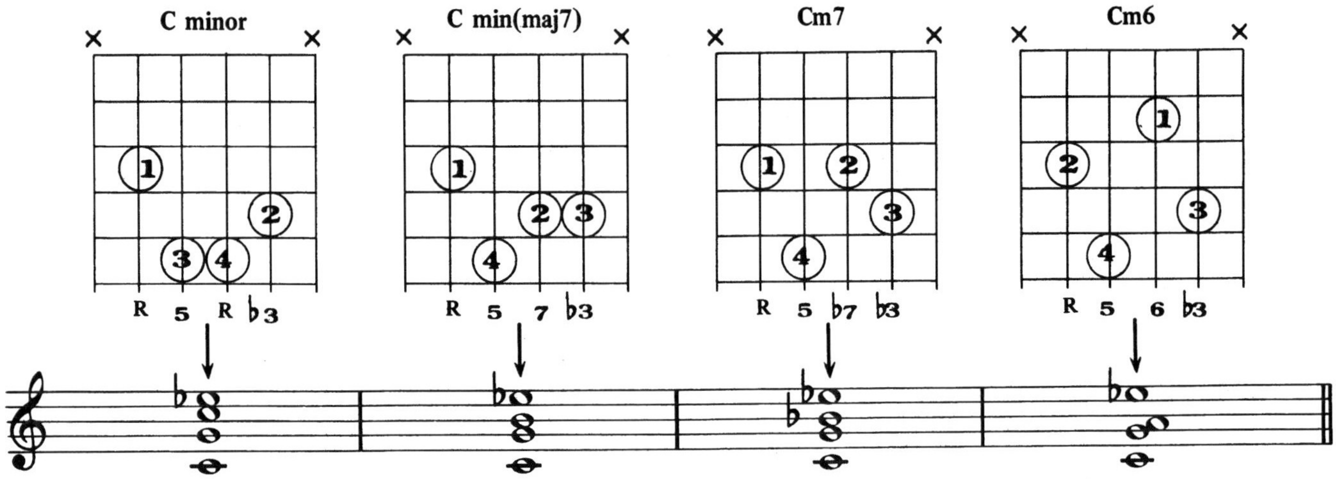

Same progression using "G" roots—

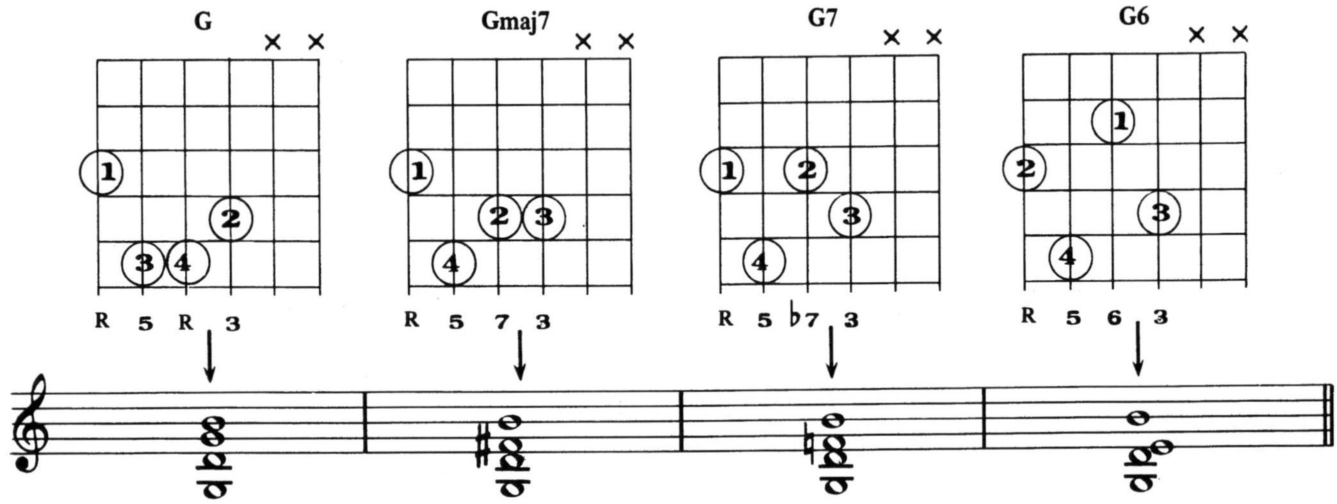

Same descending chromatic line in the second voice under the melody – works well on major – Gm6 is difficult using above pattern—Example below presents a more practical fingering using minor form – last chord eliminates double 5th and makes fingering easier—<u>Do not "sound" 1st string</u>—

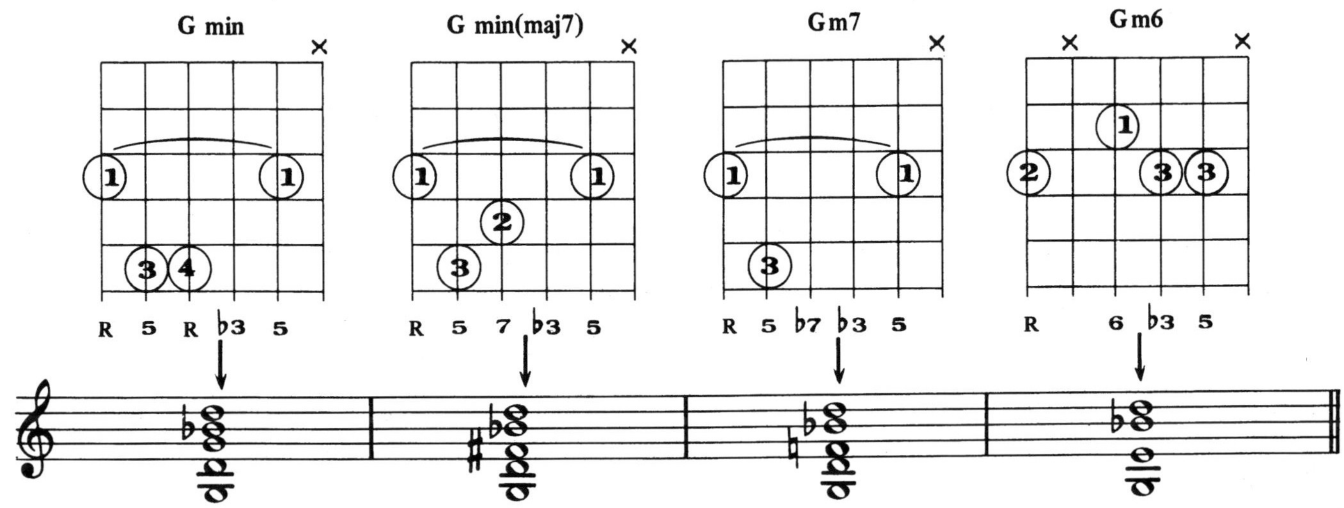

Additional forms of the minor with added major 7th

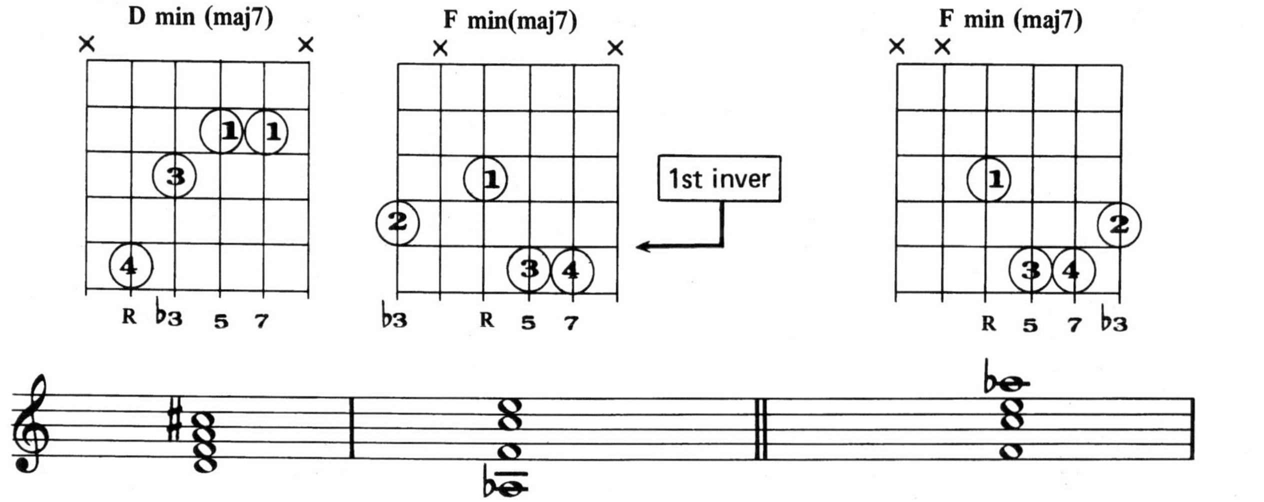

Note the relationship between the upper three notes of this chord (♭3 – 5 – 7– to the augmented triad built on the root of the relative major chord. Using this concept for substitutions provides some unusual opportunities for movement.

Example (using F+ as Sub. for Dm maj7)

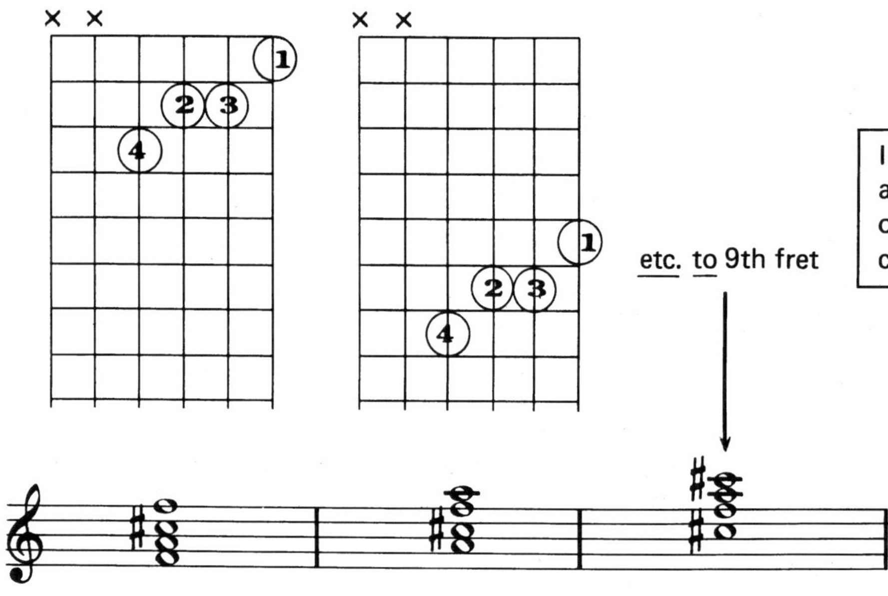

Inner string forms may be utilized also— This provides movement opportunities without getting into complicated fingerings—

9TH—11TH—13TH CHORDS

Three additional scale tones may be utilized to complete our chord nomenclature—These tones are found through an extension of the scale by another five tones beyond the octave—

These extensions are easy to remember. The 9th tone is one whole step above the root; the 11th is the same as the 4th; the 13th is the same as the 6th—

If we add another 3rd to our 7th chord, we have a 9th chord

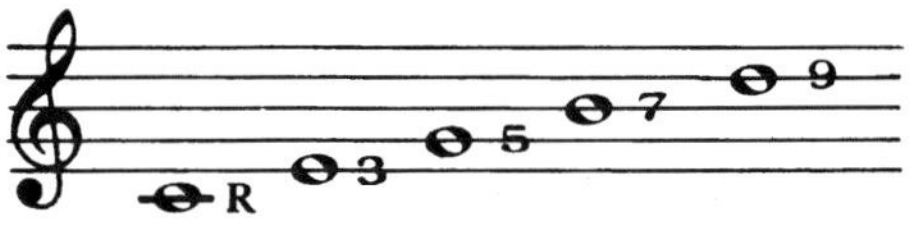

The ninth itself may appear in three forms.

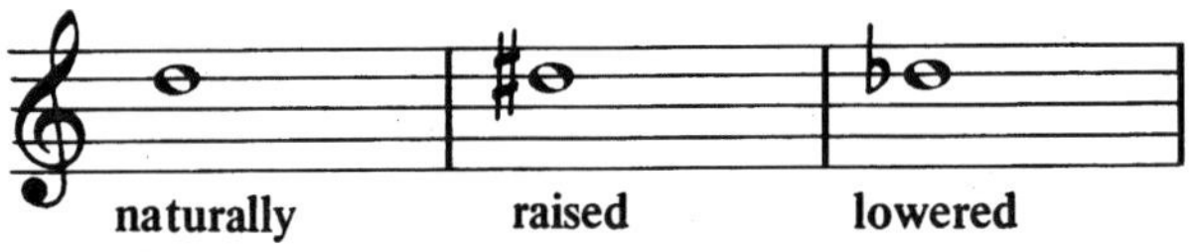

It must have the seventh, in some form, for support. Added to a basic triad, it becomes a suspension:

Example:

Let's look at various kinds of 9th chords— How they are symbolized, and the nature of the other tones in the chord.

Ⓐ C9 – R – 3 – 5 – ♭7 – 9
Ⓑ C7 ♭9 – R – 3 – 5 – ♭7 – ♭9
Ⓒ C7 ♯9 – R – 3 – 5 – ♭7 – ♯9

These are the forms of the dominant 9th chord, built by adding the 9th to the dominant 7th chord— Two other alterations would be possible if we alter the 5th tone in either direction. Each form above would give us 9 dominant 9th chords—

As follows:

Ⓓ Cmaj9 – R – 3 – 5 – 7 – 9
Ⓔ C6/9 – R – 3 – 5 – 6 – 9

As follows: 5ths could be altered, but with care—

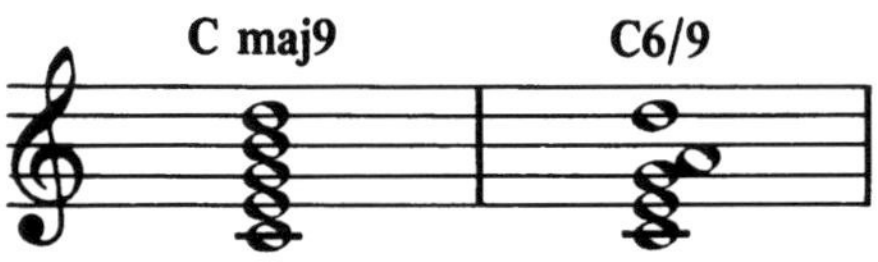

Ⓕ Cm9 – R – ♭3 – 5 – ♭7 – 9
Ⓖ Cm9♭5 – R – ♭3 – ♭5 – ♭7 – 9
Ⓗ Cm6/9 – R – ♭3 – 5 – 6 – 9 } 5th tone alterations possible
Ⓘ Cm 9maj7– R – ♭3 – 5 – 7 – 9

As follows:

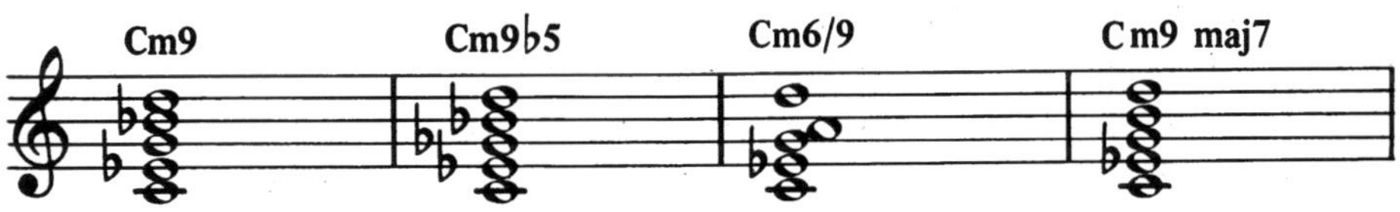

The complete 5 note 9th chords are not always possible— Most suitable voicing for guitar eliminates either 5th or root tone—Very few forms of the 9th are available in closed position—

Lets take a look at the forms available on the guitar fingerboard—

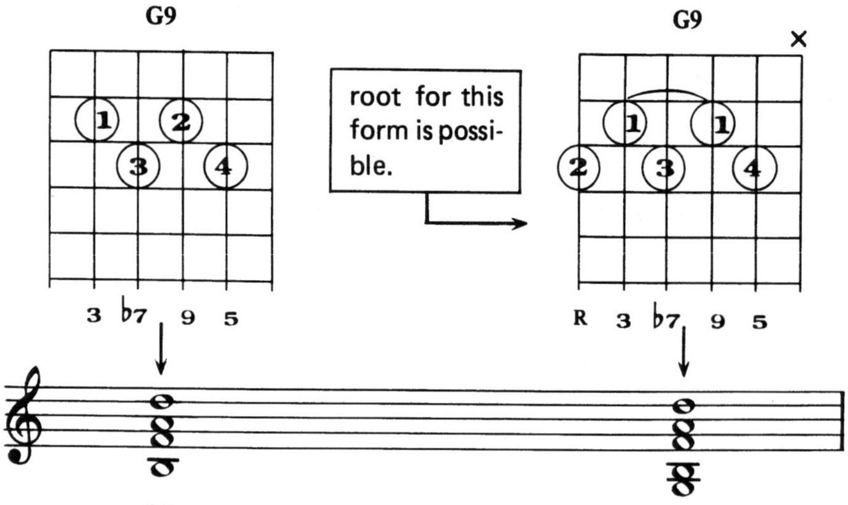

The form without the root is best form for altering. G9♭5 or G9+5 would be easily available with 2nd form—also—

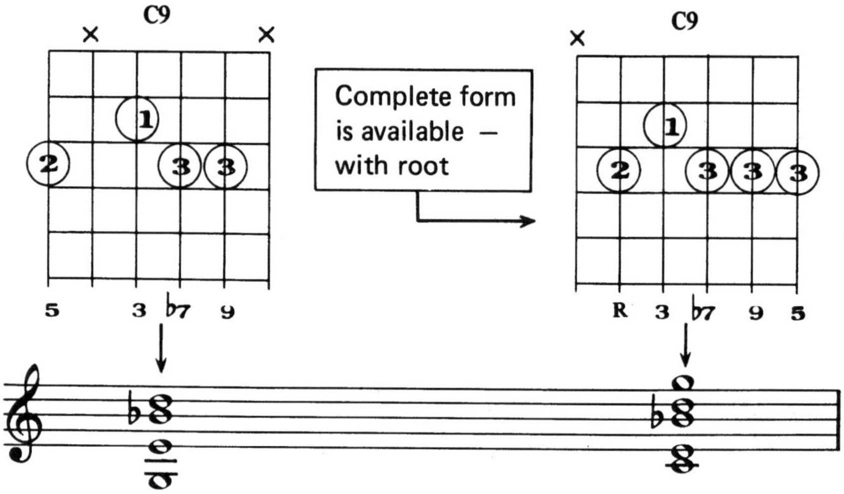

The form without root is best for alterations—

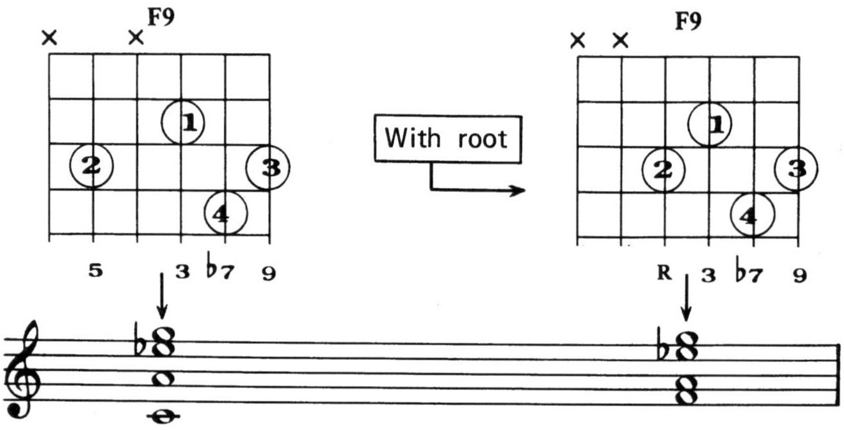

The previous three 9th forms will cover most any situation at any place on the fingerboard. Almost all alterations are possible. Try some of them

With higher extensions it becomes most important to remind you of the sounding range of the guitar – don't add the 9th tone on the lower strings – unless for special effect—

Dominant 9th Chords Across the Board [Incomplete forms with root and no fifth]

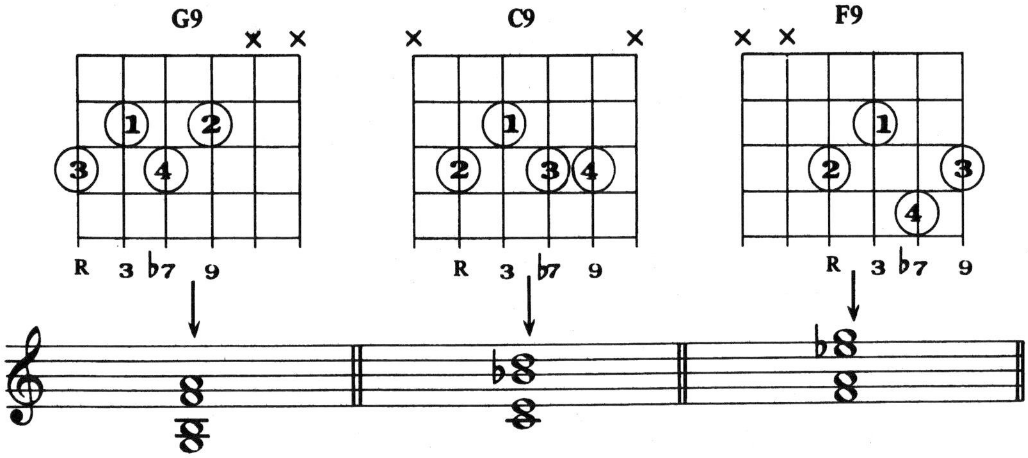

Each form will transform to minor 9, to 7♭ 9, and to 7 ♯9, Try them all with alterations—

Here's a good, closed position dom. 9th using the top three strings open –

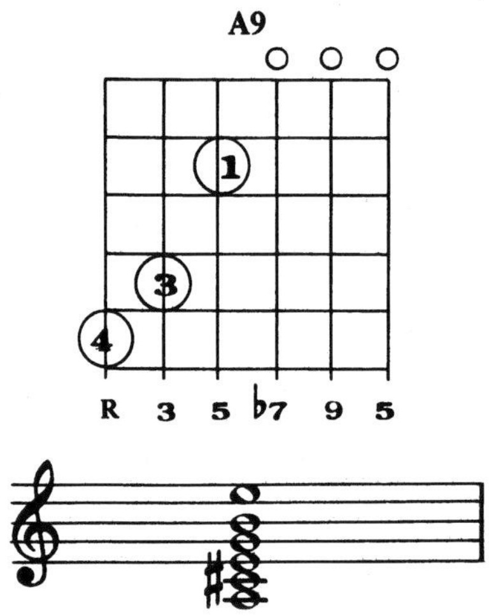

This is a beautiful sounding 9th— Cannot be moved, due to acute fingering problem.

> There are many chordal possibilities using open strings with position fingerings which will be discussed in section titled "Open string possibilities".

Some Alterations on the Dom. 9th chord

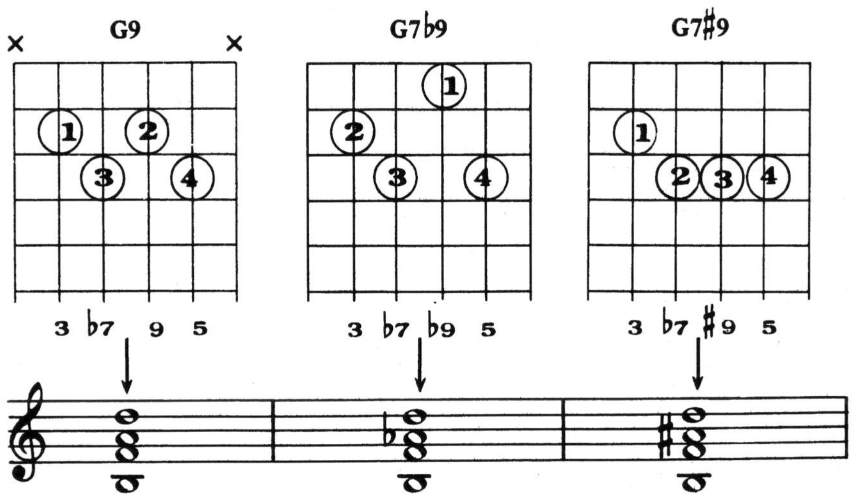

The 5th tone may be raised or lowered on each of these chords – Giving you six more forms G 9+5; G9♭ 5; G7♭ 9+5; G7 ♭9 ♭5; G7♯ 9+5 G7♯ 9♭ 5

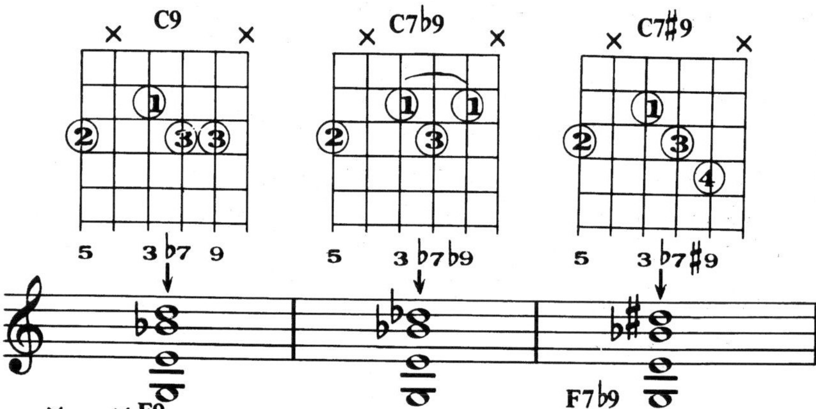

The 5th tone may be raised or lowered on these— (+5 gets a little shaky) ♭5 will give you forms which will resemble G♭7 chord— Try them.

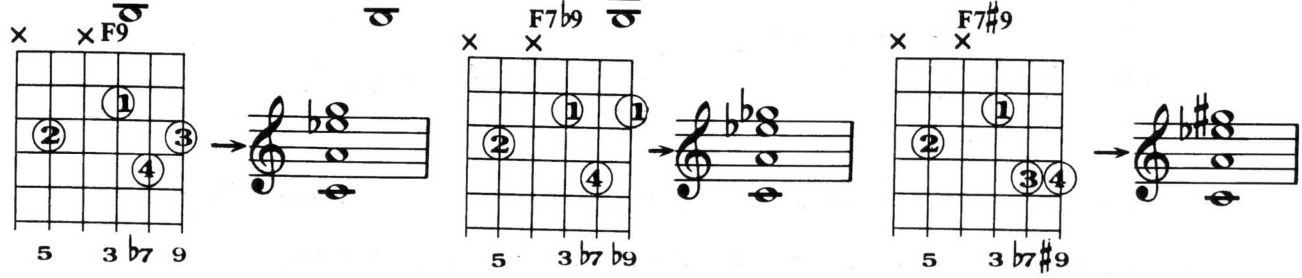

The 7♭9 chord in a series, across the board.

G7♭9 **[will be Dim.7th chords except where root is included]**

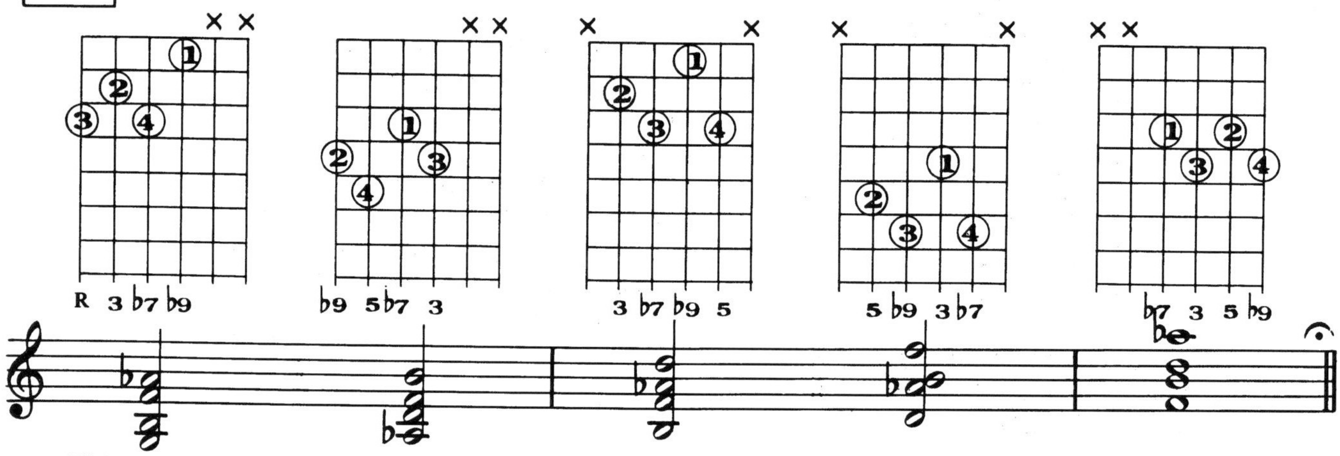

This can be done other ways— This fingering keeps you within a short fret span – covers all melodic possibilities—First chord is only one with root included. [6 fret span]

C7♭9

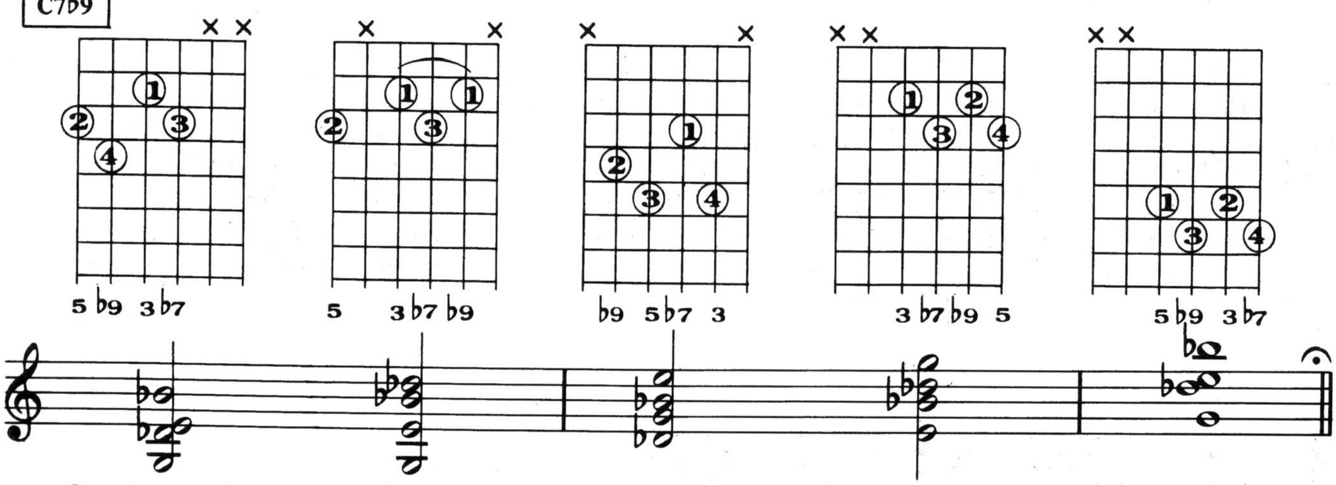

Spacing on 2nd chord does not conform, but enables us to keep series in a 5 fret span. No root included – covers all melodic possibilities—

Theoretically, the ninth tone is possible in almost any position in the chord — It is best when it is above the root of the chord — however, even this is possible if handled carefully —

Ex: Different voicing possibilities — (closed positions)

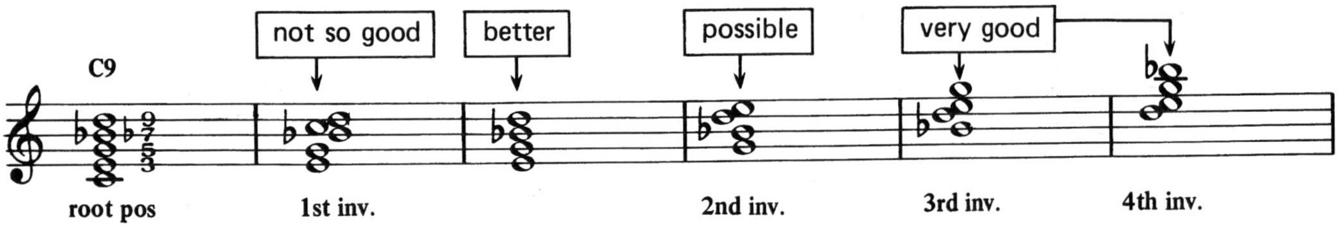

The 9th and the 3rd tones placed next to each other is a good voicing consideration. Just remember that this combination needs support above — 5th or 7th — some of these are possible on the guitar —

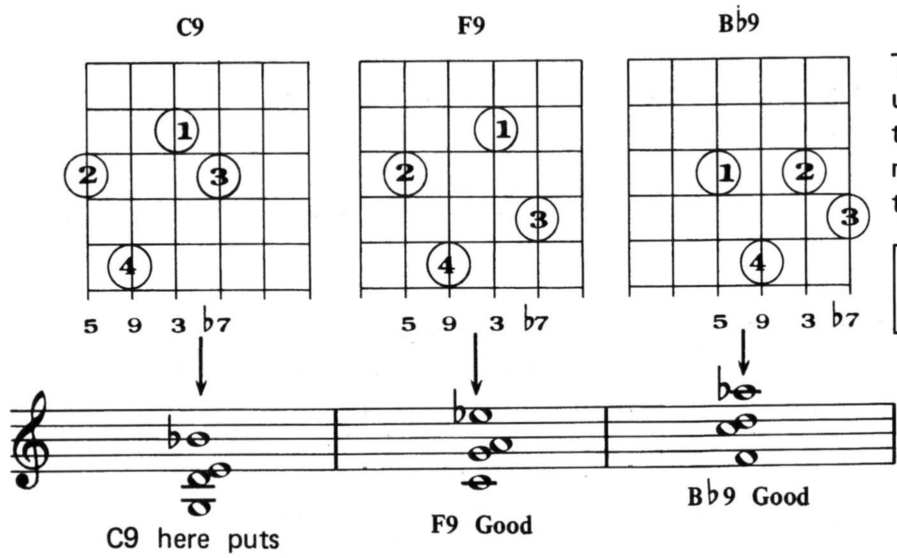

C9 here puts
9th tone too low.
handle carefully.

These three have the same tonal set-up with 9th and 3rd adjacent. Use the 1st one with care — It becomes more functional as it moves up the fingerboard.

Some transformations are possible! Try then —

Smaller forms of 9th — easier to play

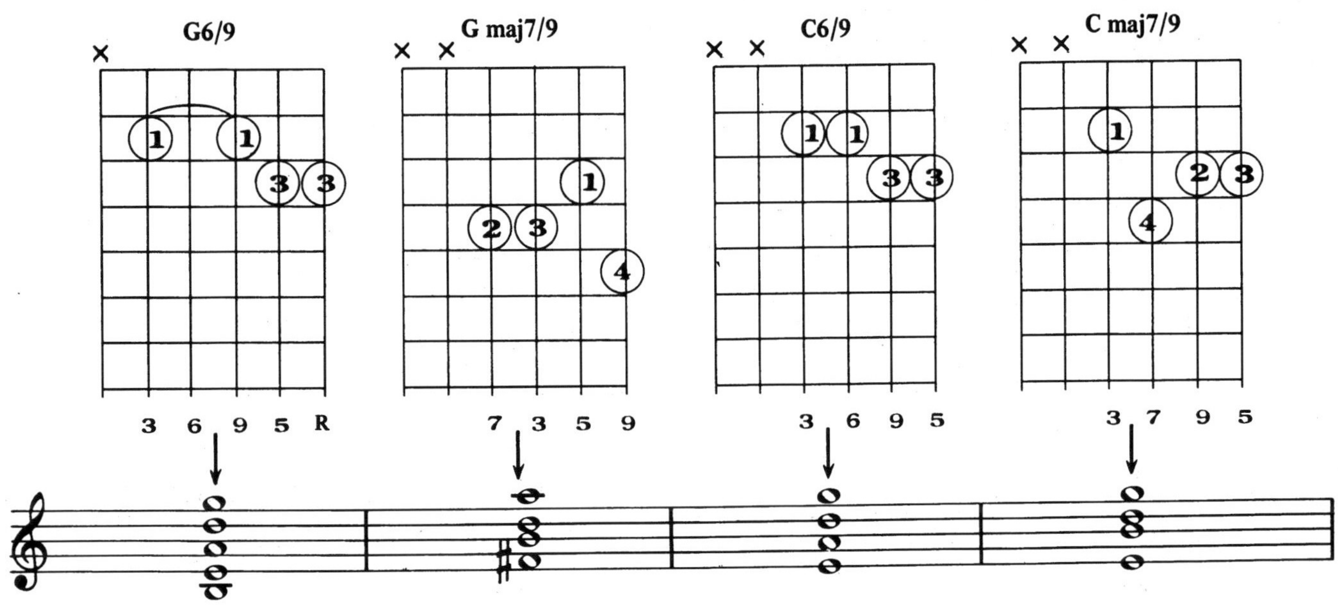

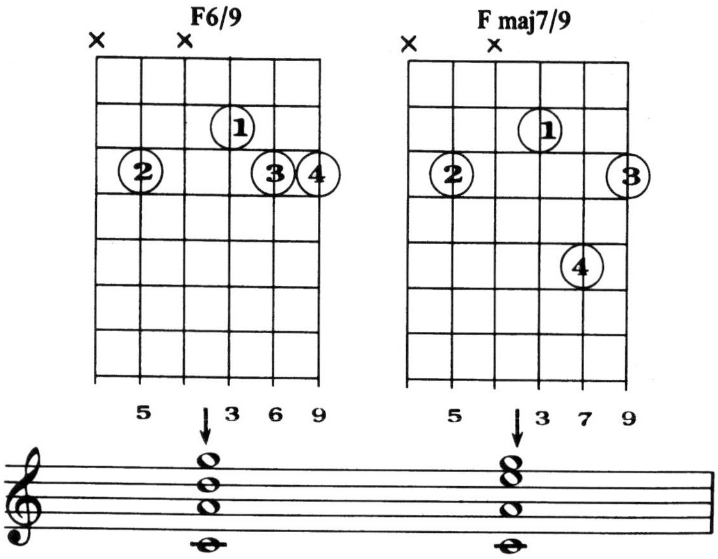

Note root above ninth in G6/9 form – good sounding due to interval construction – (use of 4ths) note similarity of maj7/9 forms to iii m7 – good for substitution purposes__ Root of "F" form available by moving 2nd finger across to 4th string (same fret)

These are good forms for "comping" – are also good as arpeggios and very good for chord solo purposes__ Remember__ Learn the tonal functions of the notes contained in each chord. Transformations are possible__ Try them__

There are some very good, closed position, 9th forms available. Most of these are hard to finger, but are possible.

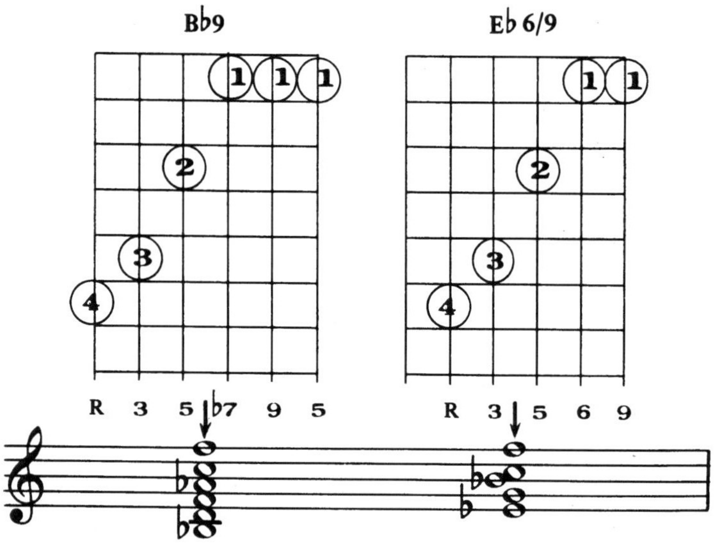

These are possible, but need a lot of practice. If you like, just eliminate the root tone, and refinger the chord – you then have a 1st inversion form on the fingerboard. [Bass player can easily supply root] Remember, these are possible.

They would not be good rhythm chords –

Let's look at some more of the large forms in open position (1st__ using the "F" barre form)

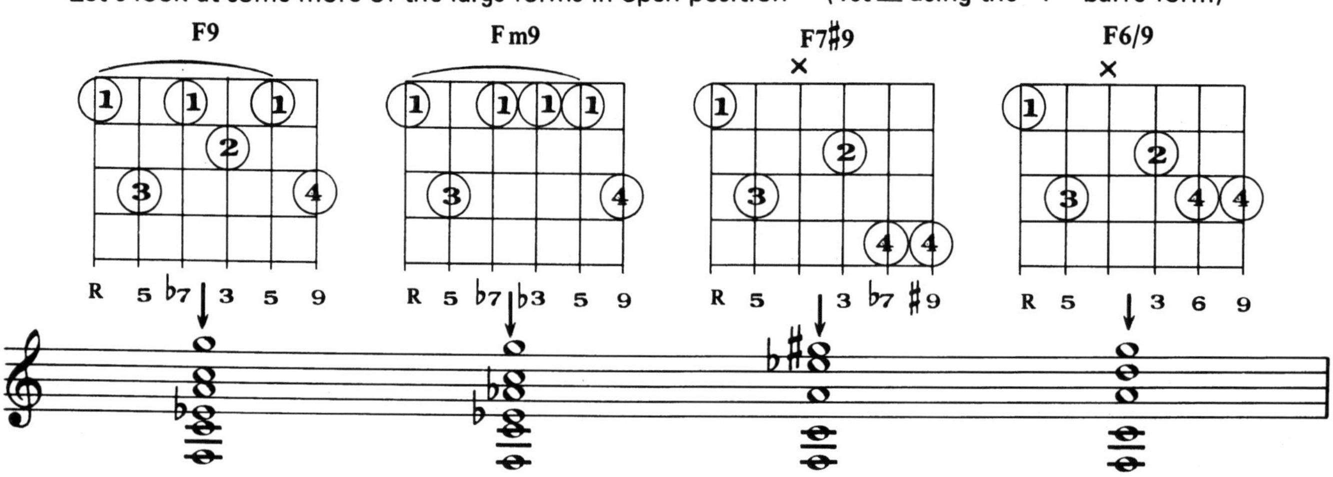

Larger forms of the 9th chord (cont'd)

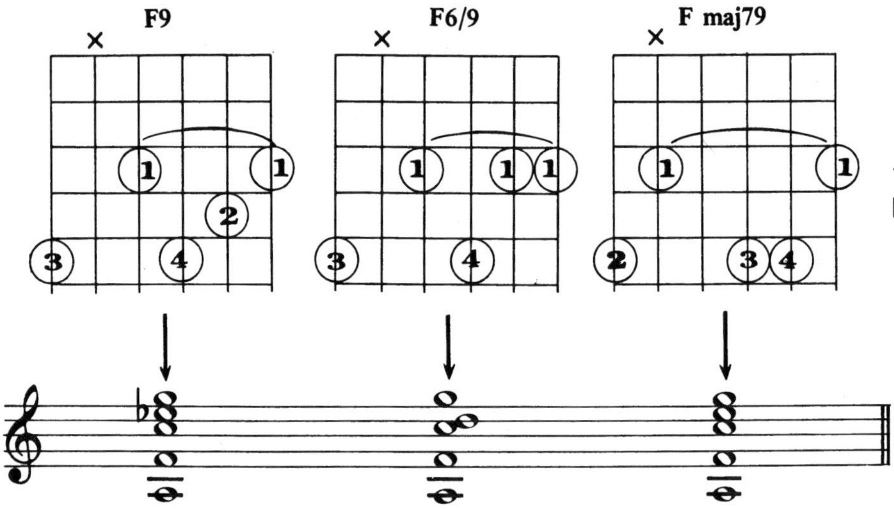

All 1st inversion forms – (3rd tone in bass) note 10th form as bottom three notes—

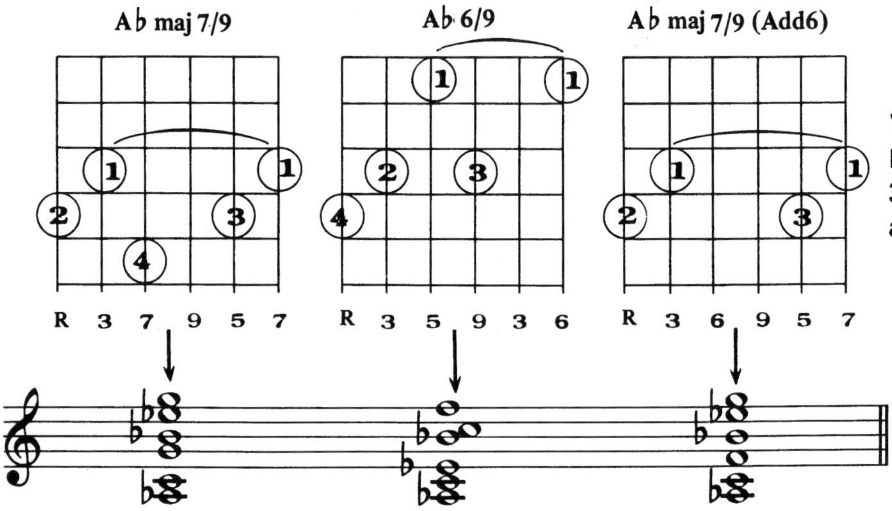

Very rich texture in these forms – Notice doubled tones in 1st two – 3rd form has major 7 and 6 tone along with 9th—

These are not good for rhythm purposes— They are good for sustained effects as ballad accompaniments, and are good for intros, modulations, and endings—

More large forms (using "C" root) – note the use of the thumb to make fingering possible –

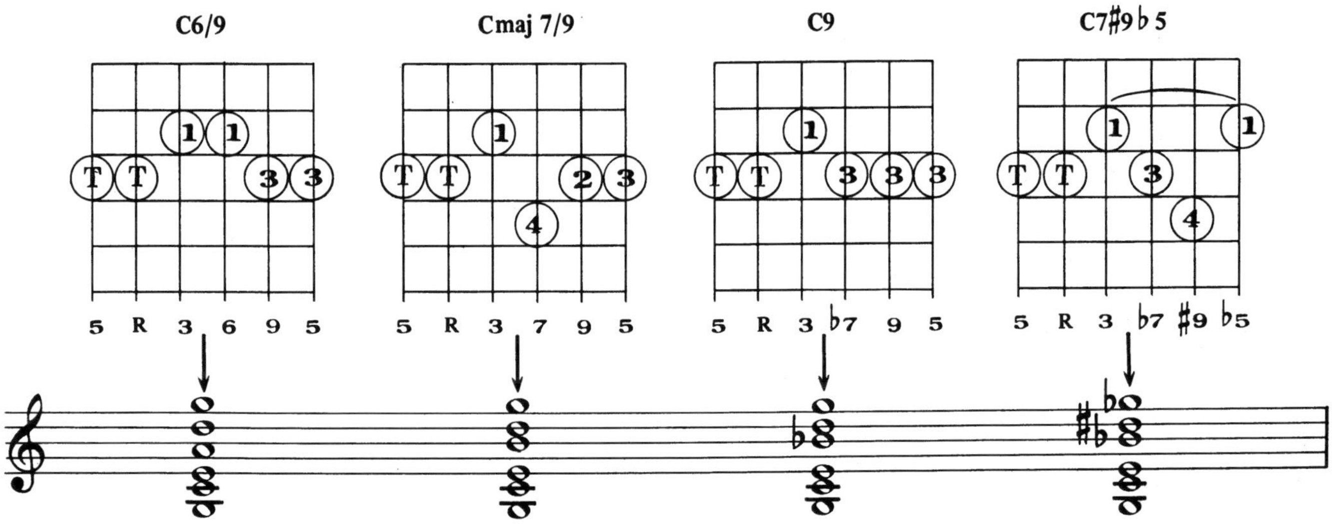

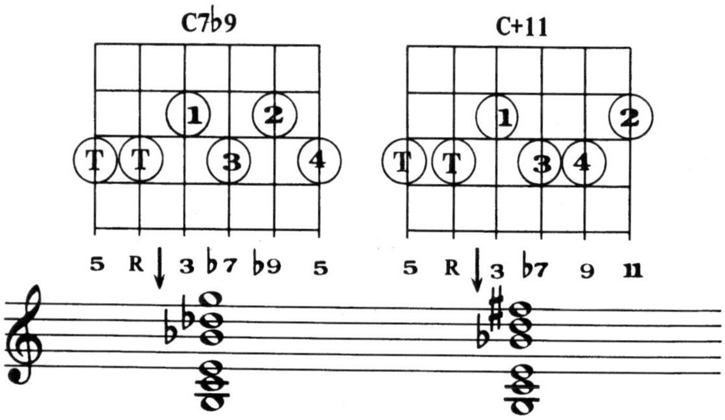

I've included the +11 with these forms because of presence of 9th in chord and because of use of the thumb__ These forms have value which make them worth the learning effort__ They are excellent for special effects, good for "chord-harmonics"__

Example of usage:

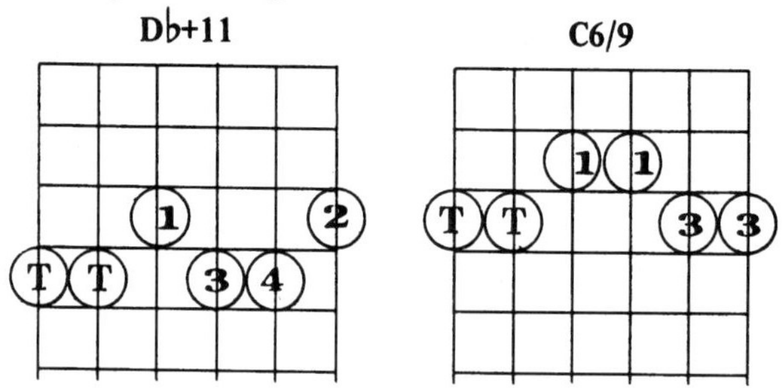

For V-I ending, this is a beautiful substitution__

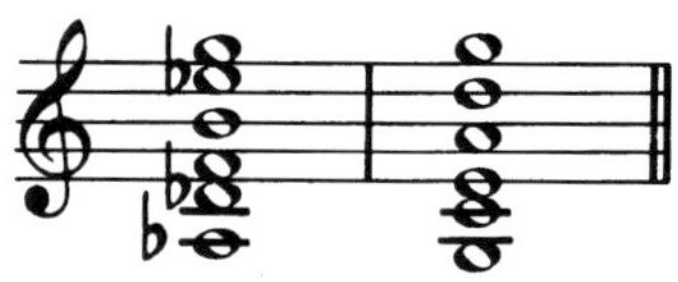

try as harmonics

Another "Closed-Form" – this time an altered 9th [notice how smoothly it resolves]

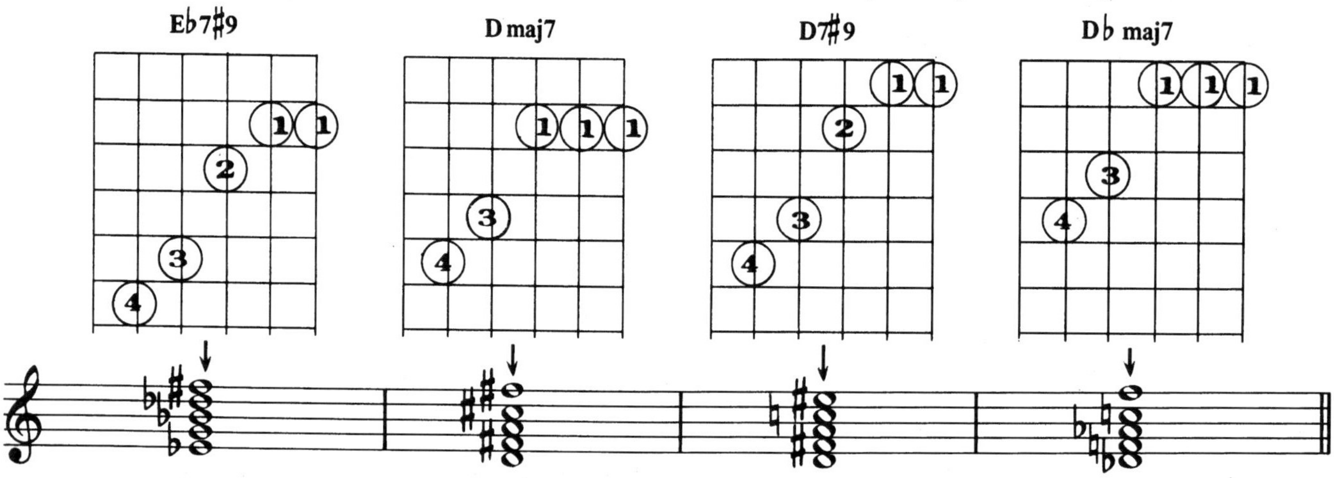

Listen to this ♯9 move into a tonic 6/9.

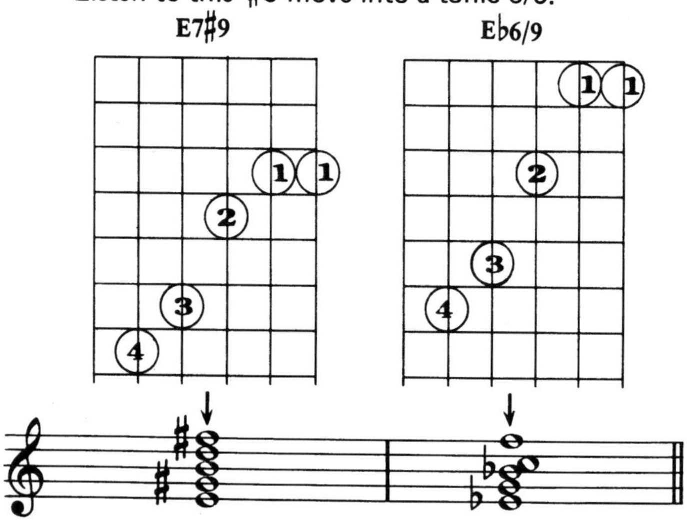

These fingerings are not easy – with practice, they <u>are</u> <u>possible</u> and provide excellent sounding chords__

Dominant 9th chords may be transformed to min9 chords. Simply lower the major 3rd one fret — Try this on all previous 9th chords —

For example :

Note all three forms without root included. Transformation to min9, via 3 also gives you major 7th form on root a minor 3rd above the root of the dom.9 chord This is a good device for substitution purposes.

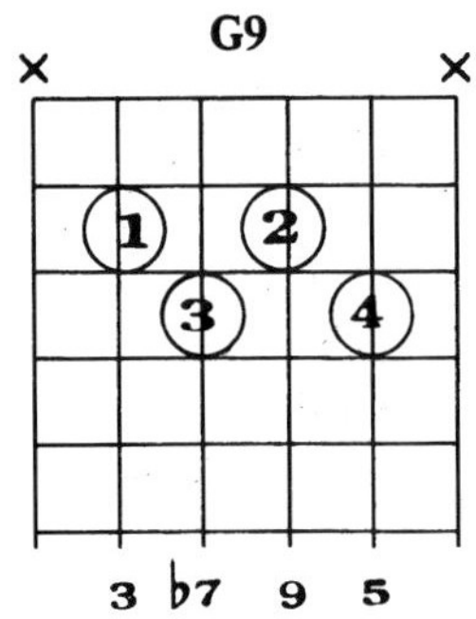

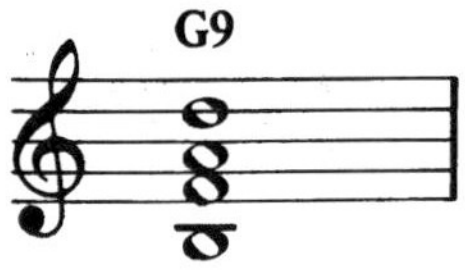

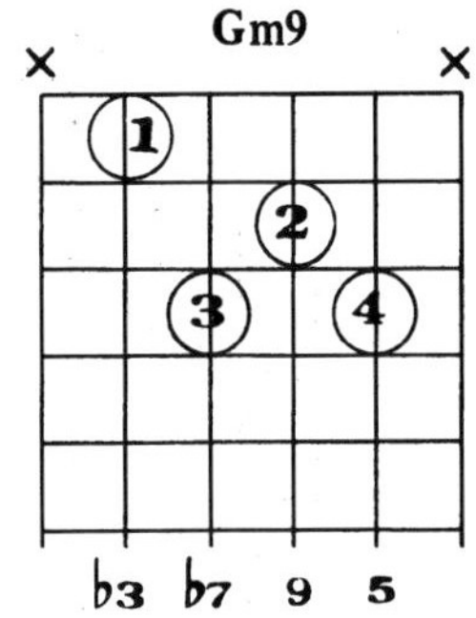

Also B♭ maj7 root pos.

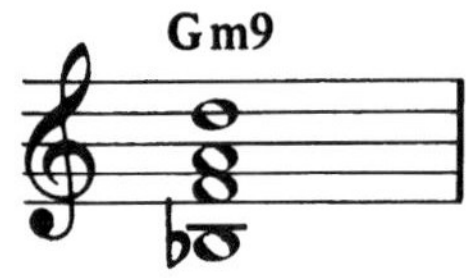

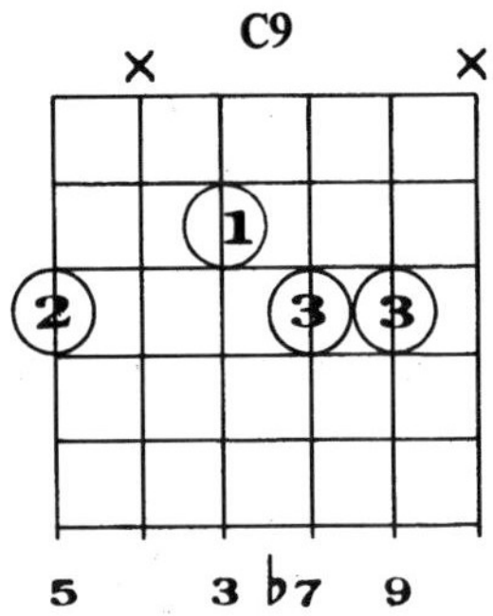

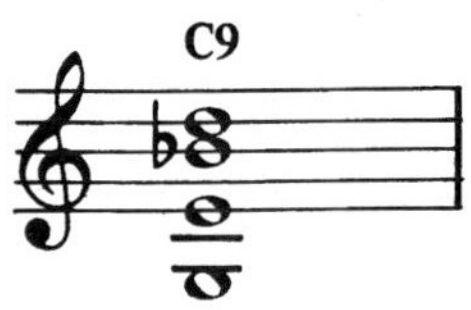

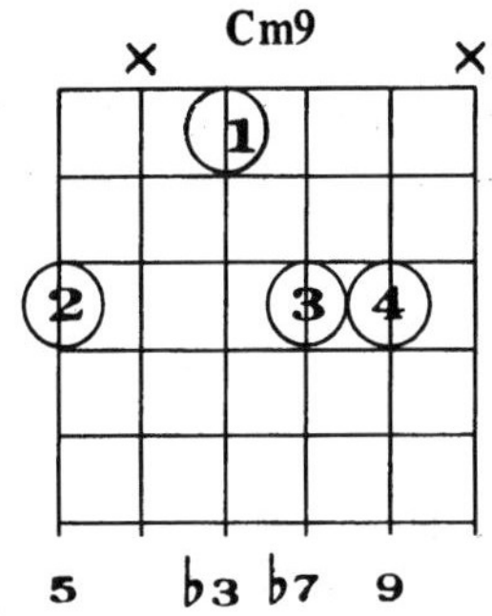

Also E♭ maj7 1st. inversion

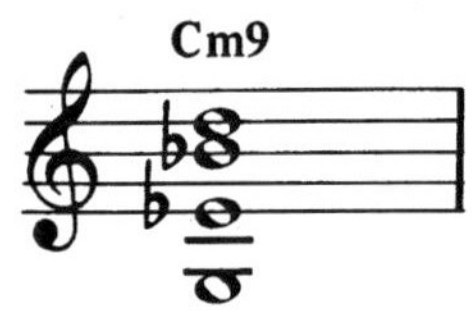

Make alterations on previous 9th forms — some will work — some won't.

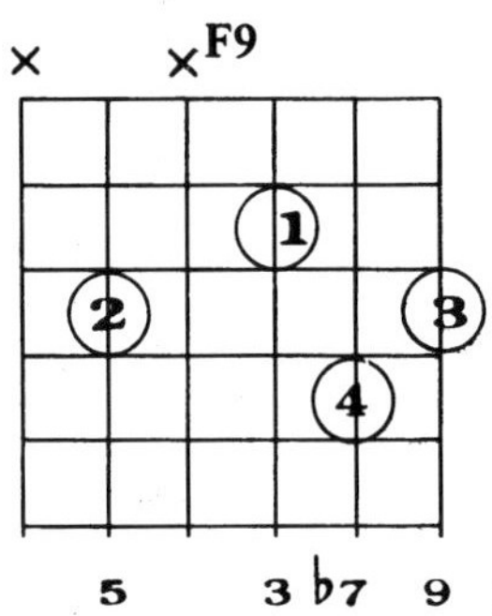

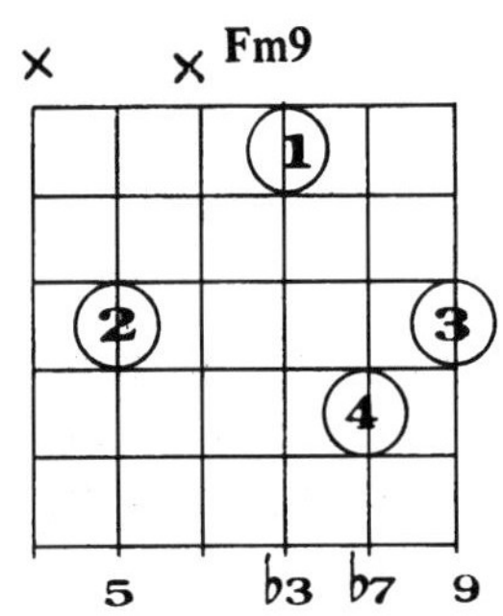

Also A♭maj7 1st inversion

Minor 9th forms — cont'd

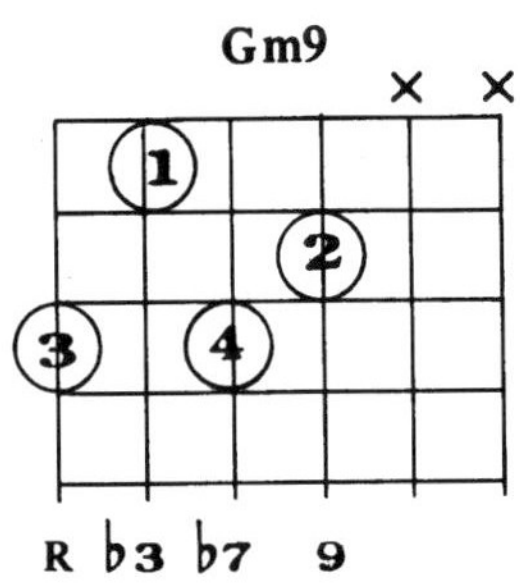

This is a good "low" form, utilizing the bottom 4 strings. Transforms to m6/9 nicely.

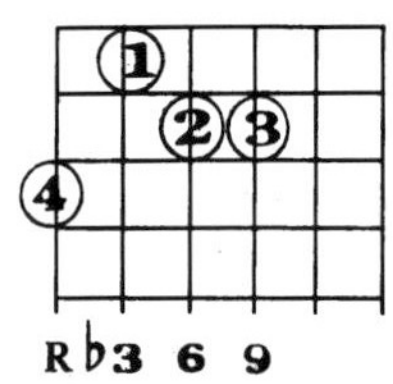

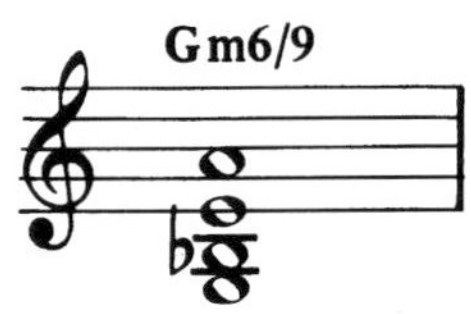

Previous Cm9 transforms to min6/9 also —

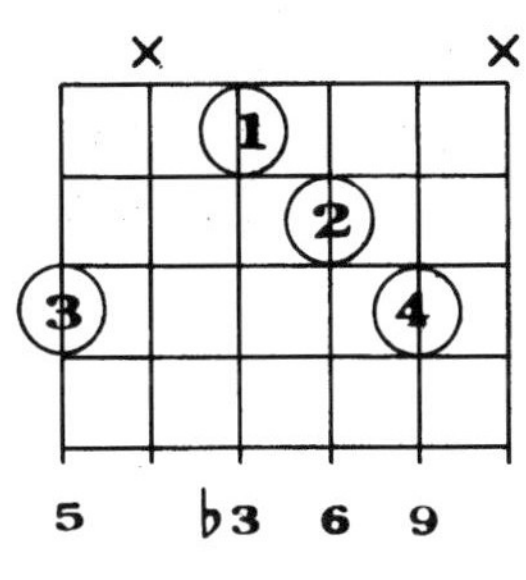

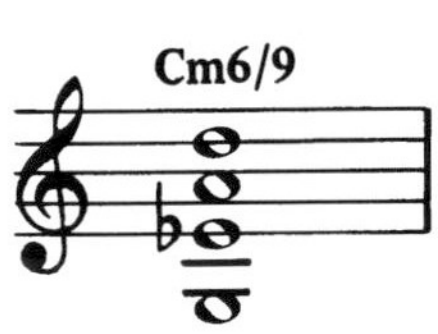

Move 3rd finger across to (5) string if you want root in chord —

Think of this in relation to E♭ root – it then becomes E♭maj7♭5 (1st inversion) (good for substitutions)

Ebm6/9

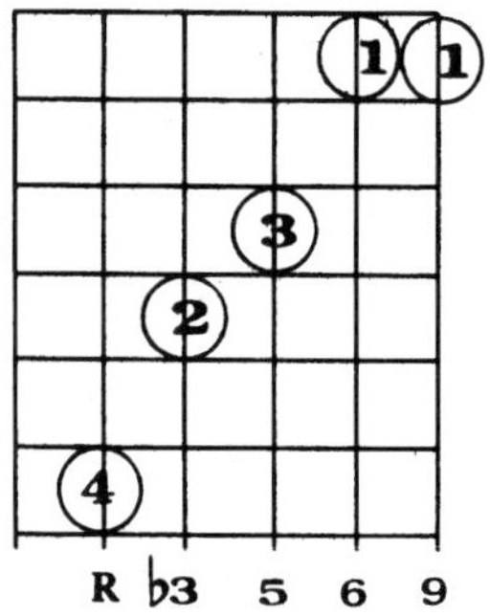

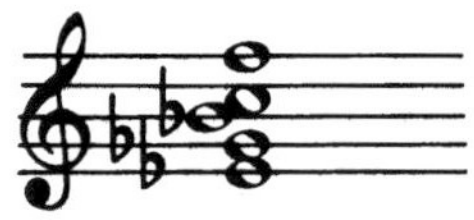

Here's one involving quite a stretch – It's possible and practical__ A beautiful, closed position voicing – [also works with Ab as implied root – an Ab13 with the chord 5th included.]

There are many possibilities, via alterations on any of the forms you know__Remember the importance of knowing, and understanding, tonal functions__

Two good forms of minor 9th chord (Actually a suspension; doesn't include minor 7)

In open position

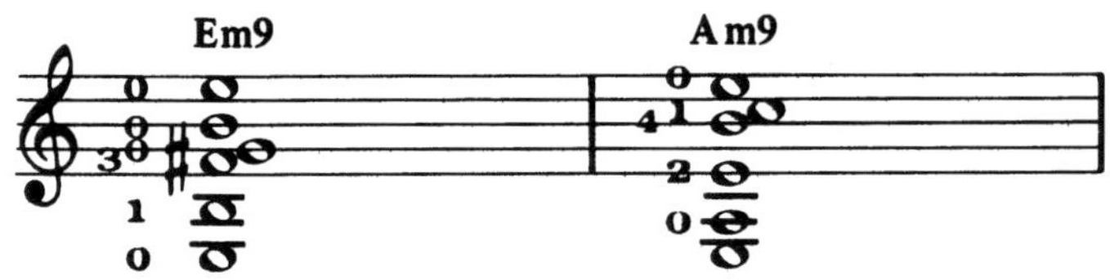

The minor second interval in both of these forms give these chords a unique sound. Em9 may be fingered 2-4.

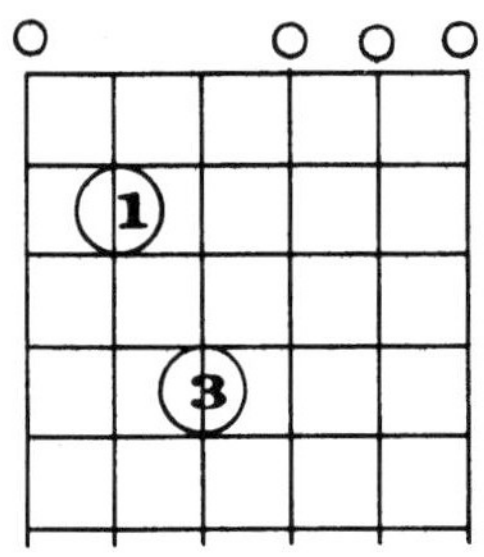

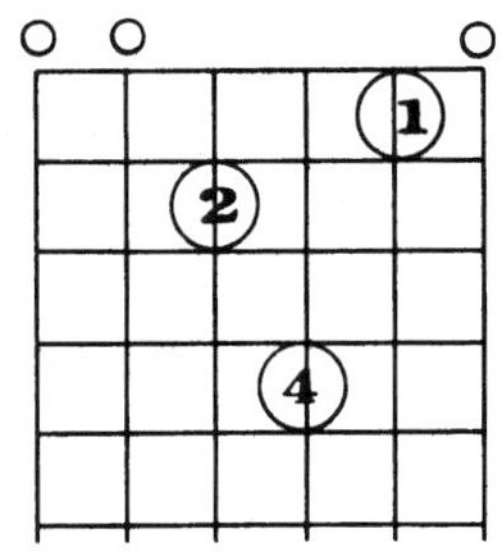

Moving these forms up the neck involves the use of the barre and they become extremely difficult__

Fm9

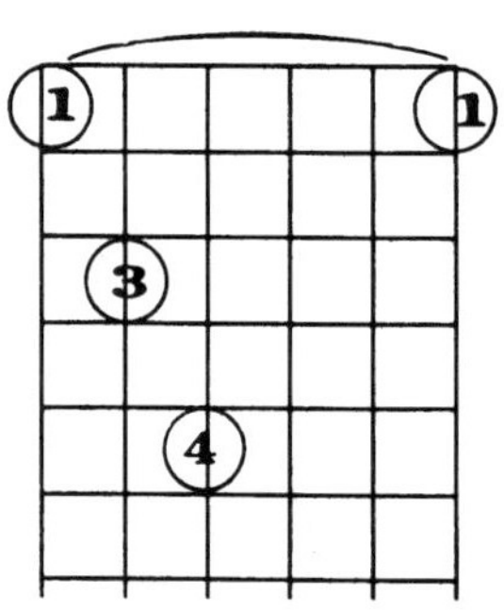

Bbm9

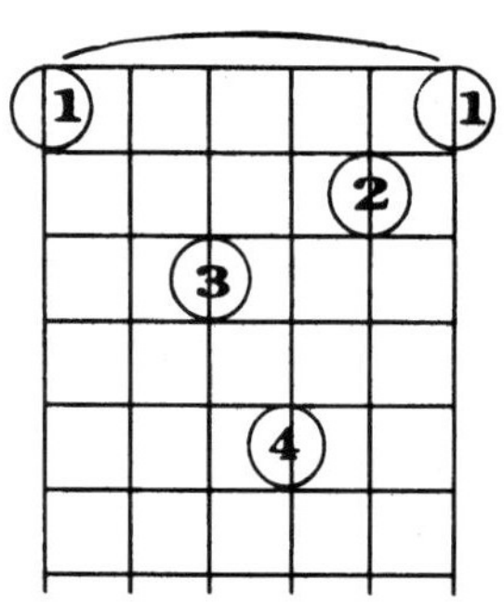

Practice changing back and forth, moving up the neck one fret at a time. The farther up the neck, the easier they will become. (Due to frets being closer together.

These are well worth the effort – they are beautiful for ballad accompaniments.

11TH CHORDS

The addition of the 11th tone to a chord gives it the feeling of an unresolved suspension. This is most commonly indicated in the chord symbol as sus4. The 11th may appear as part of a tonic chord but its best use is as an extension of the dominant. (The minor 11th is another common form of usage.) I think of the interval as follows: (1) If the chord contains ♭7 as an active tone, and perhaps 9th tone also, call it an 11th chord— (2) If the chord does not contain these tones, call the chord by its name and add sus4 to the symbol.

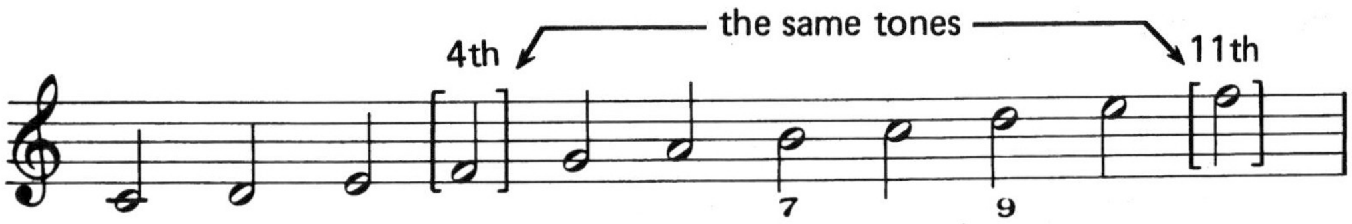

Theoretically, each additional extension needs the support of the preceding extension(s). For example the 9th tone would give the 11th proper support—The 11th tone is a 3rd step above the 9th and it may appear in its natural form or raised ½ step. In this case the chord would be indicated by +11 addition to the symbol.

This symbol would assume the presence of the 7th & 9th— also chord 5th— If the chord 5th is not present, call the chord ♭5

C11 chord in closed position.

C+11 – clos. pos. with "G" omitted call chord C9♭5.

In major form, the 11th theoretically replaces the 3rd tone— In minor form, it will replace the 5th tone— These would be the normal resolution tones, and you'll find many examples of usage which will contradict these statements— Let your ear decide.

An excellent way to think of the dominant 11th is to picture a m7 chord built on the 5th tone of the dom.7 – for example : D11

Build a minor 7th chord on "A", the 5th tone of the D7.

We would have to re-voice this for guitar as follows.

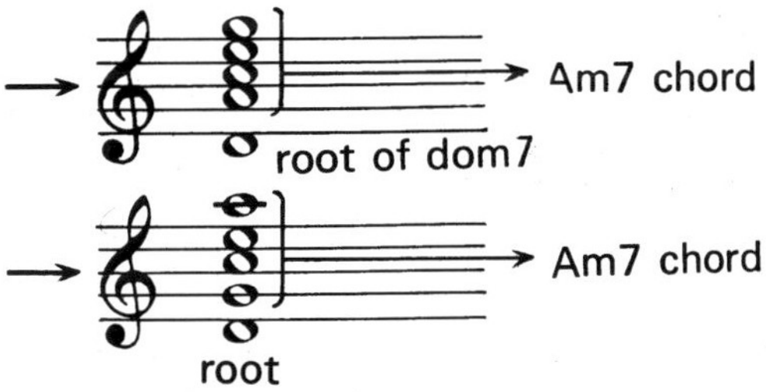

Very easy to finger:

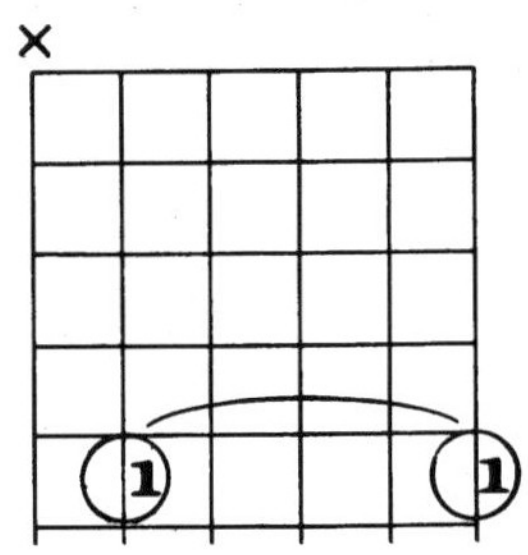

Ordinarily, would resolve to either D9 chord or to tonic G chord—

This gives dom7th or dom9th chord a most sophisticated flavor. Note no 3rd present. with this in mind, substitute 11th chord in places where you use 7th or 9th in their dominant forms. If melody note is 3rd of chord, don't use dom11th!

Used with tonic chord as sus4, the sound will be like plagal, or "amen", cadence in church music— very good effect when used this way—

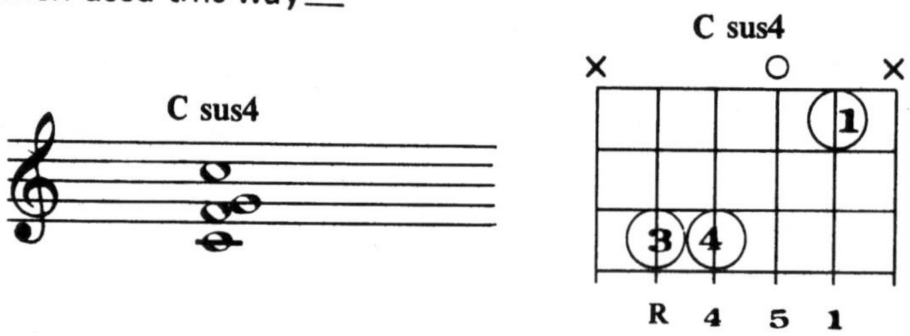

Sus 4 (F) will resolve into the 3rd tone (E) of the C chord :

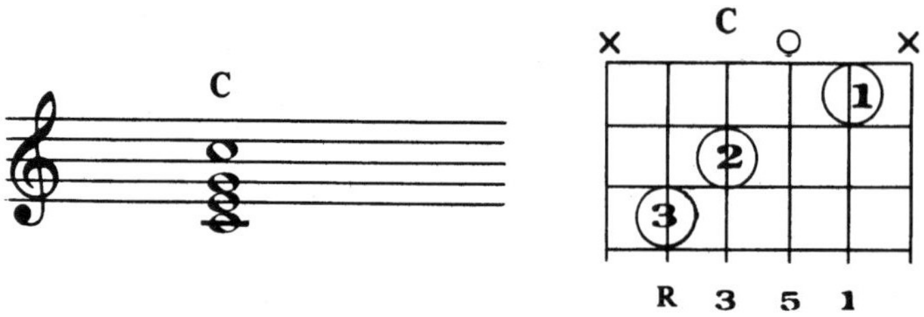

Good guitar voicing for F sus4:

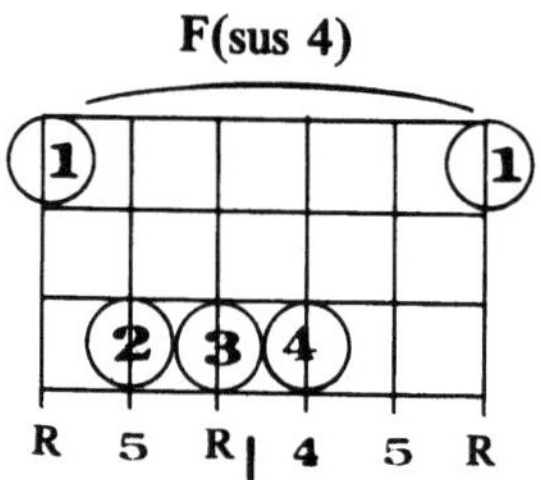

Resolves to:

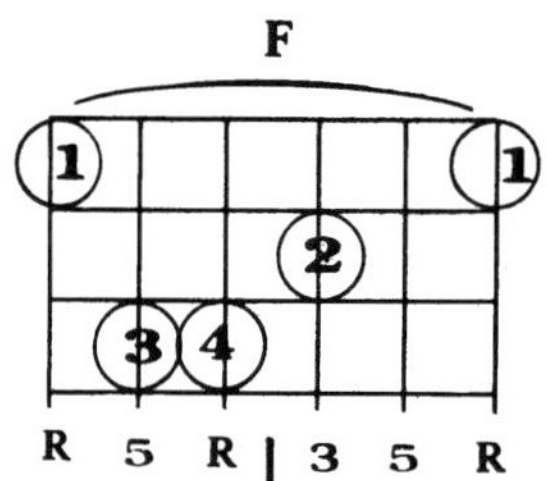

Sus 4 resolves to 3rd of F chord—

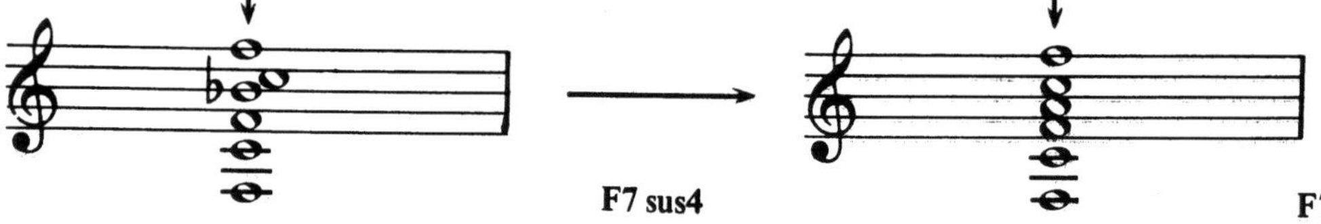

Here's same chord with ♭7 added

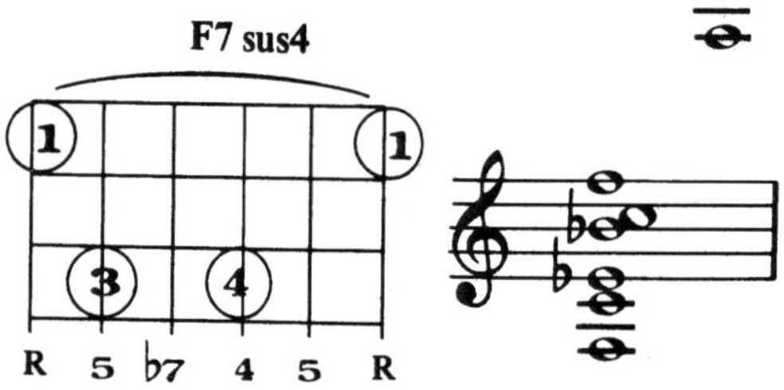

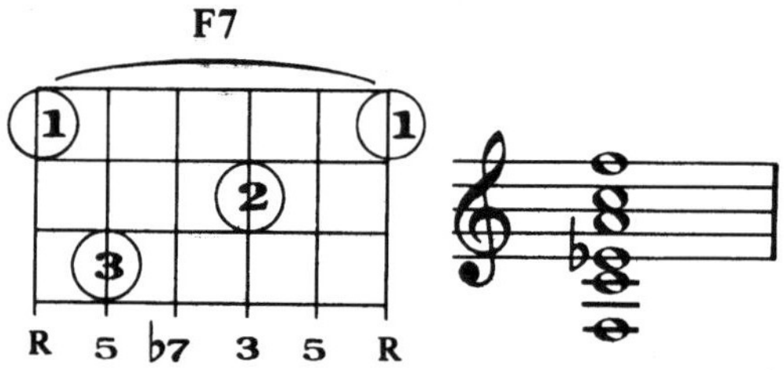

The best usage of the natural 11th is as a part of a dominant chord. As a four note form its best components are ♭7 – 9 – 11, along with the root. A good way to remember the chordal form is to think of a major triad one whole tone back from the given root.

Example : G11 Build major triad on F,

one step back from root G

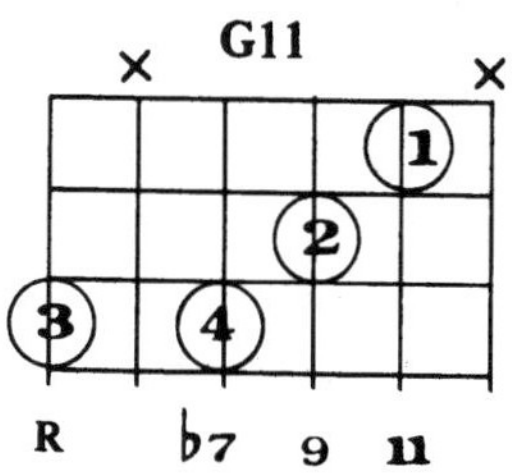

or

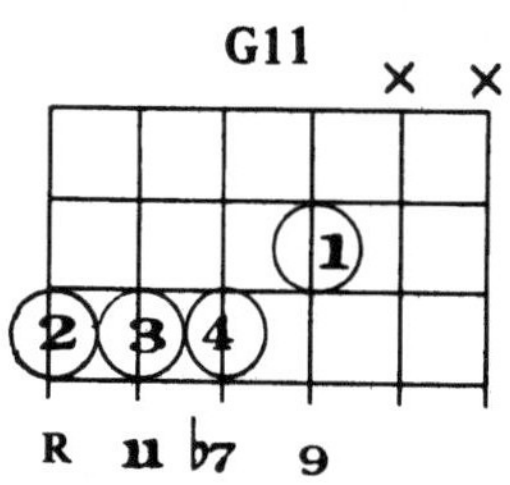

This is low! (use with care) –

Example : C11 Build major triad on B♭

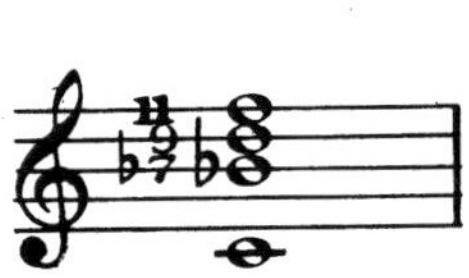

C11

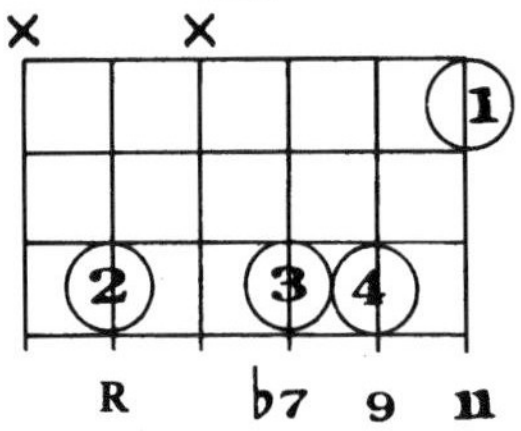

C11

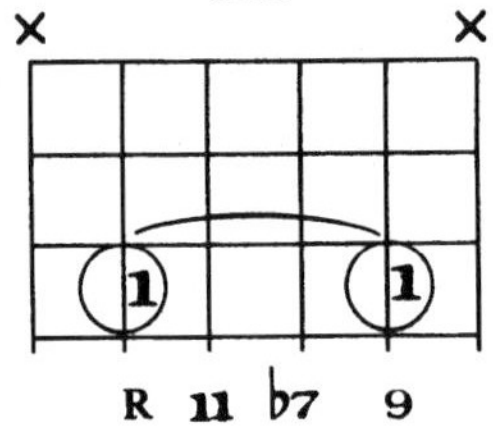

B♭ triad inverted, with C root

These two forms will provide usable forms of the dom. 11th, available in any position— One with root on (6) string, and the other with root on (5) string—

Some minor 11th forms:

Gm11

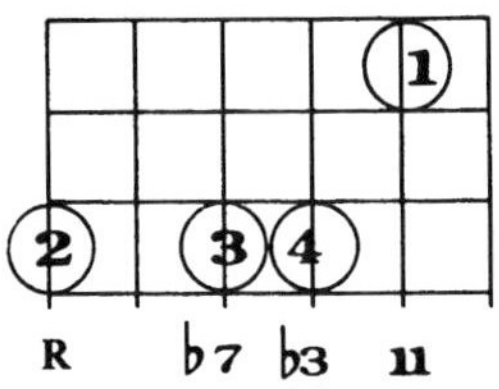

This form contains the minor 3rd (B♭) this may be substituted for a C11—

Cm11

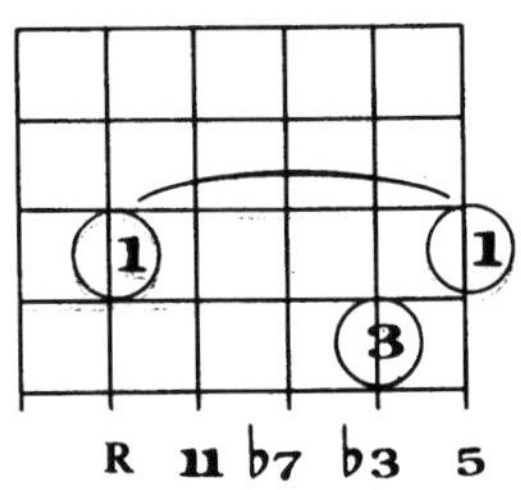

This form contains the minor 3rd (E♭) – This may be used also as an F11—

Without including 3rd, the 11th form may be used in either major or minor context – from the same root tone—

F11 or Fm11

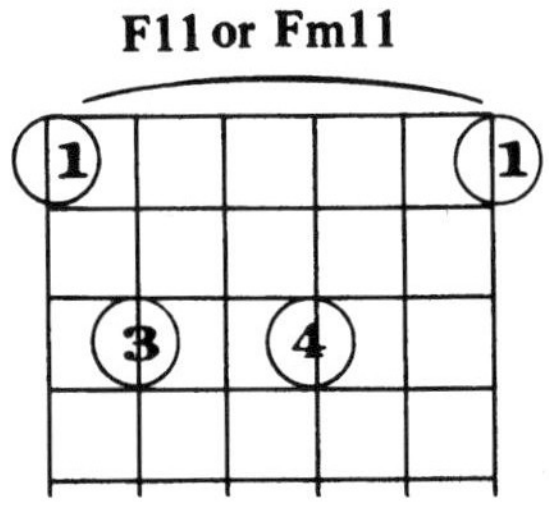

B♭11 or B♭m11

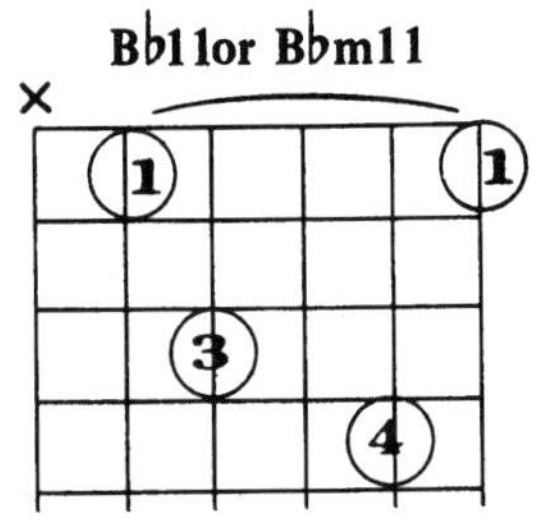

E♭11 or E♭m11

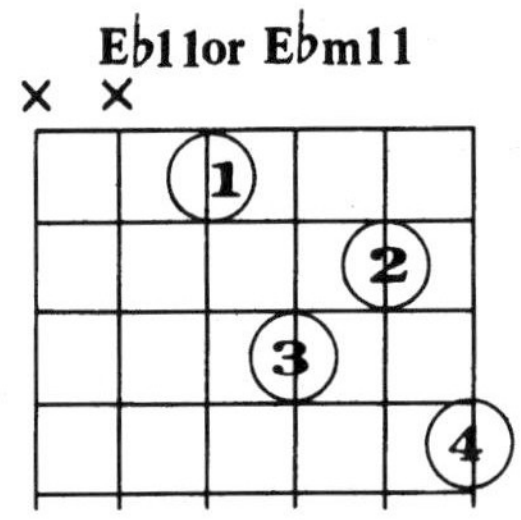

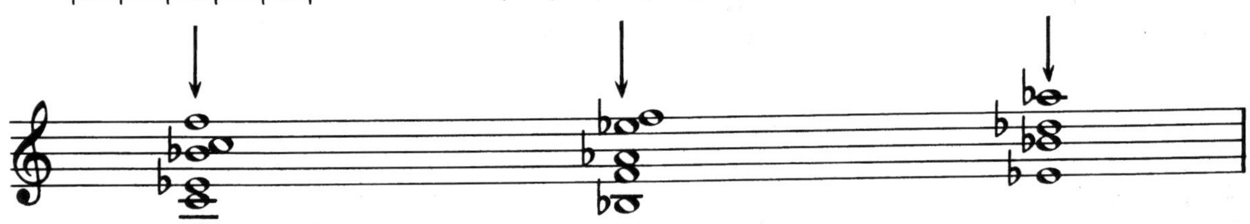

Note

11th tone may resolve down ½ step to maj. 3rd, or down 1 step to min. 3rd –

To find other forms, take any 4 note dom7 and replace 3rd tone with 11th (one fret higher)

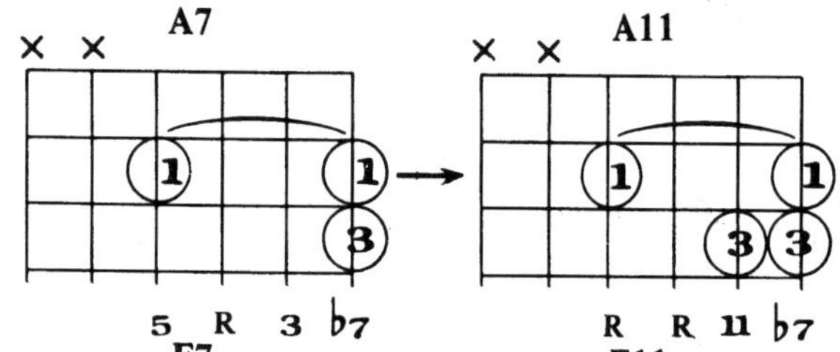

also use as Am11

(also A7 sus 4)

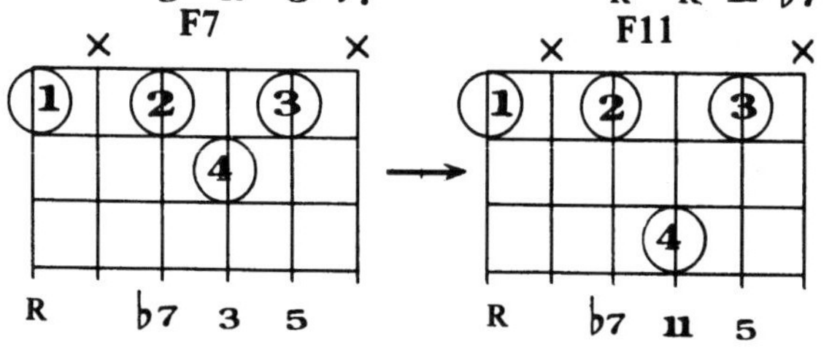

also use as Fm11

(also F7 sus 4)

There are many possibilities available_The following two forms will give many "miles" of use.

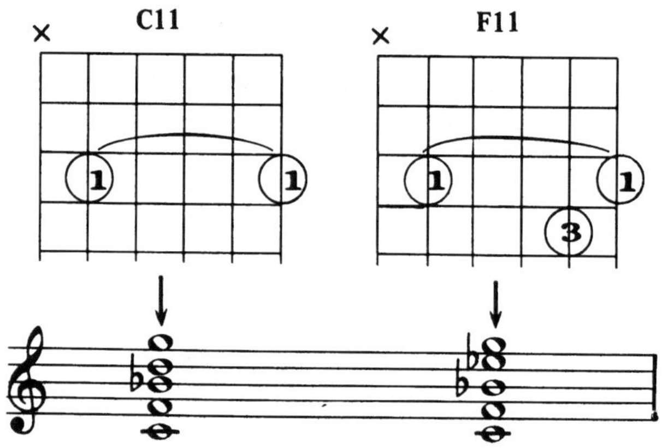

Since neither of these forms include 3rd, you could use as m11 form also _ Try them!

The 11th, in its augmented form, is used more in dominant to tonic resolutions than in its natural form. The qualification for this chord is generally considered to include the natural 5th along with the +11 [+11 sounds the same pitch as ♭5]

Example :

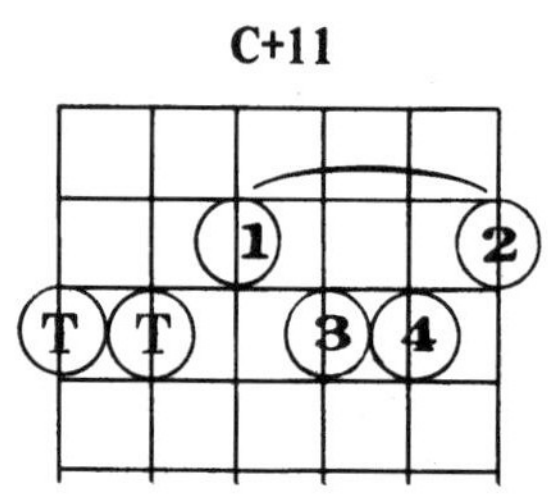

Note utilization of thumb to finger this chord
Also note B♭ + triad as upper three voices.
Consider for movement possibilities.

Like most chords with added, "high", harmonic extensions, most of the voicing become unusual and cumbersome – including both chord 5th and +11 becomes a most impractical rule for the guitar fingerings which would be available For general usage you can substitute, in most cases, a 7♭5 chord built on the the same root as the +11. [If we consider the dom 9 with ♭5 we end up with a "whole tone chord", like the aug.]

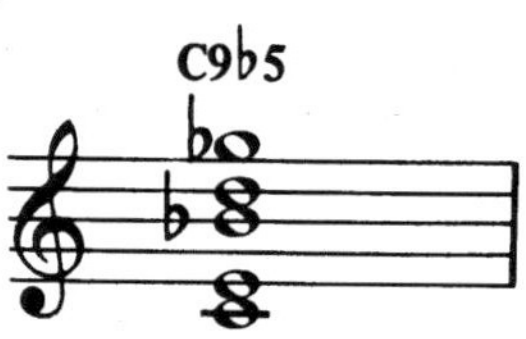

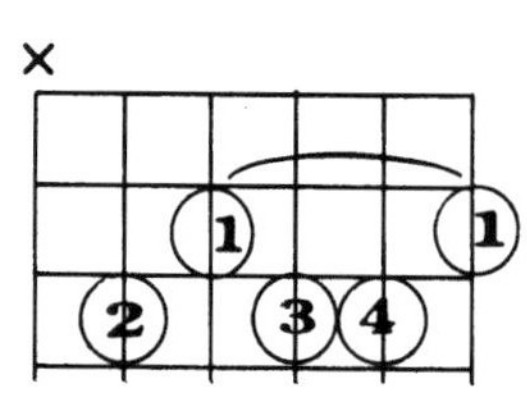

This works just as well as complete form given above_

Note Upper four note chord (on top 4 strings) form a G♭7+5_

The tri-tone (E — B♭) appears in each chord as active, or color tones__ The two tones reverse their functions in relation to the particular root, either C, or G♭

Example :

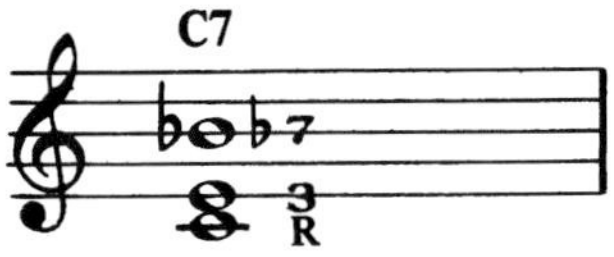

or

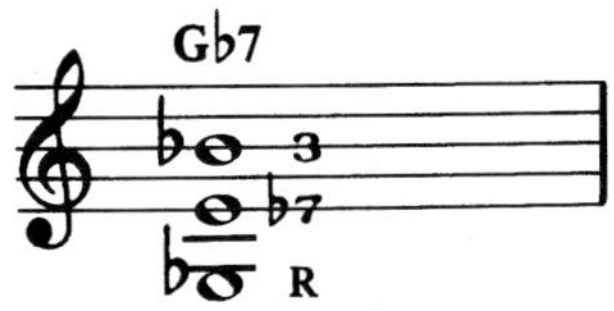

If we are on our way to an F chord, both become equally valid resolutions__ Thinking symmetrically (dividing the octave exactly in half from any given dom. 7th root) we can use this device as an effective substitute for the dominant 7th__

REMEMBER__ Any tone of the chromatic scale will work, or function, as a member of the dom. 7th chord__ (with possible exception of major 7th interval) even this, as passing tone on a weak beat, will sometimes work__

Example :

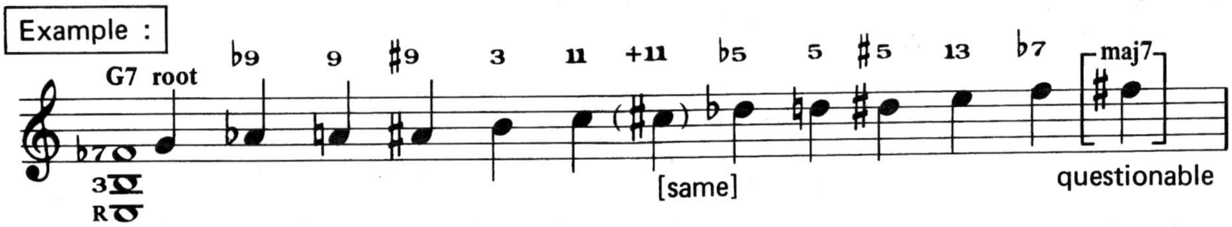

Now Let's examine our octave division in terms of the dom7 substitution we mentioned.

Half way point of G octave is D♭ →

Add higher extensions to the G7 chord and then analyze them in terms of the D♭ 7

Add to G7	Function in D♭7	Functions as
A	9th	♯5th
A♭	♭9th	5th
A♯	♯ 9th	13th (B♭)
D♭	♭5th	root
D♯	♯5th	9th (E♭)
D	5th	♭9th

This is a most interesting concept to develop. See section titled "whole tone chords" and do some experimenting via the dominant 7th chord__

Two good forms of +11 which will handle most any situation__

[root on (5) string]

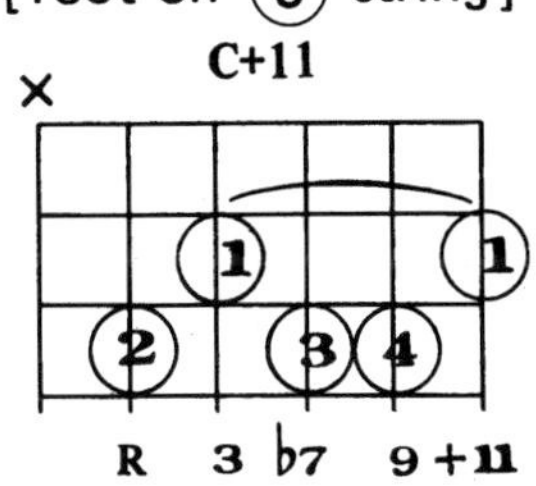

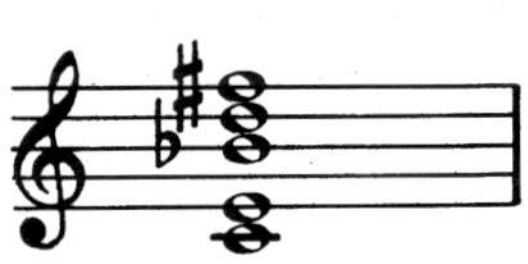

[root on (6) string]

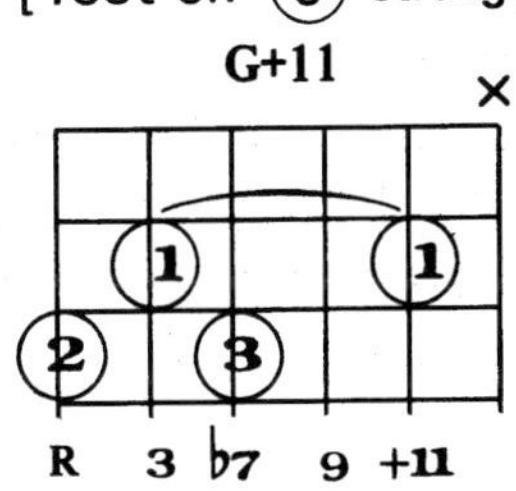

Notice, we left natural 5th out in each case.

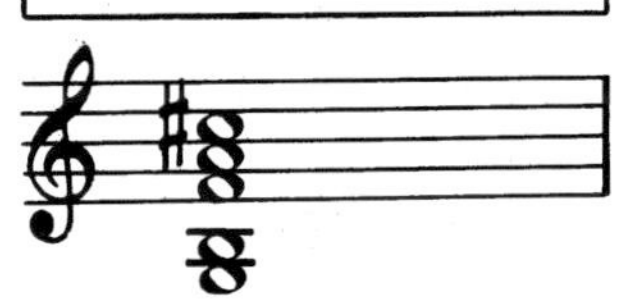

Your best approach route, and in the interest of simplifying matters for sight reading, is to substitute a 7b5 chord for the +11 — Just remember one thing – keep the 7b5 in root position.

Example

Here's the easy route – and also effective!

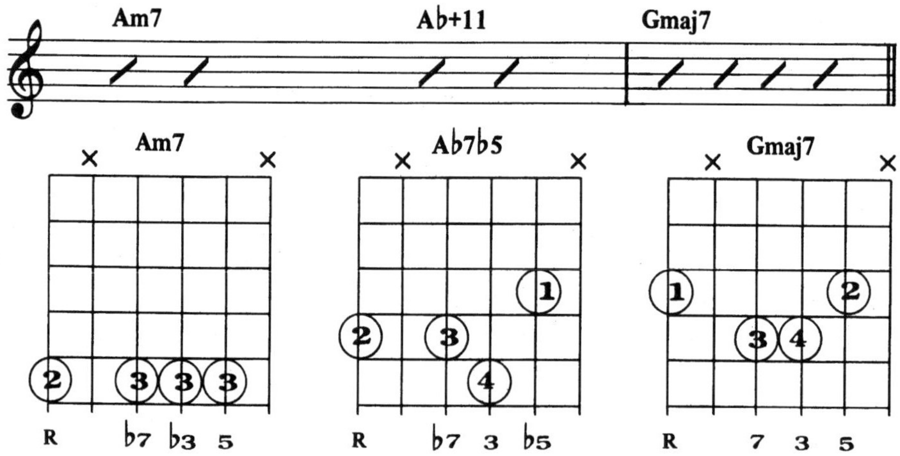

By substituting Ab7b5, you've kept a smooth line moving and have eliminated potential leaps and/or fingering problems on +11 chord.

Here's another, with roots on (5) string.

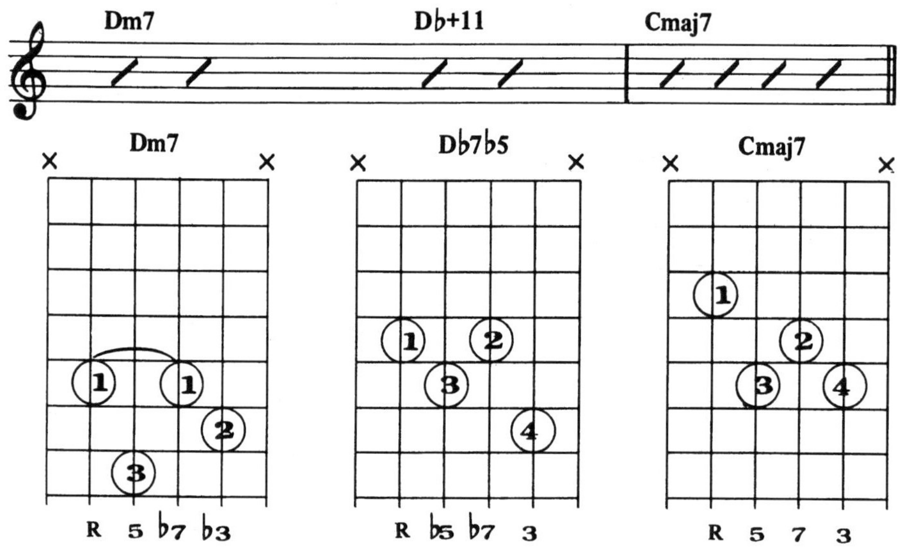

The previous four string forms, and the two five string forms, will handle any situation. [If you have time to "work out" your part you could use fuller +11 if desired.] I think you'll find the examples given to be most adequate — Don't limit yourself to these few, even if they do function consistently — Experiment! Remember, if playing rhythm is your responsibility, use the smallest, easiest, form possible. Concentrate on contributing to the "time" — Don't "bog-down", or "hang-up" the rhythm section — If you're in a small group, look for prettiest, fullest sound you can find — If you work with piano player, work out progressions which supply fullest, possible sounds.

Forms are easy — Knowing tonal functions and how to use the forms is the hard part. This becomes more important with the high extensions – experiment with substitutions on tunes that you are 100% sure of! Use the large, dissonant forms, with care. Constant use of these forms soon causes boredom — Use them selectively for contrast, surprise, etc — Know what you're doing!

13TH CHORDS

The 13th chord will complete our discussion of the three harmonic extensions available above the 7th chord. It will appear as a form of the dominant chord only__ The qualifying factor is the presence of the ♭7 in the same chord, and for best sound – absence of chord 5th – it will not function as part of a minor chord. [It is the same pitch as scale tone 6, and without the ♭7 it is the added 6th on either major or minor chords.]On the dominant chord the 13th appears as the next 3rd step above the 11th__

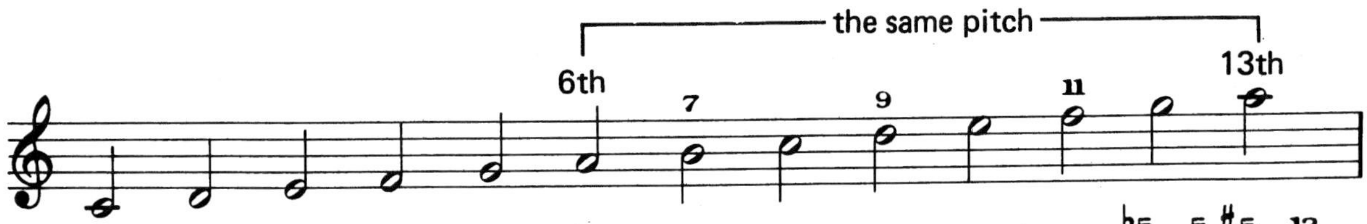

Example :

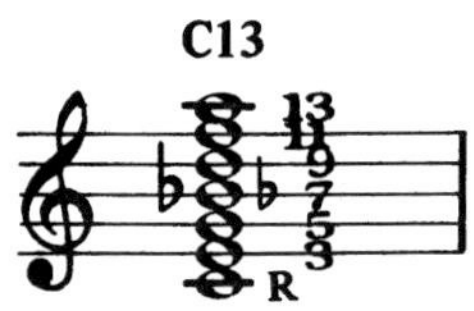

Theoretically, the 13th sounds best without the 5th – as it is considered to be a 5th substitute__

Note : G6 & Gm6 contain "E", 6th tone. G13 contains "E" along with flat 7 "F"

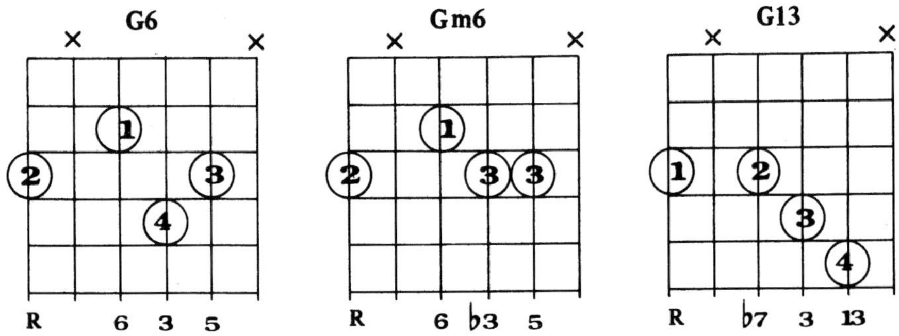

Note absence of chord 5th & presence of ♭7

The 13th may be altered in one direction only, DOWN! It then becomes ♭13, and with ♭7 would be an exact duplication (soundwise) of a +5 chord__ But – it should resolve differently.

Example:

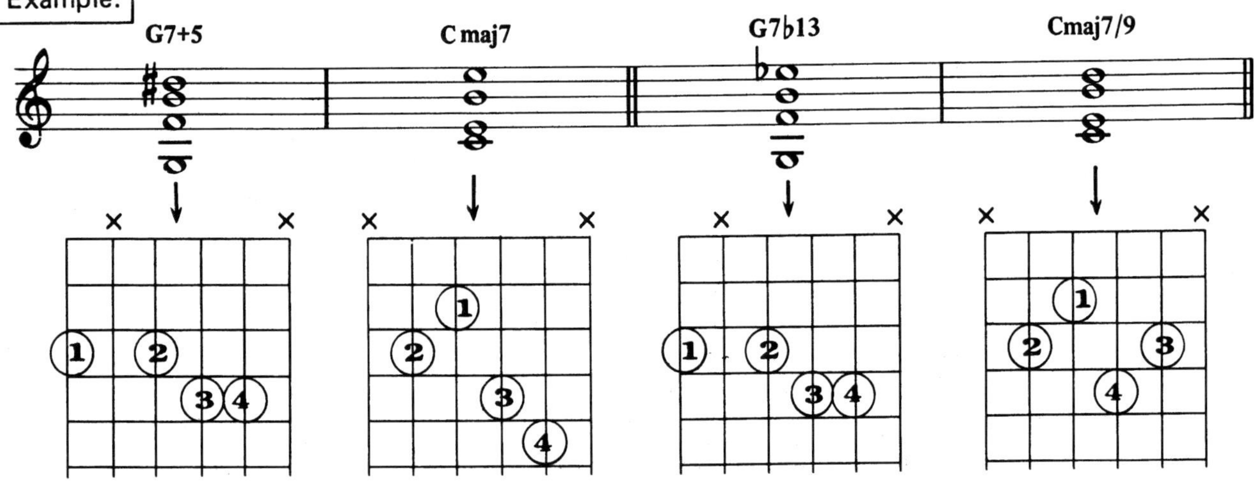

This may appear as "Hair splitting", but I feel it is a most valid approach to examination, and use of each chord__ Theoretically, the augmented interval wants to continue in an upward direction – the diminished interval wants to continue downward__Notice the double 3rd in the Cmaj7 as a result of correct resolution of tones – ♯5 up to 3rd – ♭7 down to 3rd__

The 13th chord, although the interval itself is a 3rd above 11th in a succession of 3rds to our basic triad, gives the chord more of a 4th construction sound — It could be more properly classified under Quartal Harmony – (chords built in 4ths) than under Tertian Harmony (chords built in 3rds)

Example :

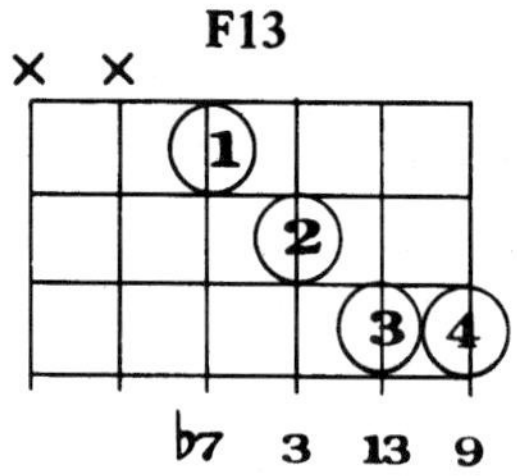

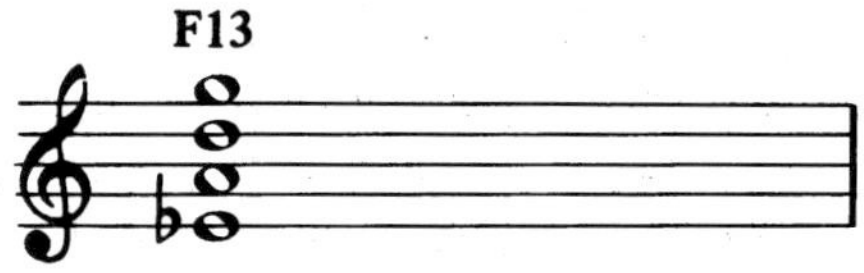

Note the intervals of fourths.—

A good place to look at the 13th chord, on the guitar, is built using A, open (5) string, as root tone.

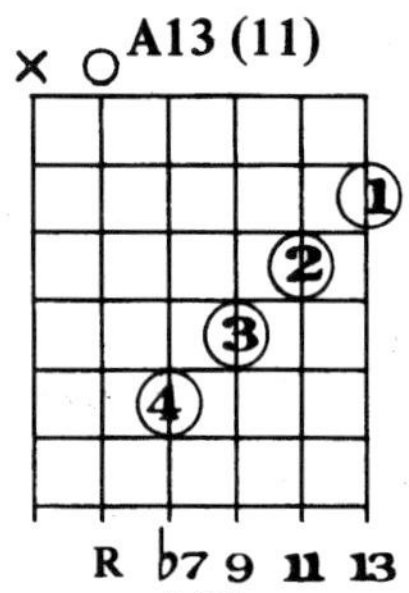

This would utilize all of the qualifying support extensions without including major 3rd – Presence of 11th gives this chord a most unresolved feeling [Use low E string as root and note m7 sound – Em9]

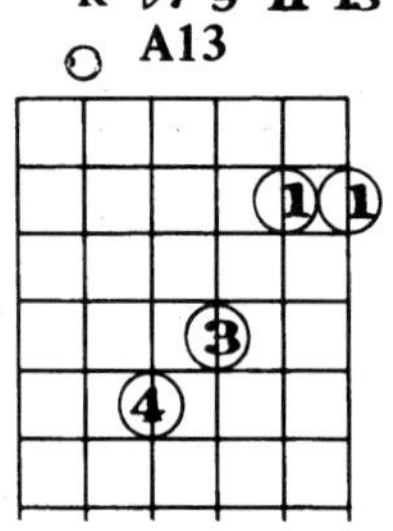

It would be letter to include the major 3rd, as given here—

This is a good, usable form and can be moved up via refingering. Could be moved down ½ step also

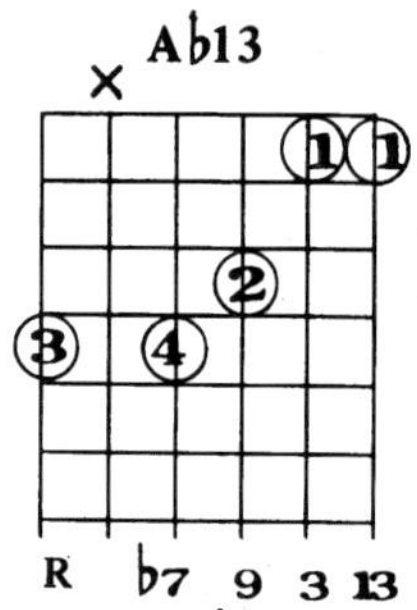

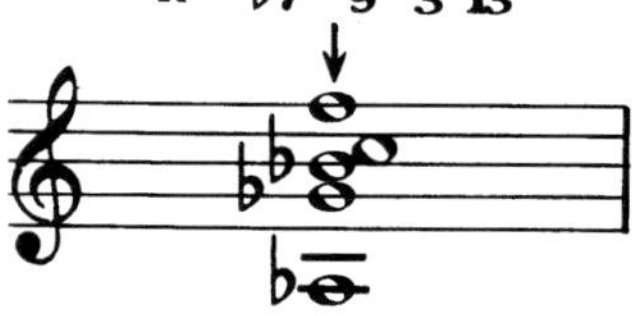

We can also eliminate 9th tone and add 13th to Dom 7th for another most practical form.

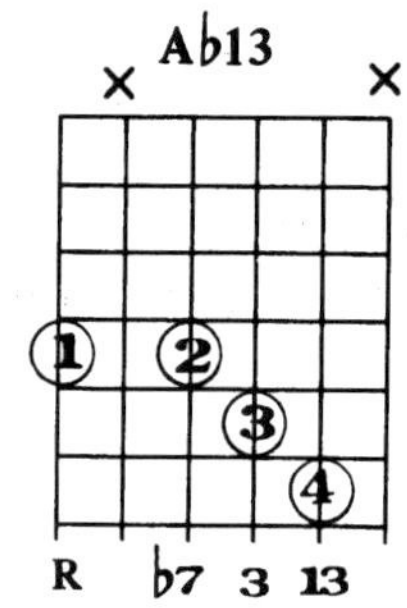

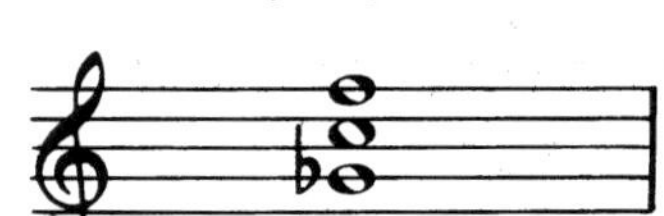

The 9th may then be added to this form – this time as the top, or melody note of the chord.

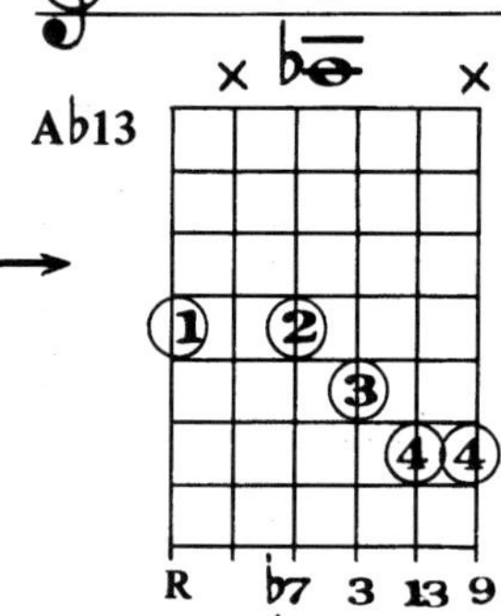

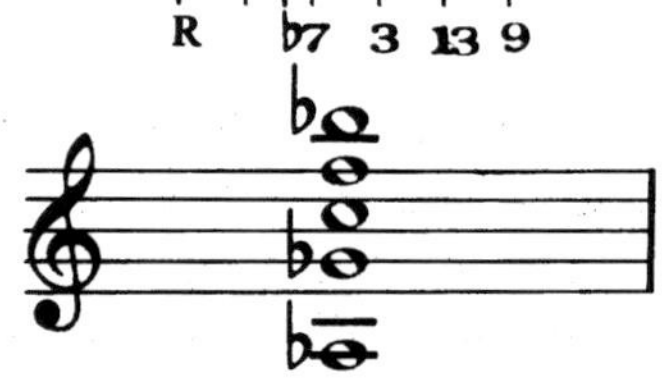

Notice 4th construction in the upper part of the chords.

Both 9th and 13th may be altered. This, again, gets us into dividing the octave in half — In other words, the chord may function over two roots. In this case the alternate root is D.

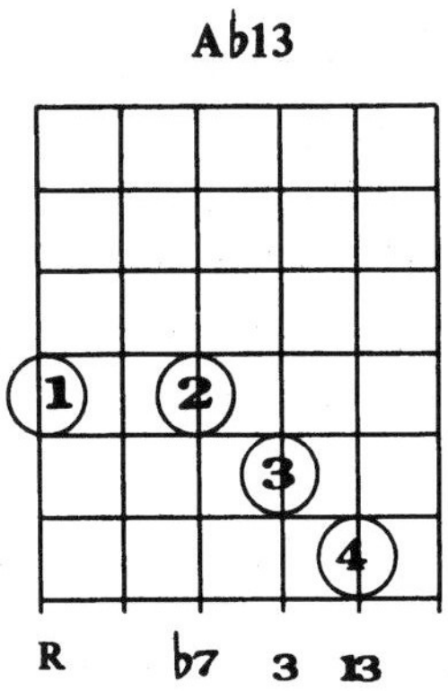

or

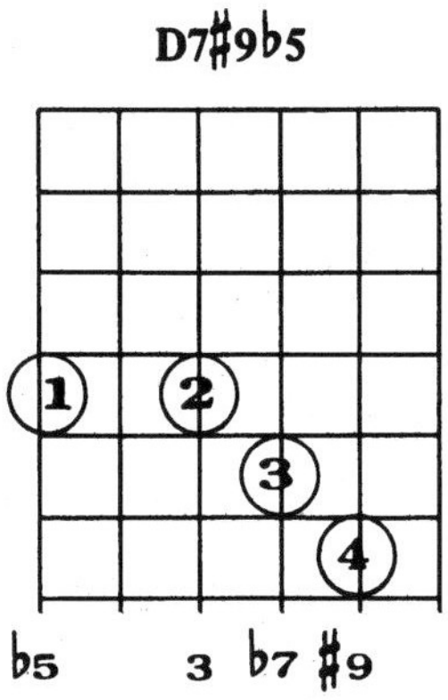

Lower 13th in A♭ and get a good D9♭5__

As mentioned before, this is a most interesting concept to study and explore__ It will provide many interesting chord lines.

Other forms of the 13th chords.

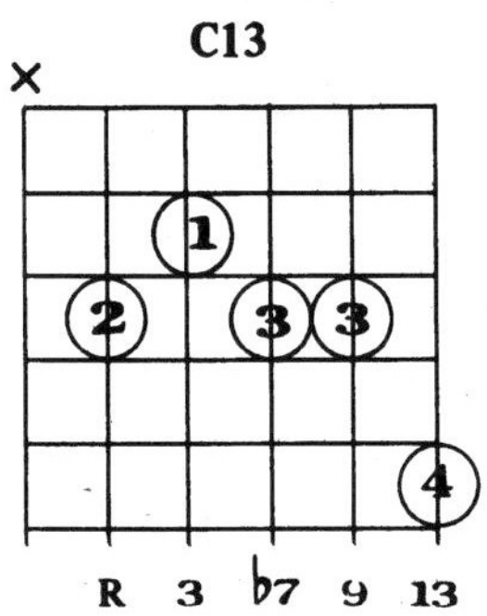

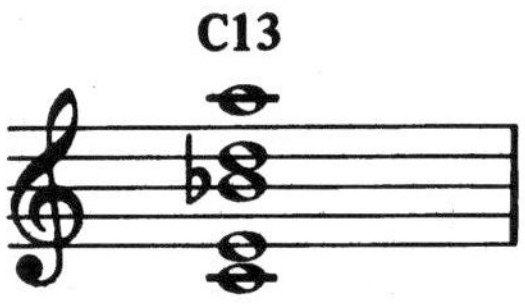

Most players move 2nd finger to ⑥ string – (theoretically not as good) how ever makes rhythm playing much easier__

Raise 9th tone and add G♭ root for excellent G♭13♯9 chord__ Symmetrical division of octave again.

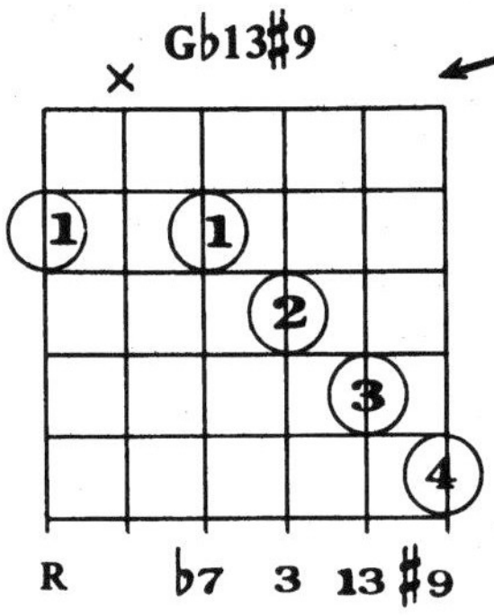

If you can't finger this one – eliminate root and use top four tones – (Let the bass player supply the root)

Two 13th forms without the root

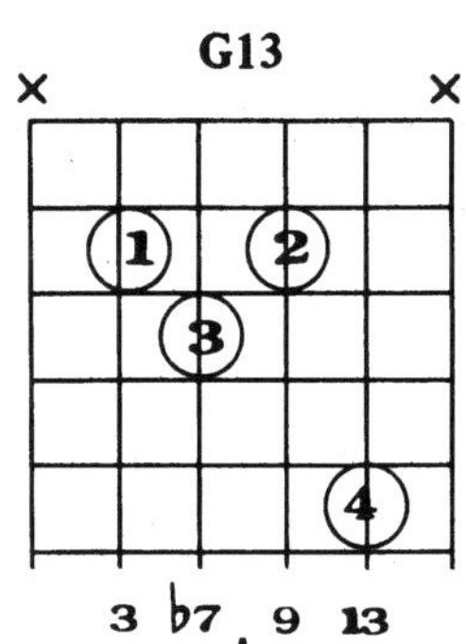

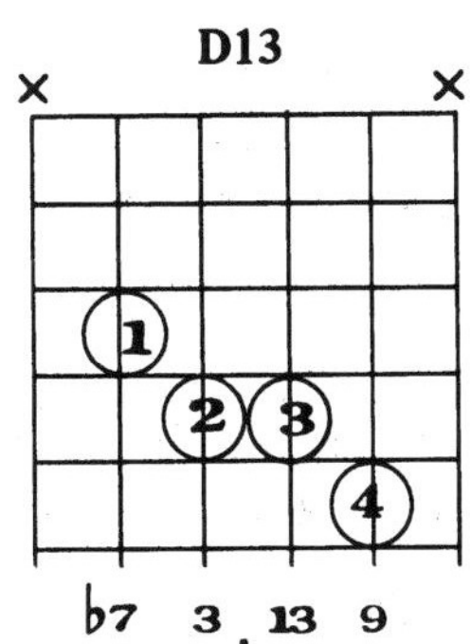

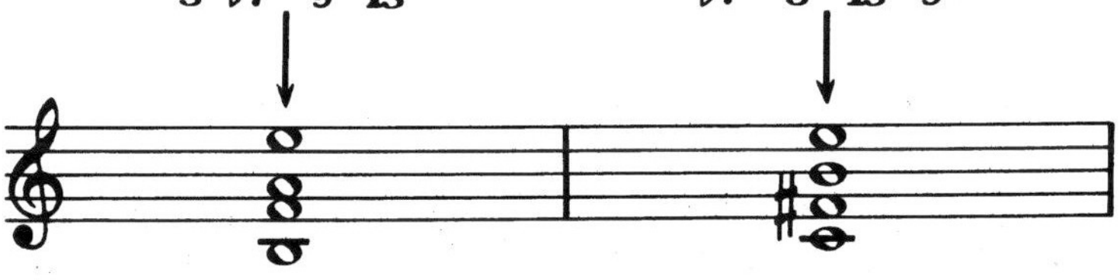

Use these two forms carefully__ Depend on bass player to supply roots__

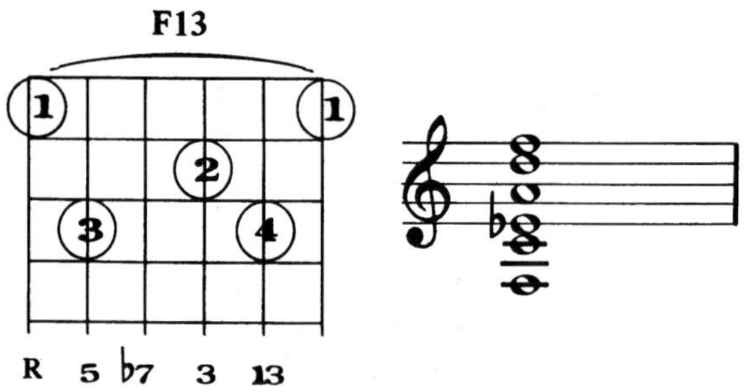

This form also includes chord 5th (C). This is an easy one to get, but does not sound as good as the other forms—

Using the super structure of this chord we have a good four string form—

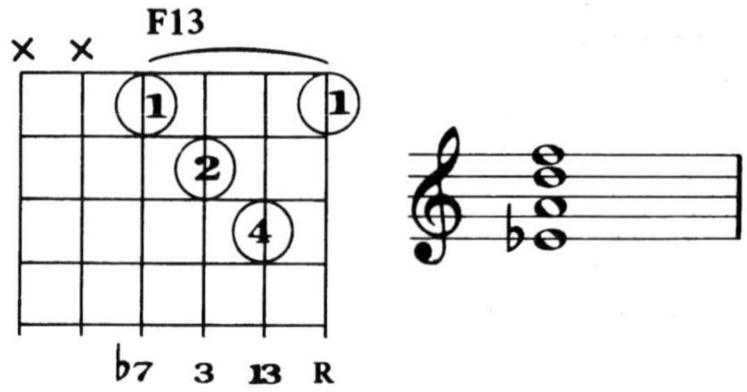

This form alters very well— Let's put it in a position where we can use open A string as the root.

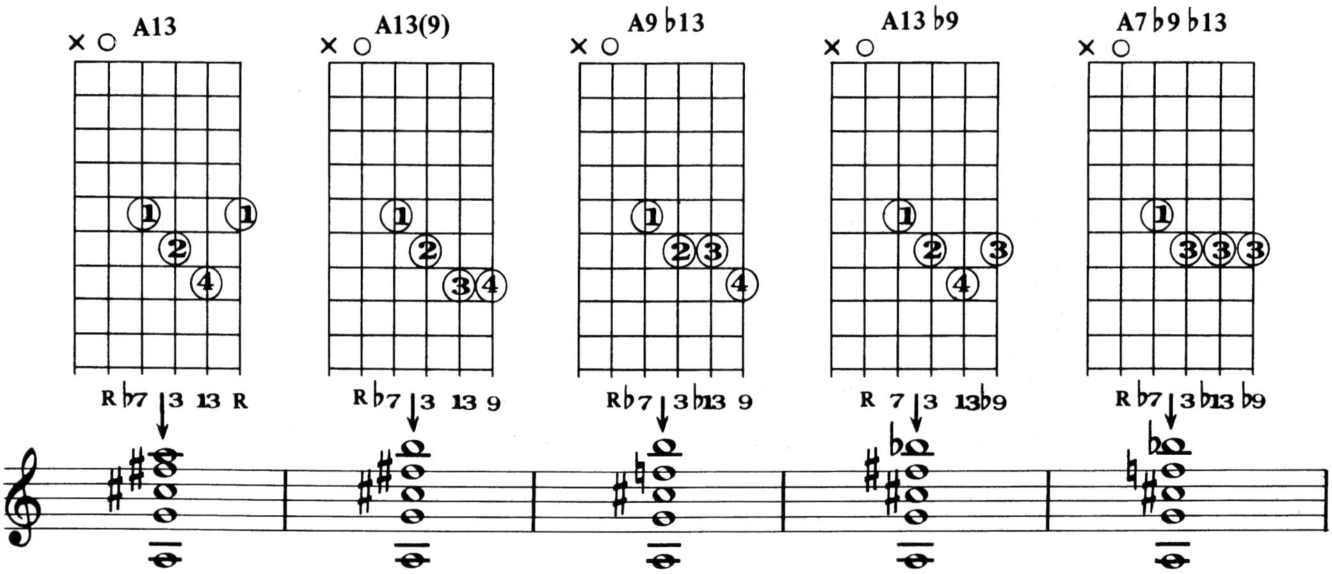

Analyze these forms thinking of E♭ as root tone. (Halving the octave again – A – E♭).

When using 13th as a dom. 7th substitution, remember one thing—Do not use if melody note is chord 5th – (Remember, 13th is a 5th substitute) use with care if melody is ♭7, as this will probably be a minor 2nd away from 13th— This is a good 13th voicing for arranging purposes, but is most impractical for translation to the guitar fingerboard.

Example :

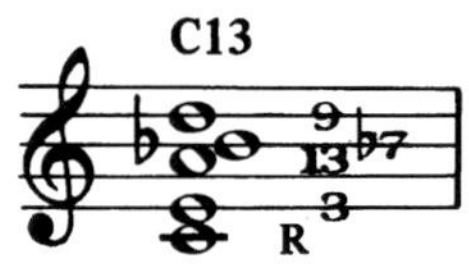

The 9th is providing support for the the minor 2nd interval.

You may be able to play the 3 upper voices at some places— Even these are hard to finger—

If you want the natural 11th in your 13th chord there are a few ways to do this— the upper extensions (♭7 – 9 – 11 – 13) form a major 7th chord one whole step lower than the given root—If you have a double jointed thumb you could play this one.

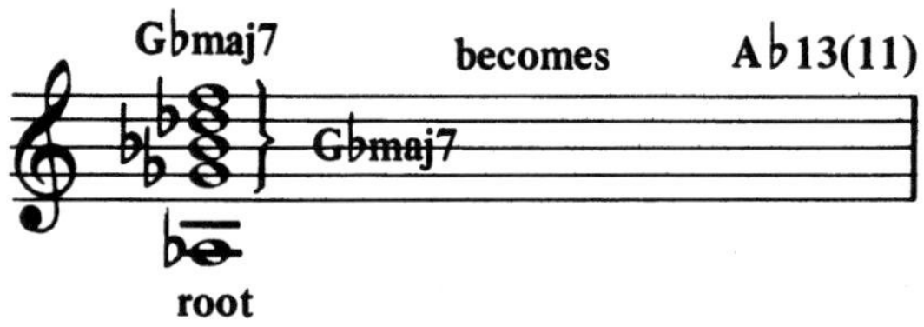

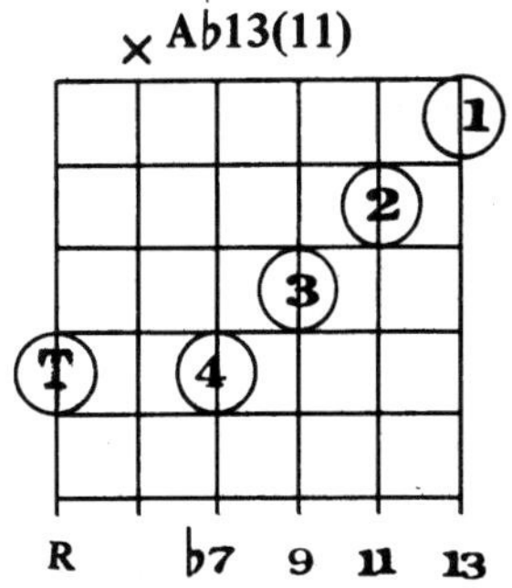

Much easier to play this next form:

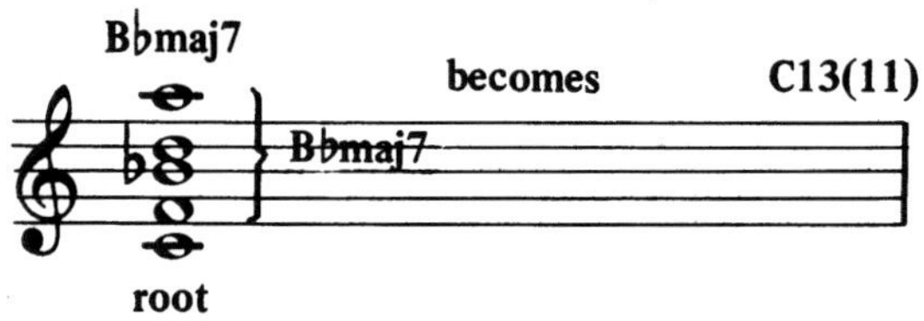

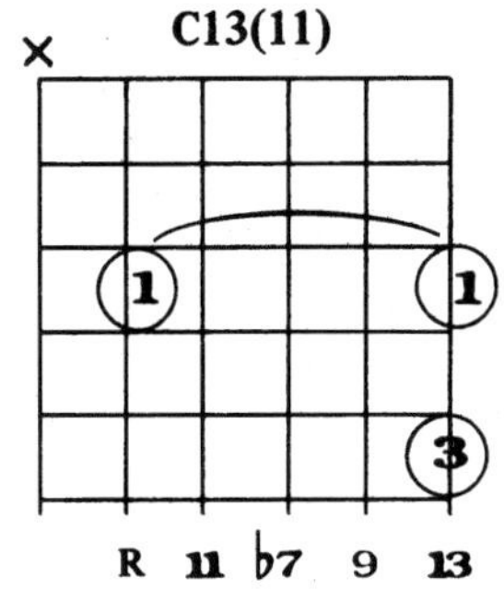

Here's another form to try :

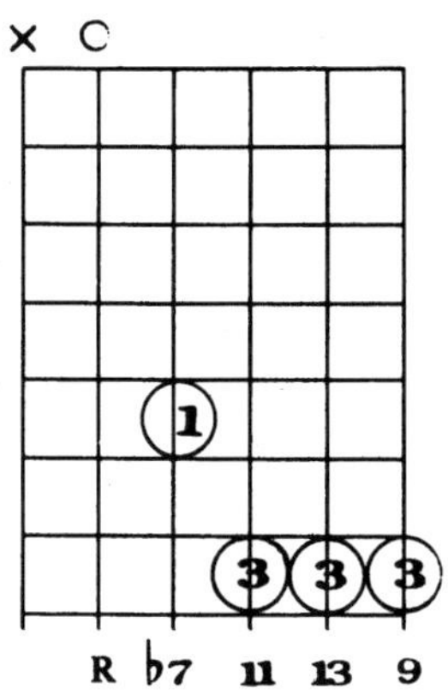

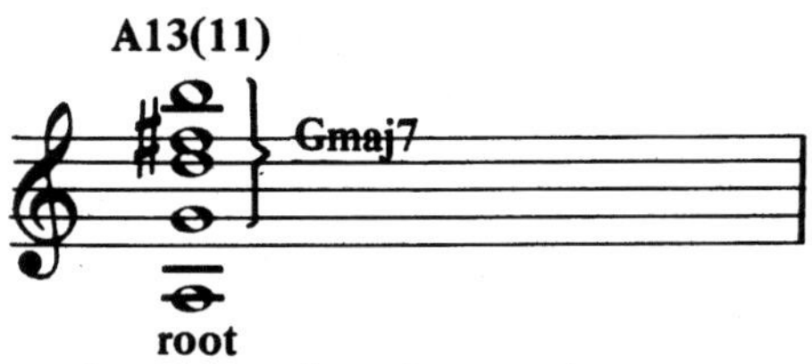

using open A string as the root__

The b5 or +11 gives 13th a unique flavor

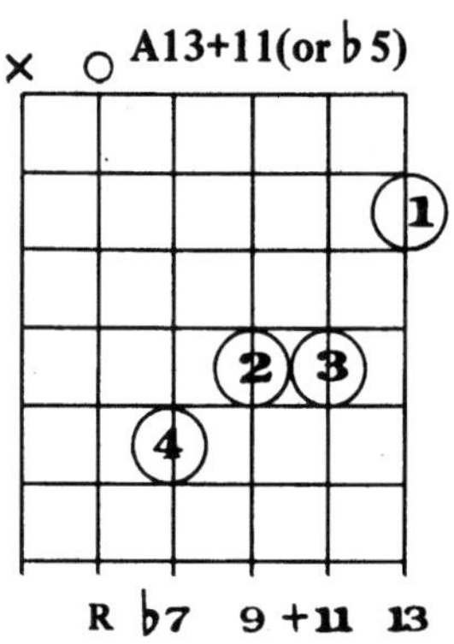

Notice top three notes are a major triad built one whole step higher than given root. A good point to remember__

The upper extensions, 9 – 11 – 13 and their alteration are most beautiful additions to the dom.7th__ They are most sophisticated, and very rich sounding when used properly. Use them sparingly and with good musical taste__ Stay in character with the type of music you happen to be performing. Don't use these high structure chords for folk songs__ Learn to recognize the chords for folk songs – and listen to how good players, and arrangers, use them__

Use of chords with a number of alterations or with more than one extension beyond the triad —

Arrangers, as a rule, have little understanding of the guitar, Hector Berloz, in his famous "Treatise on Orchestration", said, the best way to learn to write for the guitar is to learn how to play it! (Berloz was a guitarist)— Although this would be ideal, it is highly impractical and unrealistic—One important item which should be considered when writing chordal parts is: "Don't get too complicated unless absolutely necessary"

For example:

Let's assume the arranger has scored the following chord for an 8 Brass, 5 saxes dance type orchestra →

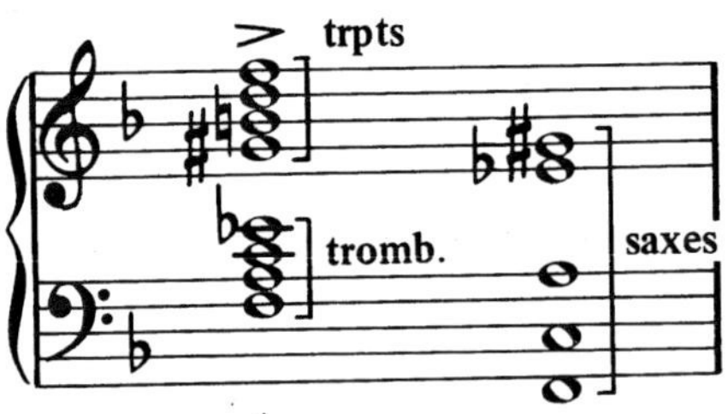

This would require a rather complicated chord symbol if he wants an exact duplication—

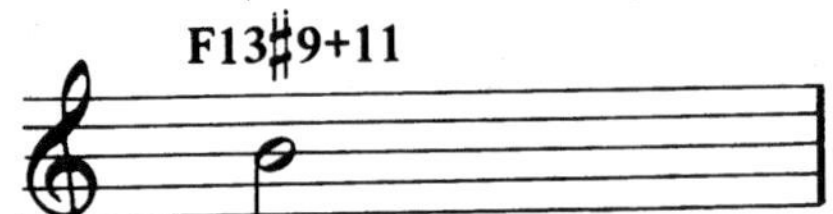

I would do one of several things:

1. Indicate a lower structure

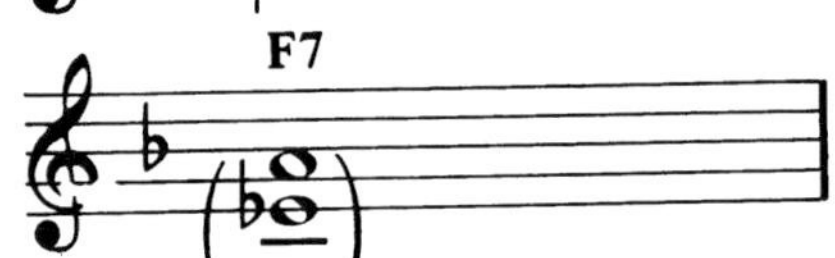

2. If guitar was integrated part of of chord, write out what I had in mind –
3. Give the guitar one bar rest.

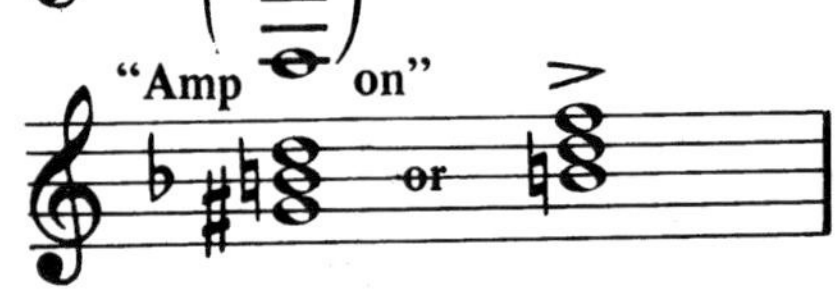

A guitarist with a solid harmonic background will, in most cases, use the chordal part only as a guide. He will lower structures, especially if his responsibility is to maintain a steady beat in the rhythm section. He will play a chord line where fingering problems and movement have been greatly minimized— Good chords for rhythm purposes are the open triads (10ths) which were discussed in an earlier section— If he is "comping" he will, probably, just play the upper structures (via closed triads) – just the reverse of the previous statement.— If you are playing with a good bass player, laying down good, fundamental lines— You can suggest many things harmonically with three or four notes—

Ex: Basic Progression

Bass player doing something like

You could do something like this →

Resulting in good sound with two forms easy to play— →

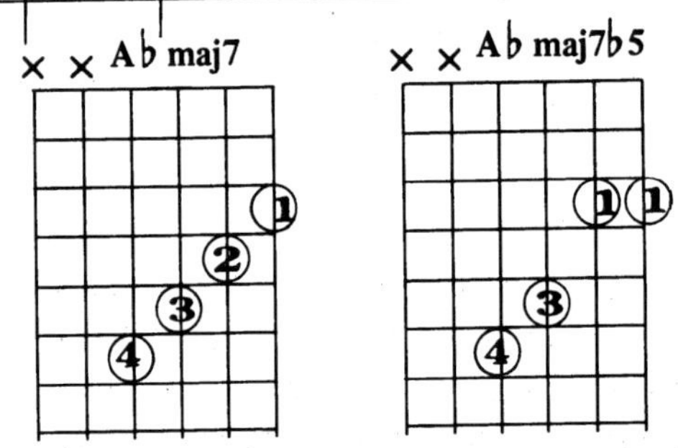

Make sure you know basic triads 100%— Let's look at them now as extensions of other chords.

Take any basic triad and assign different tonal functions to each of the tones in the chord—

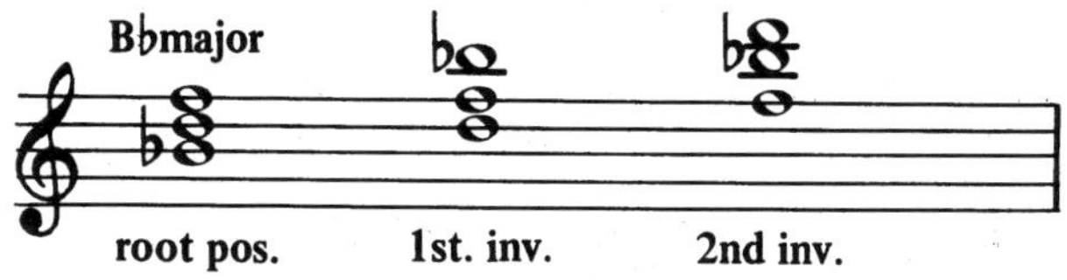

Keep triads in high positions for this to be an effective tool—

Basic Triad | Tonal Functions

F — 5 — b7 — 9 — 11 — 13

D — 3 — 5 — 7 — 9 — b5

Bb — R — b3 — 5 — b7 — 9

Use for ➤ Bb maj-G Min7-Eb maj7-C11—Ab 13 b5

Possibilities are endless

I think it's obvious here that the possibilities are endless. To be in complete command, when using this device, really requires a lot of study and experimentation. This form of substitution will give you melodic, chordal possibilities that are unlimited. Using triads, in this manner, as passing tones between other chords will give your playing a most distinct flavor— Good musical taste and lots of creativity are the basic ingredients with this device.

Here are some example progressions using basic triad forms, instead of complete chords—

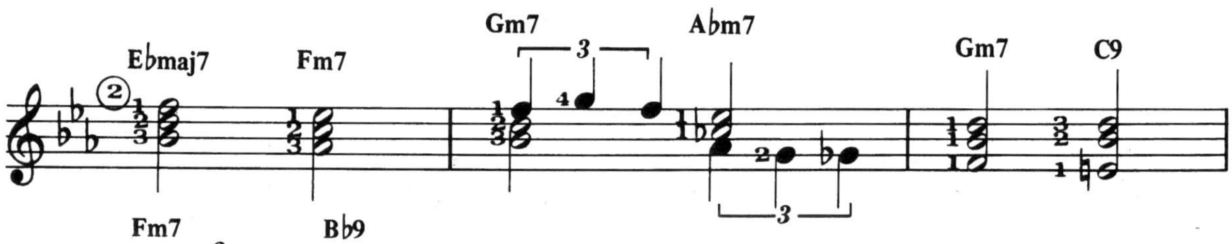

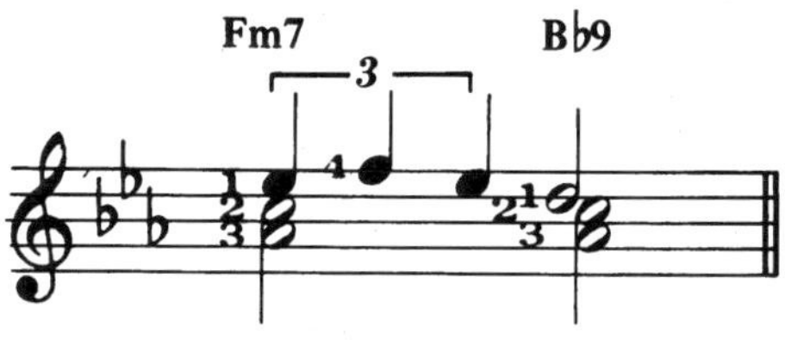

Try this with a bass player, if possible – note smooth sound and easy fingering

Last bar of above example demonstrates very good, and most effective ii→V progression. Lets make an exercise from these two chords Starting on C triad, 8th fret, and calling it Am7 –

Here is complete Am7— We will remove root and have C major Triad

It will resolve to D9 via one move—

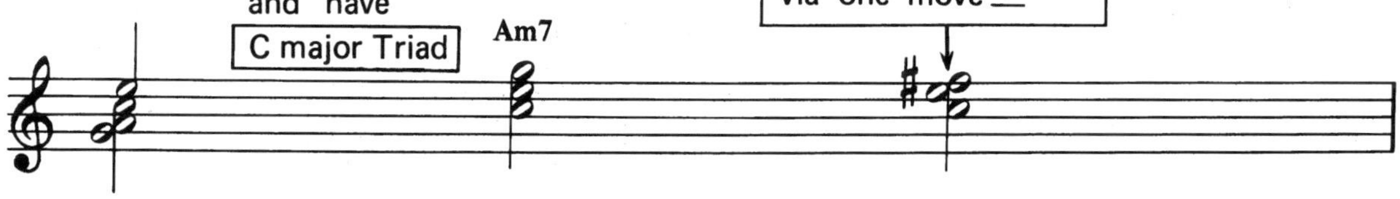

Here then is our exercise

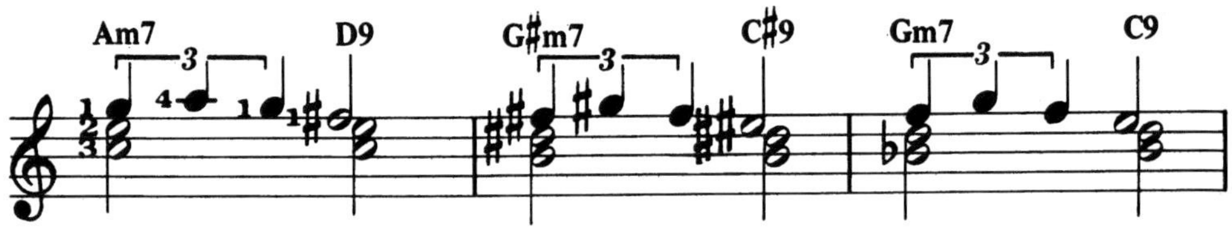

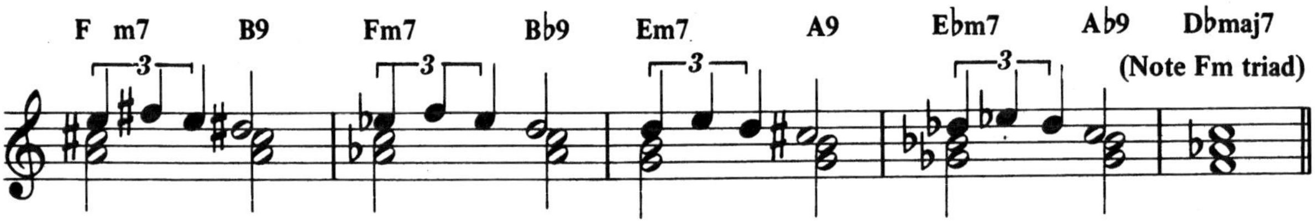

Now try inverting the triad we used before — Puts substitution into a different position.

Em7 – A9 will be our example, using a G triad as substitute for Em7 —

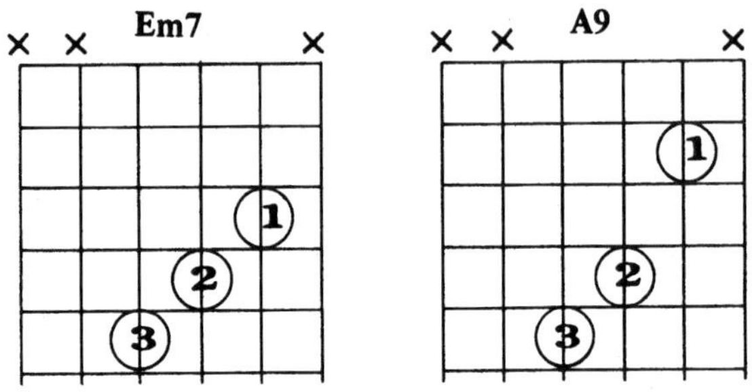

Notice – Only one tone moves – ♭7 of Em7 goes to 3 of A9 —

Keep this in mind when you invert.

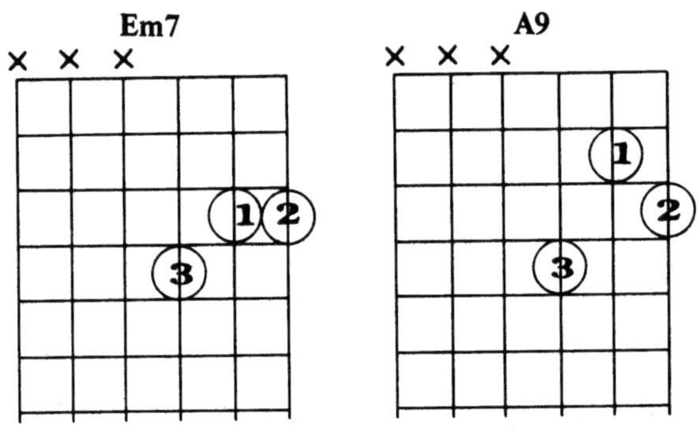

Use open "E" string and "A" string to emphasize movement

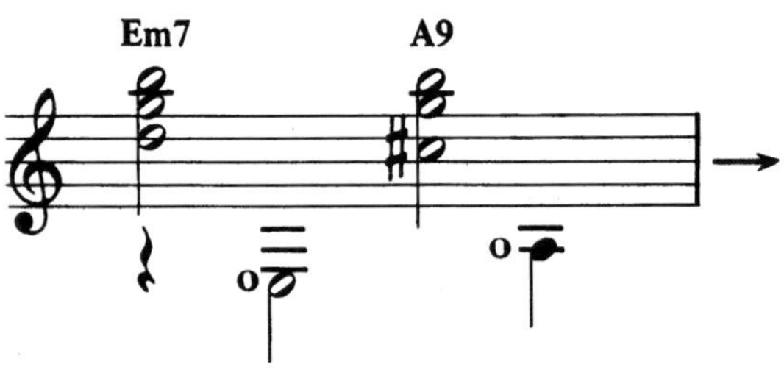

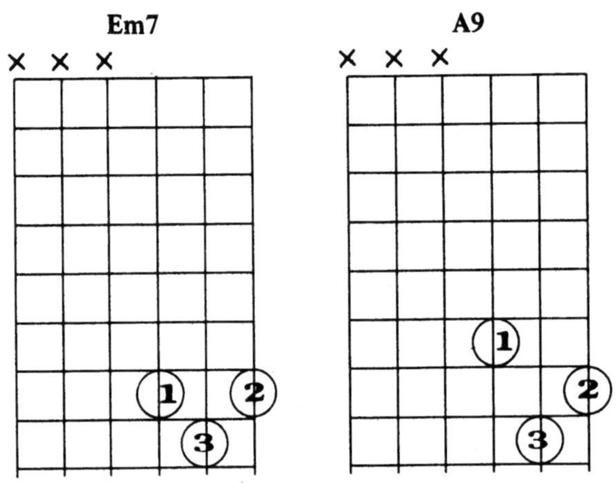

Try out above idea using other positions —

DIATONIC SCALE HARMONIZATION

In the opening section on 7th chords there was a short presentation of harmonized scales. If we "pile thirds"above each sacle tone, we come up with 7th chords : 2 major 7ths : 1 dominant 7th ; 3 minor 7ths ; and 1 minor 7th with a lowered fifth__

Example

We can call this process "Diatonic Harmony"__ Each grouping of 3rds from any given root in the scale will conform to the key signature of that particular scale__We will use large Roman numerals to indicate Major chords__ The appropriate symbol following each numeral will tell us "what kind of chord" – Example m7, maj7, etc__ Any one of the chords may be altered – if so, we use the appropriate Roman numeral to indicate this__ For example; VI 7 would indicate an F♯ , or raised 3rd tone, in the appropriate chord above__

Several harmonized scales are available on the fingerboard. They offer a systematized approach to learning all of the available chords in any given key – also – remember that each chord may be altered through lowering or raising appropriate scale tones within the chord__

Note scale degree vii__ It is a minor 7 ♭5 chord__Within the scale, it sounds like a 1st inversion of V9__

vii may be used as a good substitute for V and we will present this fully in a later section when we talk about substitution chords –

There are other instances like this within the scale : these will be discussed fully later__

> Learn to identify chords by using the Roman numeral symbol, this makes it possible to translate any chord progression into any key. Transposing chordal parts becomes an easy matter. For example if we talk about a I – vi – ii – V pattern we should be able to do this progression in any of the 12 keys.

Harmonizations are possible using any scale__ We will discuss the major and minor scales in detail__ We will briefly touch on some other possibilities so you can experiment with them__

Let's compare harmonizations on various scales__

C Major

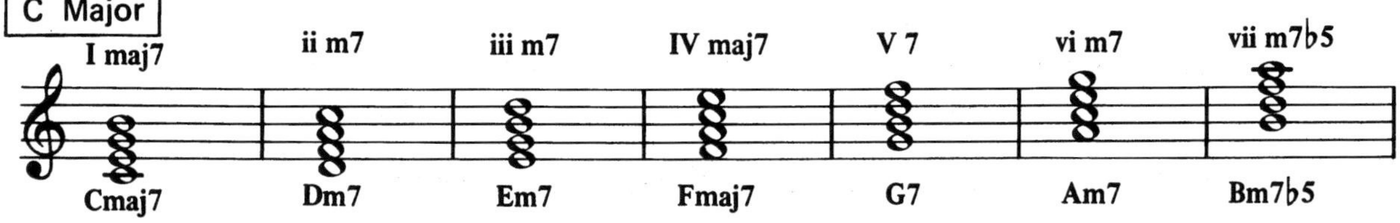

C Natural Minor Note the Roman numeral symbols

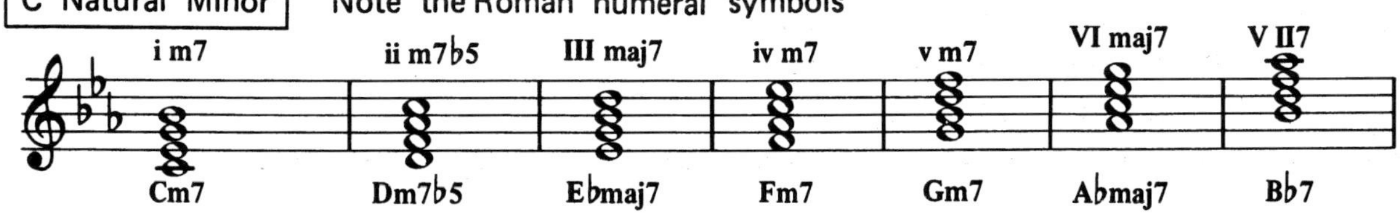

C Harmonic minor — Note interesting III chord —

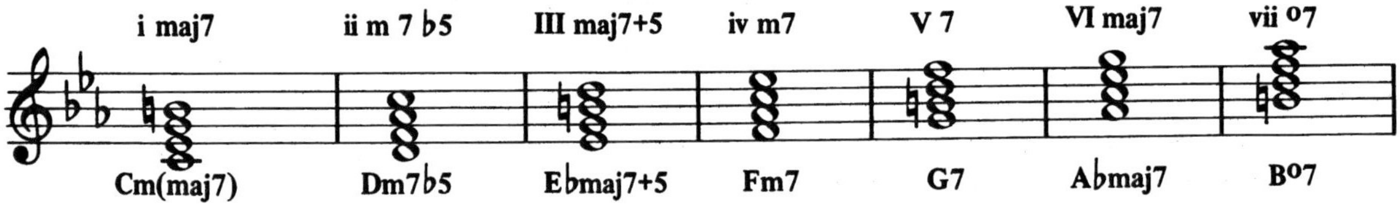

C Melodic minor — Only ascending given — descending would conform to natural minor.

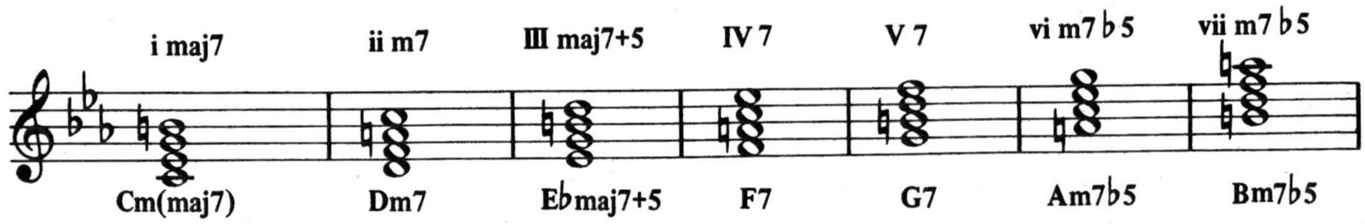

This is a good one for minor blues__

Chords may be built using other interval combinations__ A common device, used by many modern composers is to use intervals of 4ths instead of thirds__ Apply this concept to the various scales and note the interesting sounds which result__

Example :

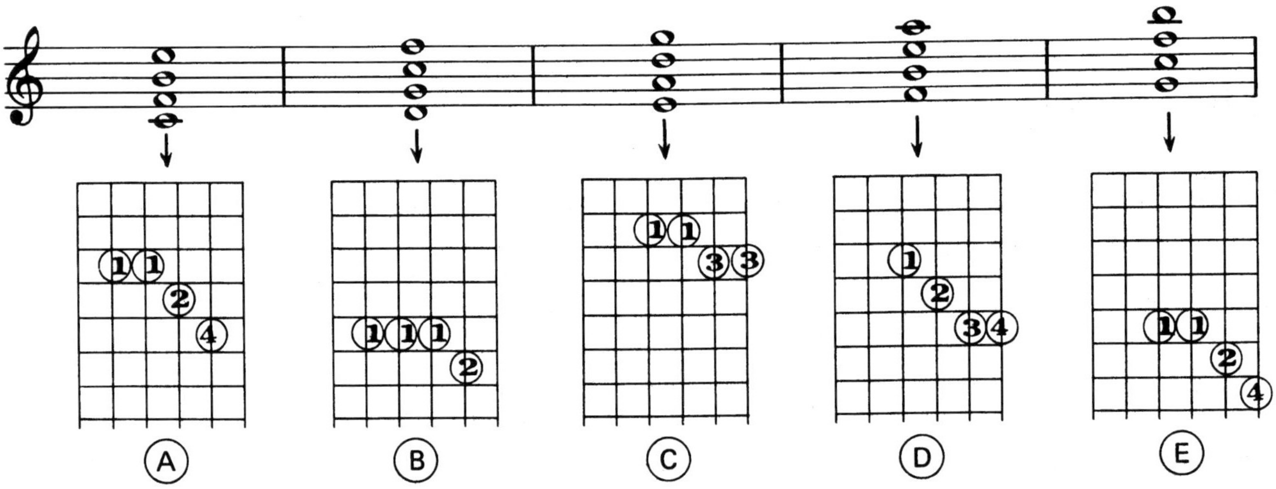

If you examine these, you'll find some very functional voicings — most excellent for regular use — they may be analyzed a number of ways and could be used in a number of ways__

- (A) Could be C maj7 with suspension — could be G13 with suspension — could be F maj7 with ♭5
- (B) Could be G7 with suspension — could be B♭6/9__
- (C) Could be C6/9, 1st inv; could be G6/9
- (D) Beautiful G9 with 13th — Also F maj7 ♭5
- (E) Could work as G7 sus4 — also C maj7 5

Possibilities are endless__Opens many doors for experimentation__Be creative__

Theoretically, chords may be built using any scale as a base or involving any distance between intervals—

You could use : (1) Seconds  etc. (2) Thirds  etc.

(3) Fourths  etc. (4) Fifths  etc.

(5) Sixths  etc. (6) Sevenths  etc.

It's obvious that most of these are impractical for guitar use Many would be possible via inversions and would provide most unusual voicings. I include the idea here for readers who may want to explore these possibilities—

The same principle may be applied to scales. There are many scales, other than our major & minor, which are usable.

EX: Pentatonic scale Note 1st chord is C6 Actually our system of 3rds does not provide for the added 6th to the tonic chord –

(Note absence of our Tri-Tone F – B)

THE HUNGARIAN SCALE

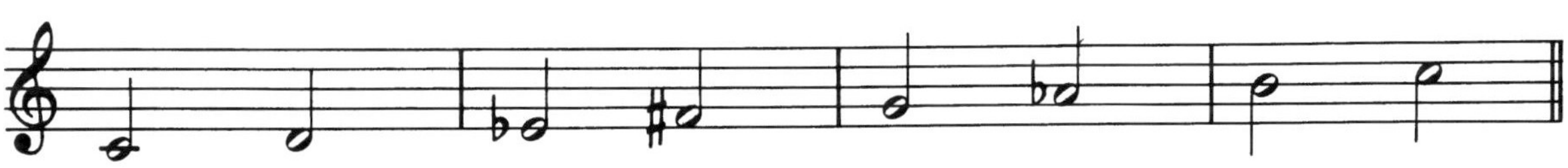

Included to demonstrate interval arrangement possibilities in building different kinds of scales. There are hundreds of different possibilities – (Far too many to include all of them here) – notice the interesting chords which result from harmonizing this scale:

i maj7 II 7♭5 III maj7+5 iv$^{o7}_{o3}$ V maj7 VI maj7 viiø7 i maj7

This offers most interesting compositional possibilities— Notice how unusual a 1 – 4 – 5 progression would be in this key – i is a minor with a major 7th; iv is a ♯IV is a $^{o}7$ – $^{o}3$; V is a major 7th –[vii 7 will "sound" like a m6— It is not analyzed as m6 chord in the scale, due to the A♭, which is ♭♭7—

Try writing a simple melody in key of C, built on a 1 – 4 – 5 chord pattern—Then add the key signature indicated by the above scale— You should end up with a most unusual sounding melody— Use harmonies indicated above—
[Try building some other, unusual scales]

Diatonic Scale Harmonization Key of C

(A)

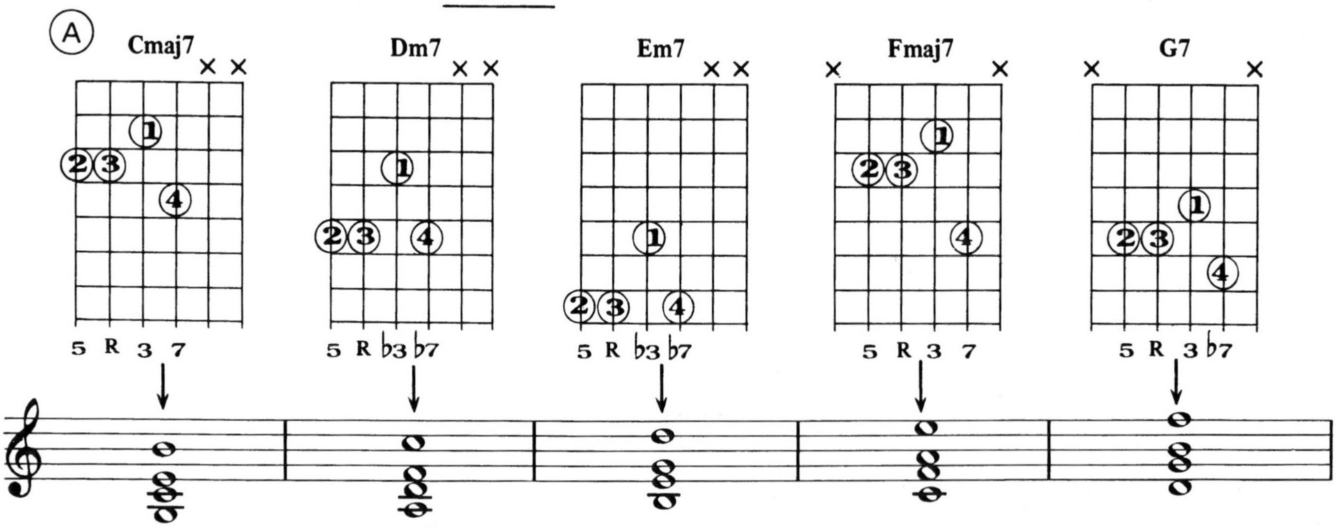

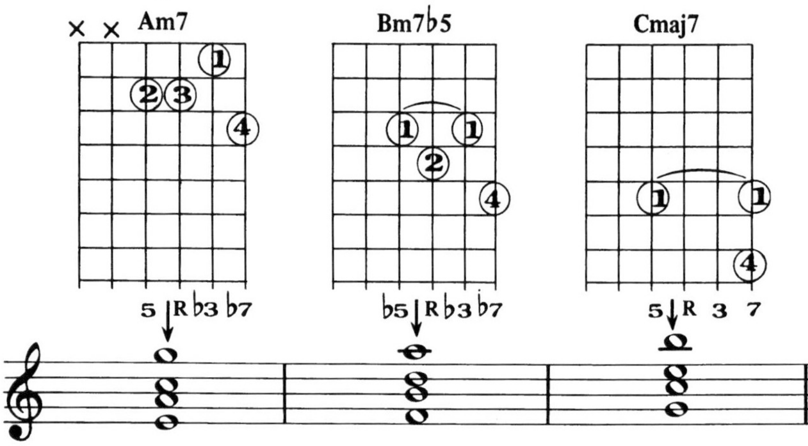

This harmonized C scale can be played within a 7 fret span from the starting chord. This harmonization can be used up to, and including key of F – starting with F maj7 – 8th fret.

Some of the voicings can be found at other positions on the fingerboard, but would extend this fingering beyond a span of 7 frets__ This is the most practical fingering for this particular scale__

> With this scale, and the one on the followng page, it is possible to paly thru all 12 keys chordally – memorize –

Diatonic Scale Harmonization Key of F

(B)

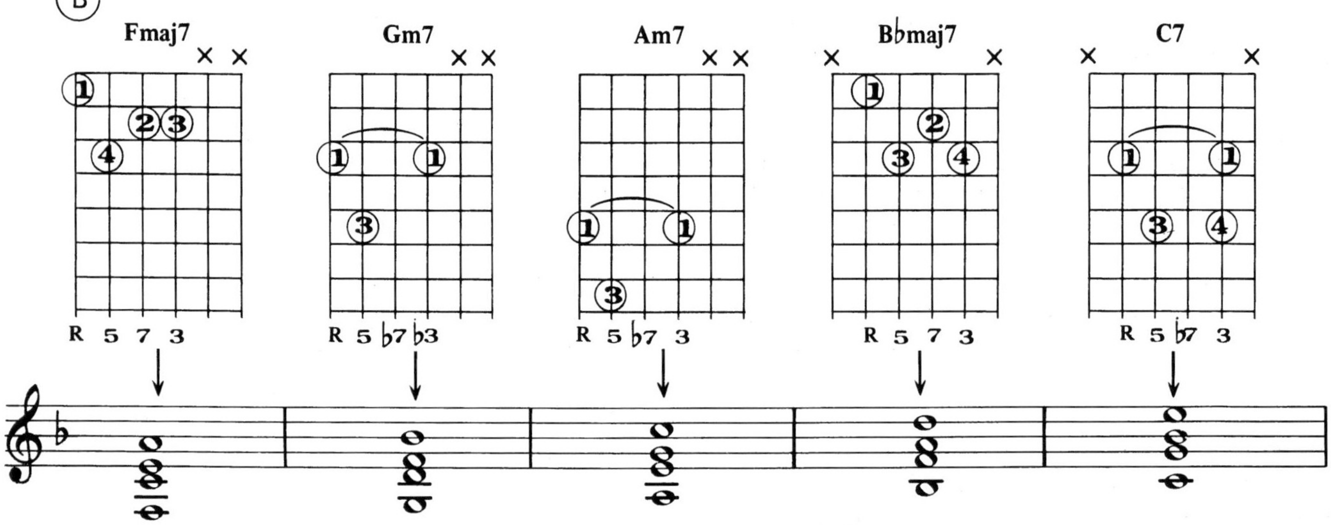

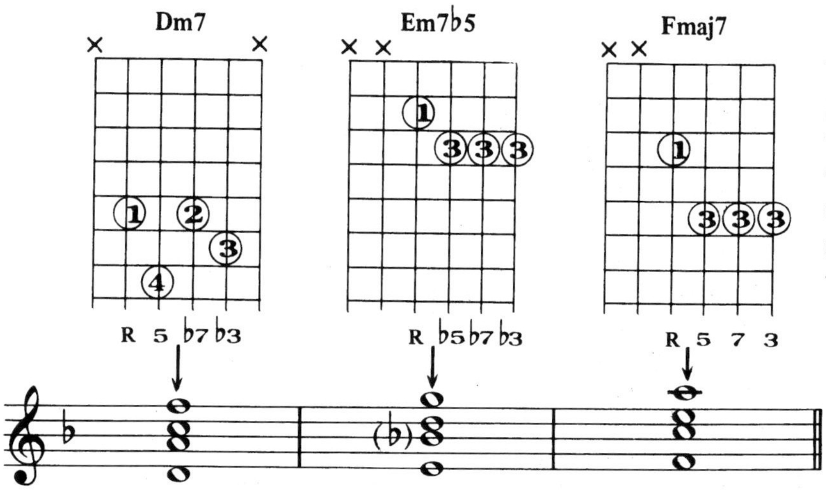

This harmonized F scale can be played within a 7 fret span from the starting chord— It is possible to use this particular harmonization up to, and including, key of C — starting with C maj7 on the 8th fret—

Some of the same voicings can be found at other positions on the fingerboard. B♭maj7 and C7 could be played on bottom four strings at frets 6 and 8. Em7♭5 and Fmaj7 can be played on inside four strings on frets 7 and 8— [It is most practical as fingered above using a minimum fret span]

Diatonic Scale Harmonization Key of B♭

(C)

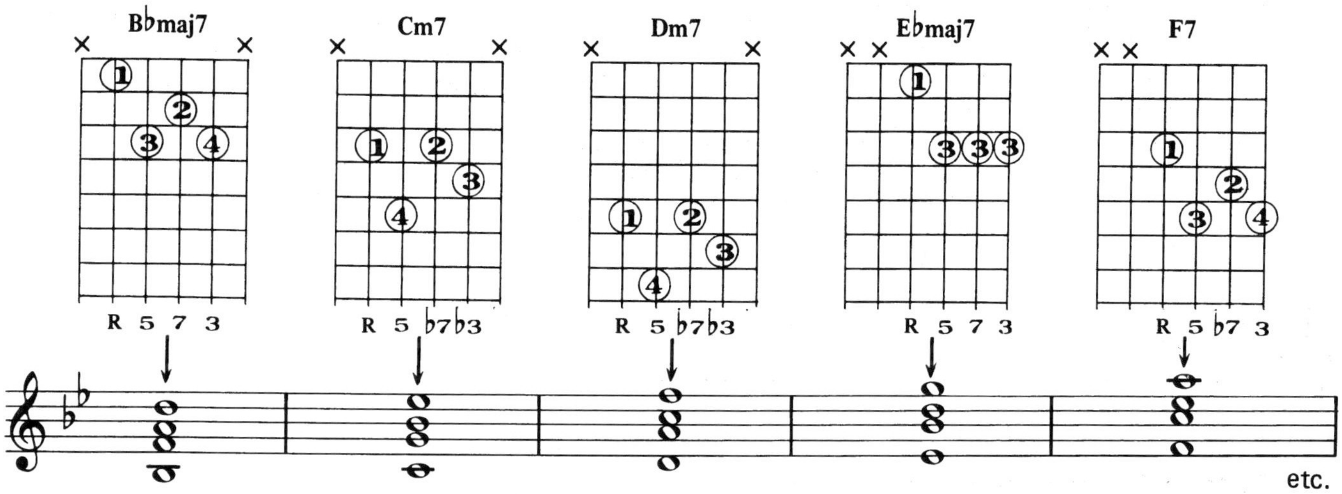

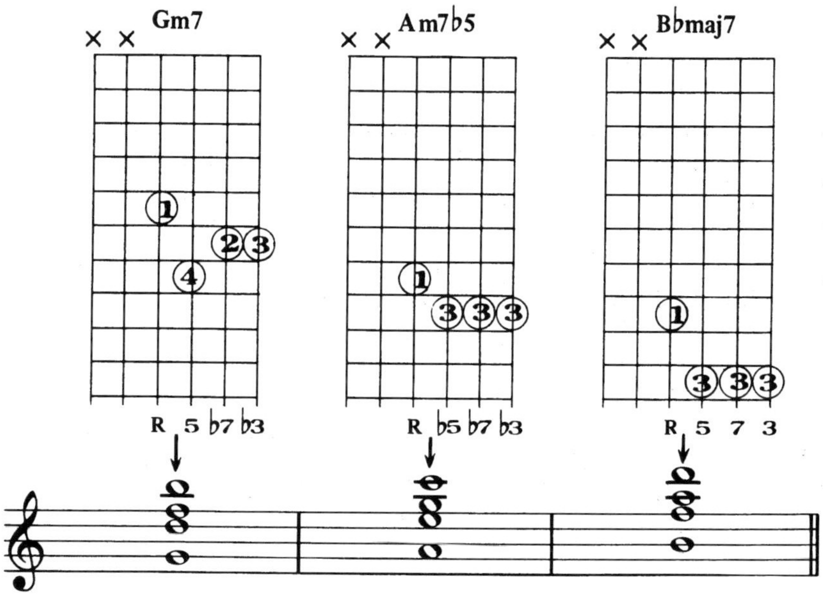

This harmonized B♭ scale covers a 10 fret span— Would be an impractical fingering beyond key of "E" unless guitar is cutaway — Chords are in a good register.

Diatonic Scale Harmonizations Key of E♭

(D)

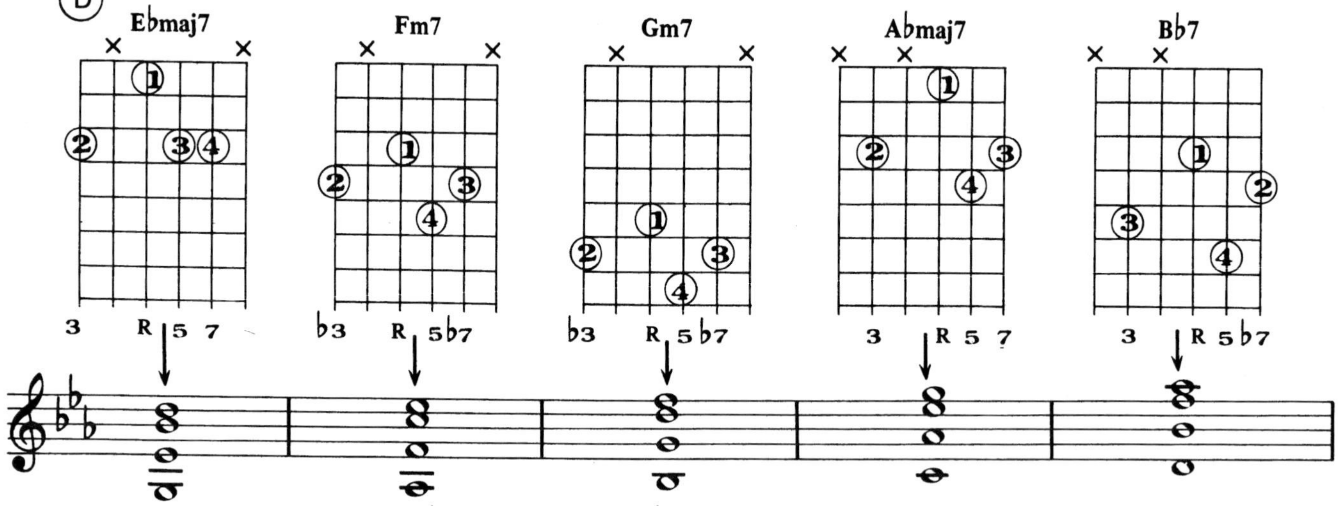

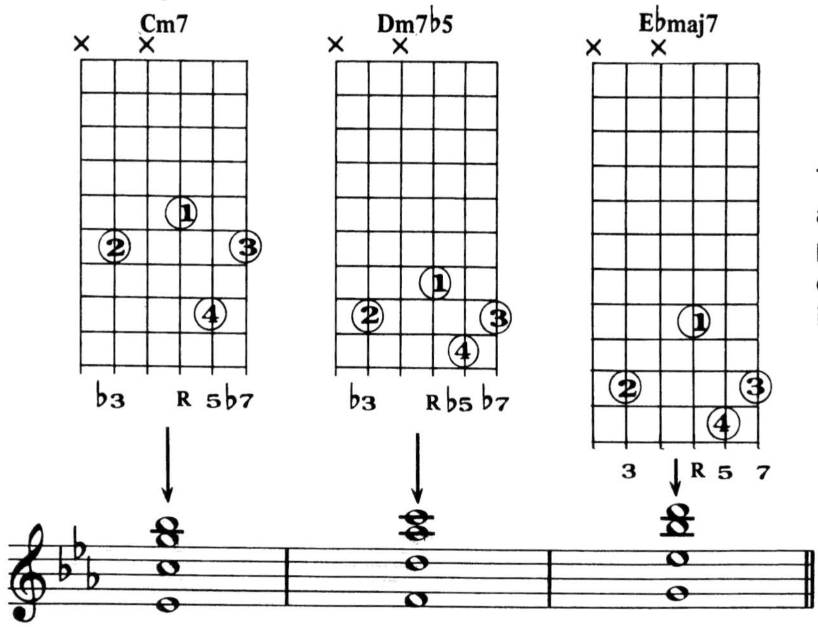

This harmonized E♭ scale covers an 11 fret span__ Would be most practical, depending on availability of upper frets via cutaway. Contains interesting inversions on all chords.

Diatonic Scale Harmonizations Key of F

(E)

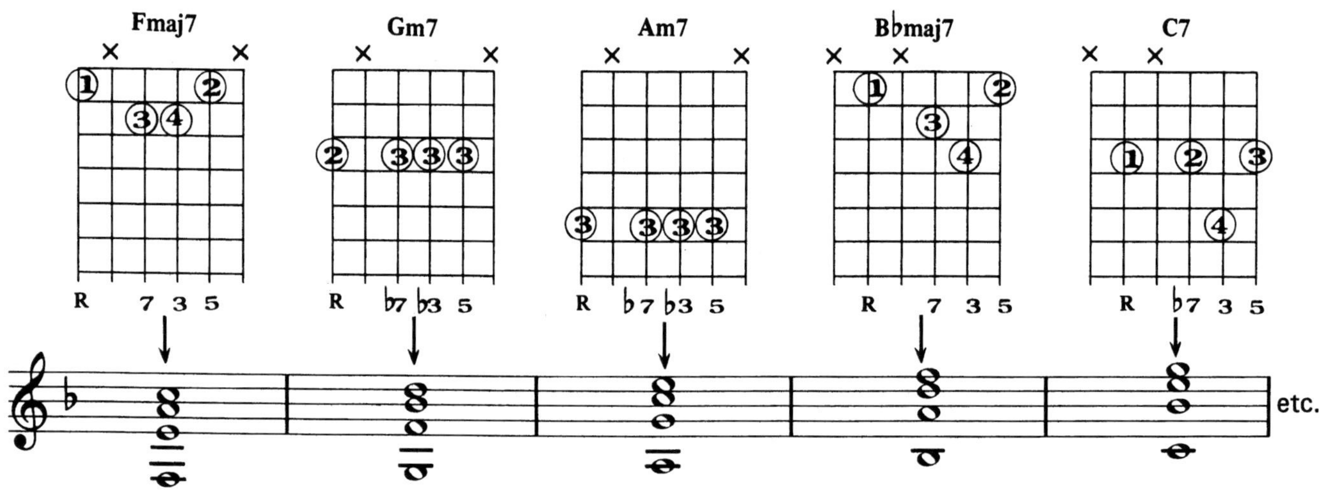

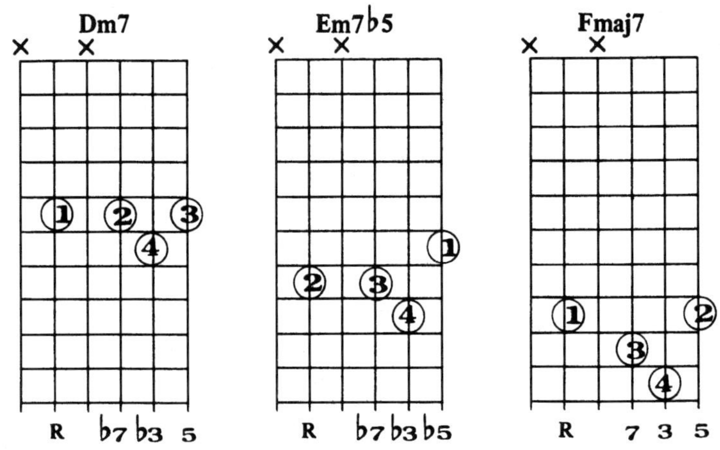

Fingering on the Bbmaj7, C7, and high F maj7 become awkward trying to maintain consistent voicing. Good way to overcome this is to refinger chords and use right hand fingers instead of pick —

Alternate fingerings

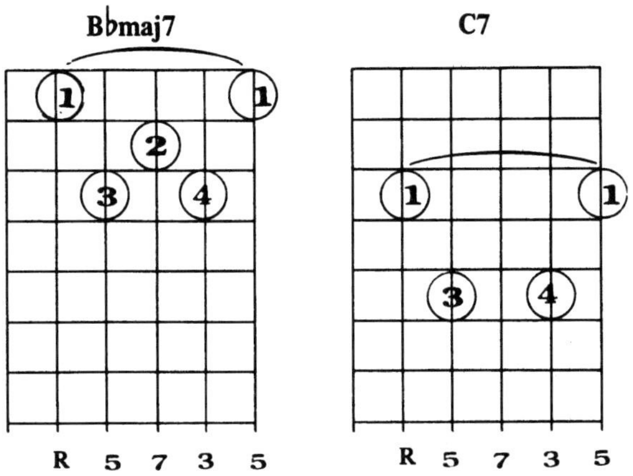

use right hand as follows
thumb – 1 – 2 – 3 – on strings
⑤-③-②-①
"A la classic guitar"

(double chord 5th with this fingering)

Diatonic Harmonization **Key of C har. minor.**

Ⓕ

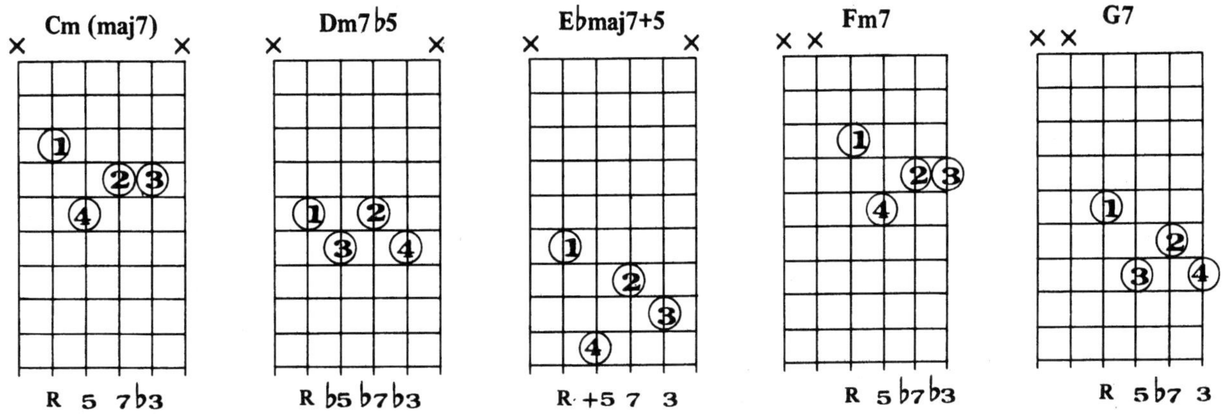

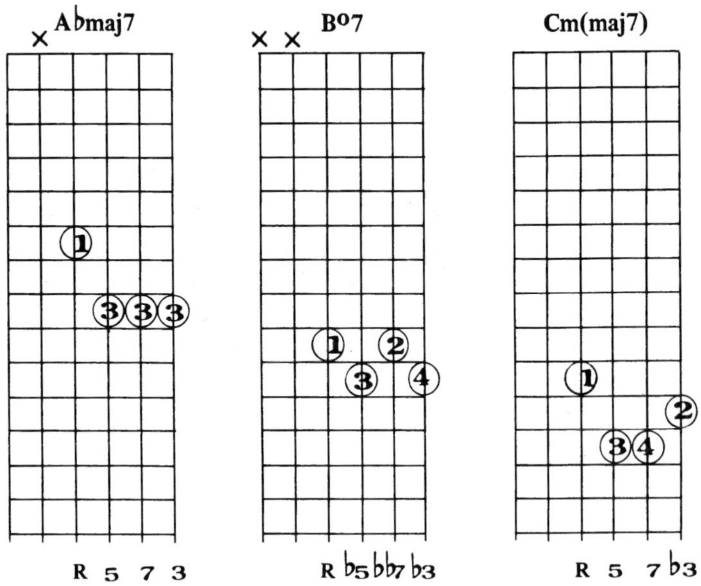

Interesting sound on the tonic minor with major 7th added. Also a most unusual III chord— major 7th with an augmented 5th—

Scale covers A 10 fret span. Lowest starting key would be B♭ min. Upper possibilities would depend on neck length—

Variations using other patterns, are possible— Use previous major scale forms— Also possible using natural and melodic minor scales— Try them— Write them—

Harmonized diatonic scales with added chromatic tones. Use of diminished chords or parallel couplings.

(1) Using diminished chords on chromatic roots—

C maj7 C♯° Dm7 D♯° Em7 Fmaj7 F♯° G7 G♯° Am7 A♯° Bm7-5 Cmaj7

Basic scale "chord fingering" the same as scale (C) in key of B♭. Diminished chords will finger naturally using the same string series as the diatonic chords—Two are marked above in accord with the particular string series.

(2) Using parallel couplings—(Going into the next chord chromatically using the same voicing)

Cmaj7 D♭m7 Dm7 E♭m7 Em7 Fmaj7 F♯7 G7 A♭m7 Am7 A♯m7-5 Bm7-5 Cmaj7

Basic fingering remains the same. Finger chromatic chords the same as the following diatonic chord. For example D♭m7 would finger the same as Dm7— Note use of enharmonic notation to make reading easier— Practice above two patterns using the different diatonic harmonizations given before.

Here are some suggested ways to practice the diatonic scale harmonizations —

Ⓐ As they are written – up and back down —

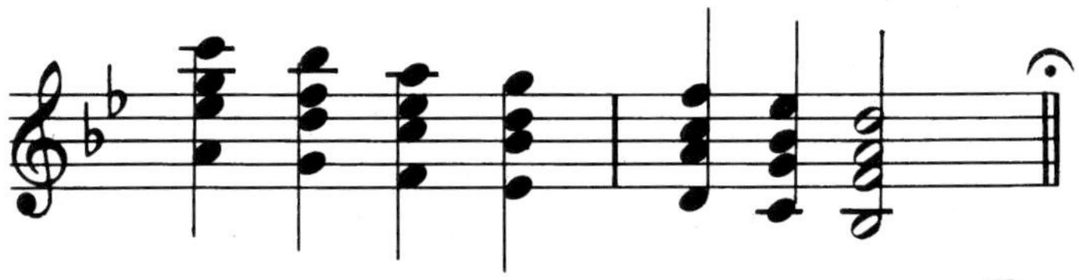

Use pick, or right hand fingers (thumb, 1, 2, 3) – Strike simultaneously.

Ⓑ Hold chord down but pick as arpeggio — (also with fingers).

etc.

Ⓒ Up three at a time then back to next scale degree —

etc.

Ⓓ Up four at a time then back to next scale degree —

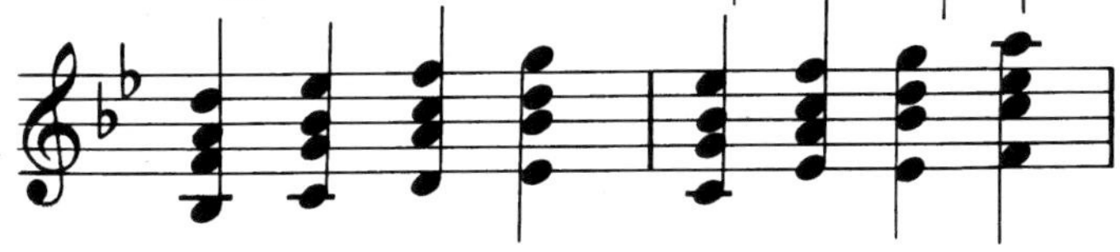

etc.

Ⓔ Do Ⓒ & Ⓓ as 16th note arpeggios on each beat. Use pick or do with right hand fingers.

Ⓕ Alternate every other scale degree

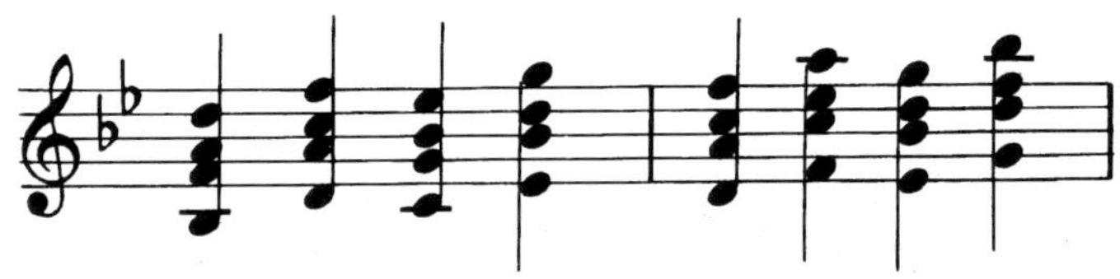

etc.

You can probably think of other ways — Enough time on these studies and you can move these around quickly and surely — Ideal "chord melody" preparation.

The diatonic harmonizations are possible in "closed position" as arpeggios — They are available in most of the fingerboard positions —

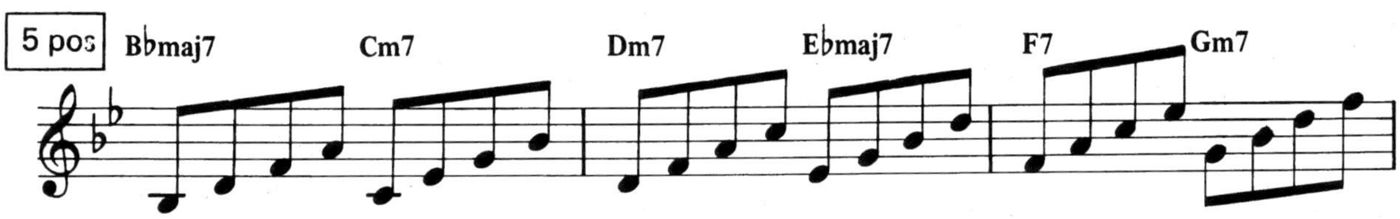

Do in other keys –

Or: Up one chord, down the next—

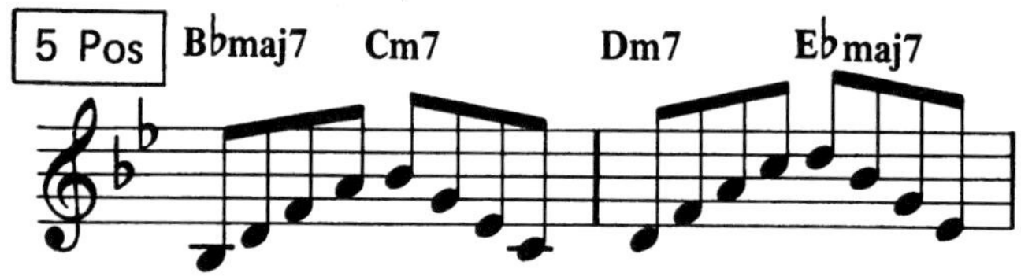

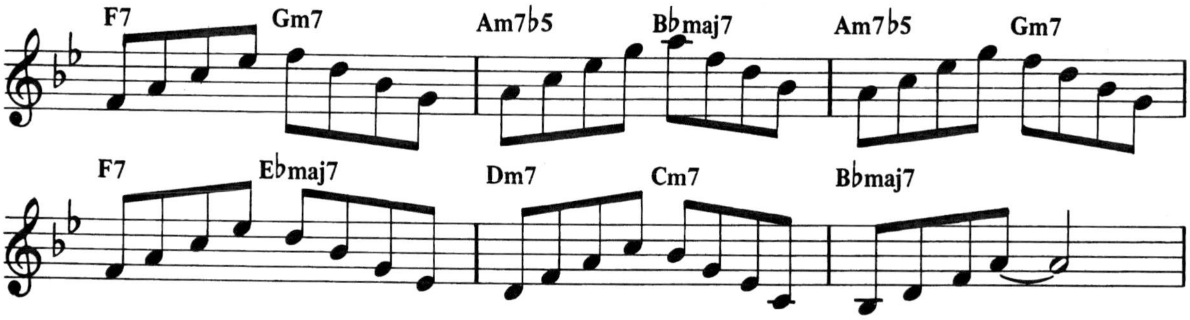

Or: 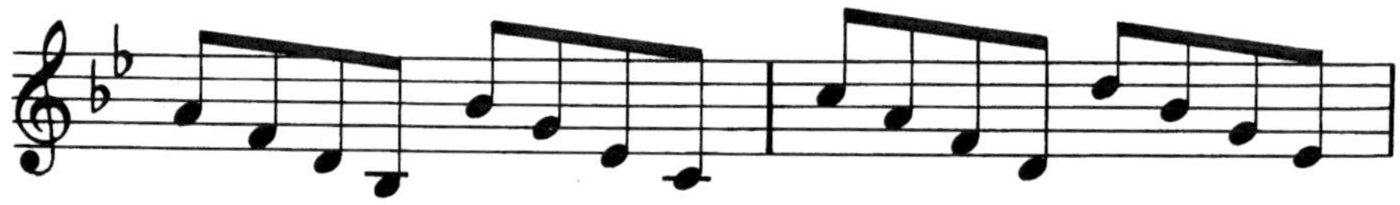 etc.

Or:  etc.

A good arpeggio "position" study is to play up the first chord, then down thru scale to next chord.

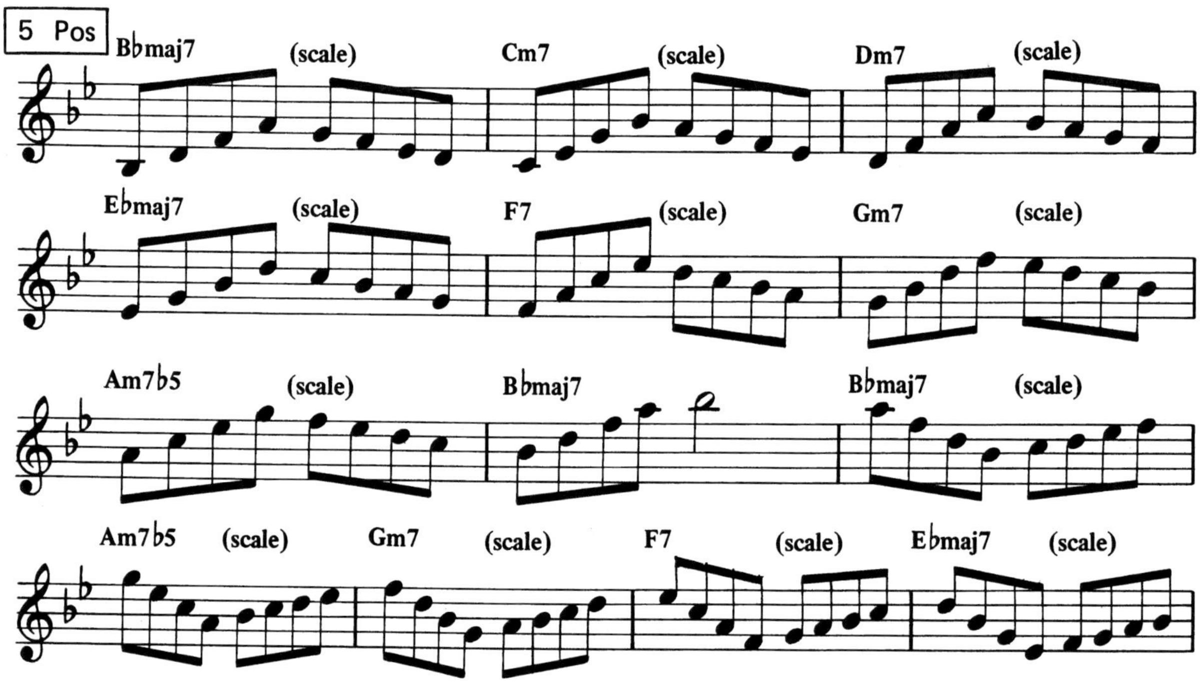

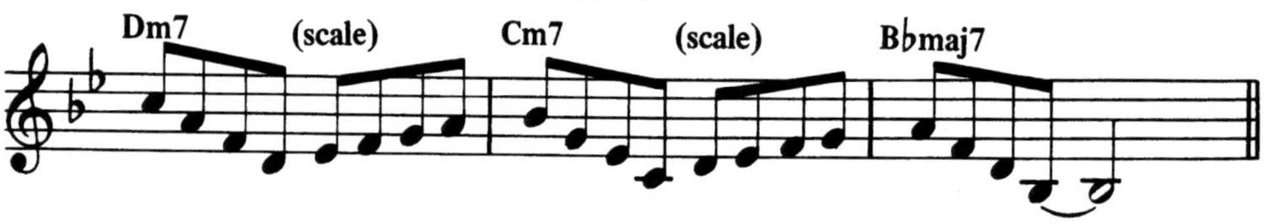

Do in other keys

This is good with someone playing chords along with the exercise. Also good as a duet with other guitar playing 3rds— Either above or below—

This should open up some ideas for other studies using arpeggios—

Another interesting approach to the diatonic scale harmonization is the use of a dominant 7th chord to lead into the diatonic chord (Through the circle of fifths).

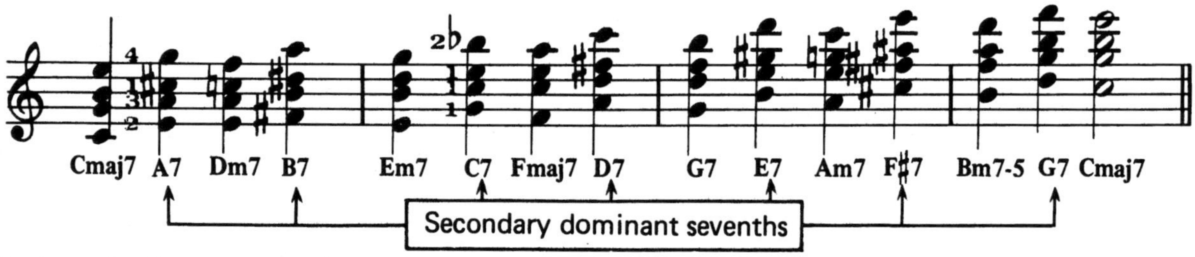

Basic scale fingering remains the same. Dominant 7th chords will utilize the same string series. Two of these chords are fingered according to the string series. Each 7th, used here as a secondary dominant, is in the 2nd inversion (5th as low note)— For further interest lower 5th tone in each secondary dominant—

This is a most interesting exercise— The secondary dominants give the diatonic scale harmonization a most unusual flavor—

Also try using root position for all chords—

For example

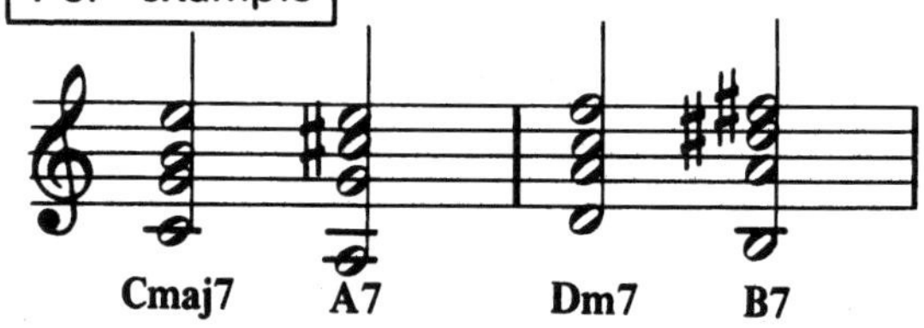

etc. up thru scale—

Here's an interesting variation on one of the previous arpeggio exercises— Note the use of accidentals on the connecting scale passages to conform to the secondary dominants—

Have 2nd guitar play chords while you play single notes.

Work out the same type exercise using the diminished chord—

etc.

Then use the parallel couplings—

Enharmonic notation makes reading easier

etc.

Modal harmonies (all related to tonic "C")

Solutions of tonic chord to V7 and return. Original in open position, with a ½ step higher to demonstrate position fingering.

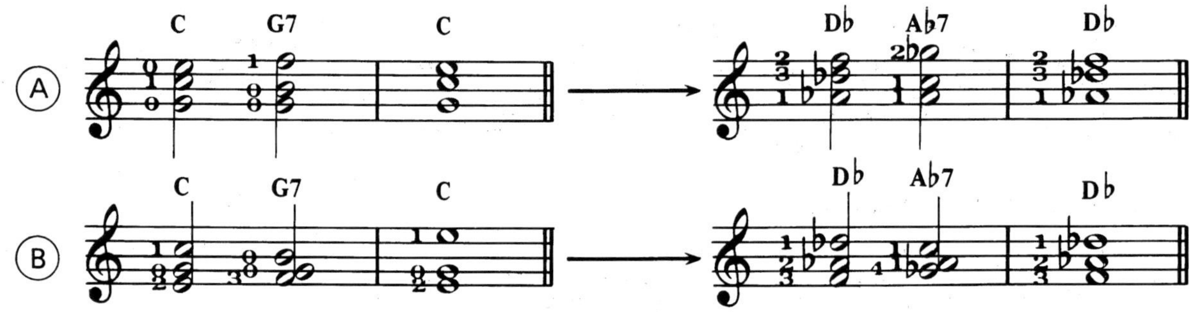

(C)

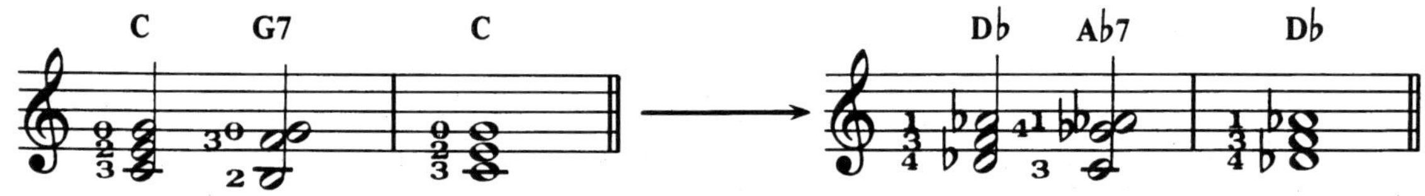

(D)

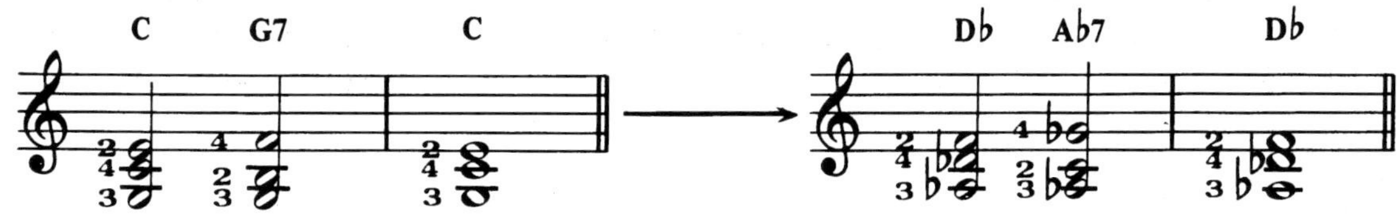

Moving (A)(B)(C) requires a fingering change into new position to compensate for the lack of available open strings. Fingering for (D) remains the same when moved due to no open strings utilized. Some examples are presented in simplest form, by using three tones (or voices) in each chord. The dom. 7th, in each instance is incomplete. (There is no 5th tone included)

The following "practice routine" on each pattern.

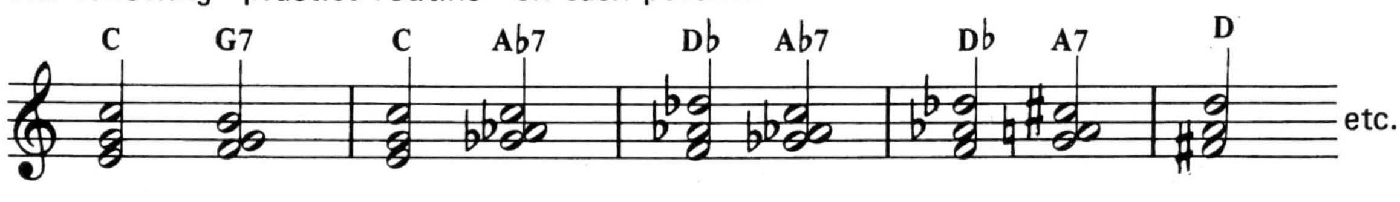

Now try the same pattern with a different melodic consideration.

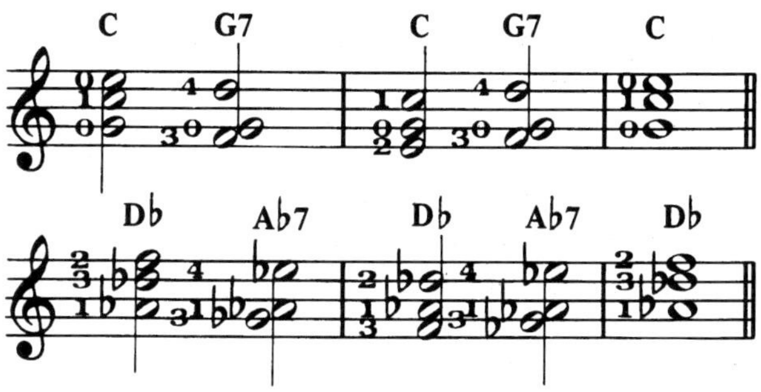

Notice lack of 3rd chord tone in dominant 7th — not offensive since b7 is included —

Let's take A four note chord in another key —

Moving this one is easy since all chord tones are fingered. Notice "complete" dom. 7th chord —

Now take the same "voice" arrangement in C

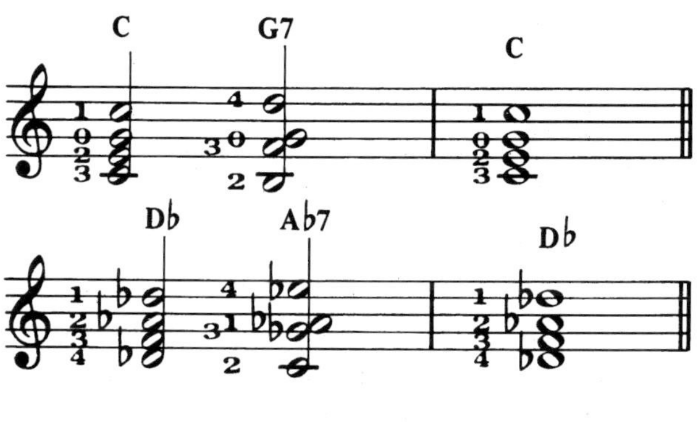

Note that moving this pattern requires new fingering, since open strings are no longer available —

A series of chords, moving from one to the other, is what we call a "progression". These chord progressions can be analyzed in terms of tonal cycles. These cycles are measured by examining the bass-root movement. The cycles which govern the majority of movements are cycles of 3rds, 5ths, and 7ths, The cycles may be positive or negative. The positive cycles are, generally speaking, more satisfying to the ear— (Probably due to musical conditioning through repeated hearings), and are stronger.

Cycle of
6ths or 3rds
(strong)

Cycle of
4ths or 5th
(strong)

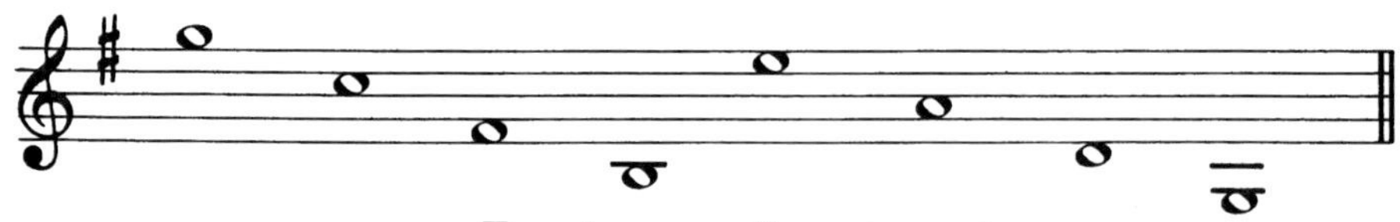

Tonal range adjusted merely
to simplify Notation.

Cycle of
7th or 2nds
(strong)

To read the negative cycles simply read backwards. Diatonic cycles would remain within the key. Chords built on these roots would conform to the key. Foreign chords to the key may still be analyzed via tonal cycles. This G to E♭ would still be positive C3 – G–B♭ would be negative.

Practicing chords through a variety of tonal cycles can begin to train your ear to hear various types of chordal movement. It is also possible to construct interesting progressions as a basis for original material. It also provides an interesting approach to learning a great many chord forms through a series of progressions—

The previous diatonic scale harmonizations given previously are all cycles of 7ths (C7)

The scale using secondary dominant sevenths could be analyzed as C3 + C5— Go back and look at it – C to A is a cycle of a 3rd, A to D is a cycle of a 5th— It keeps going through this pattern till it completes itself at the C maj7 again— [Play backwards for negative cycles]

A knowledge of tonal bass patterns is an invaluable aid to learning new material—

The following pages have some examples of the different tonal cycles. Spend some time learning them. You can gain a fund of most usable material—

Diatonic chords resolved through C3 (postive) or stronger

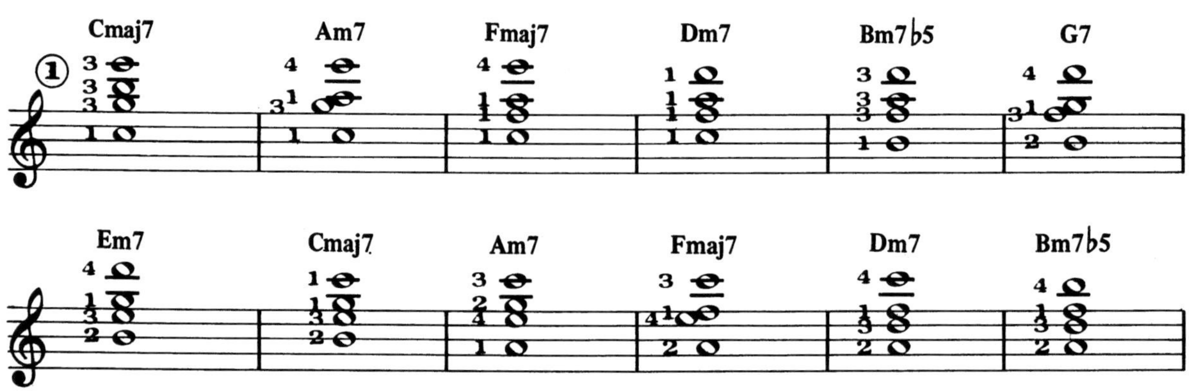

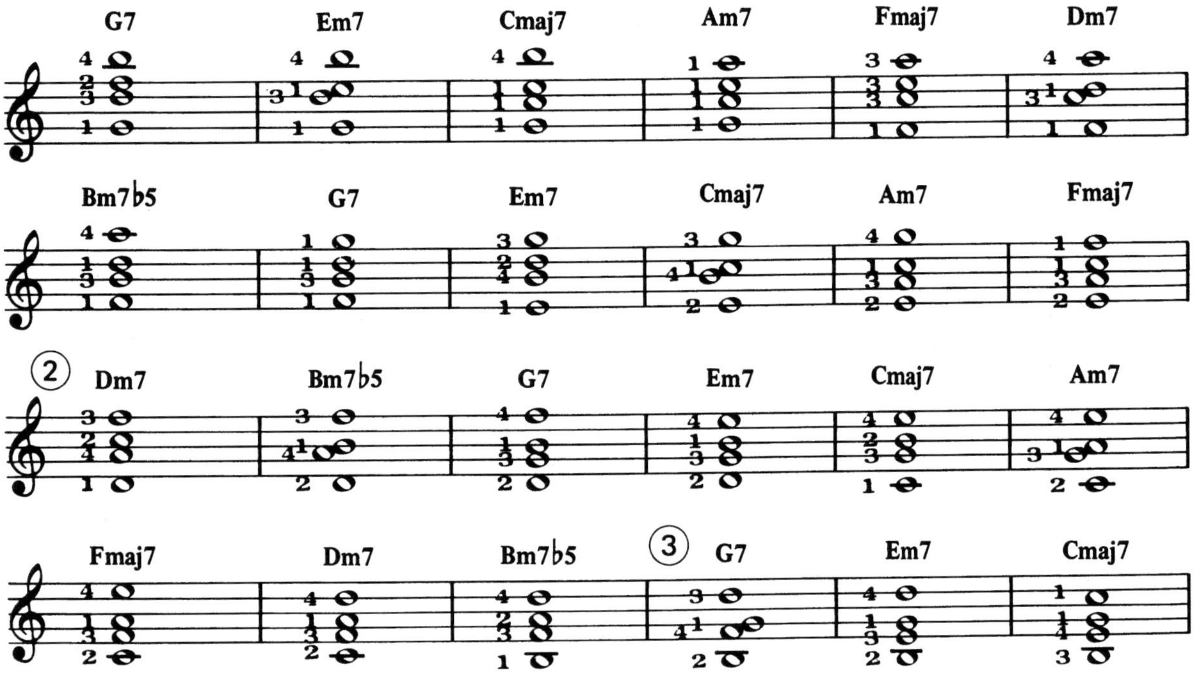

This pattern involves some difficult fingering. Do it slowly at first. Use string series and fingering exactly as marked— Good practice in learning a variety of chord forms— Listen to the circle of thirds— Try in other keys—

Diatonic chords resolved through C5 (positive) or stronger

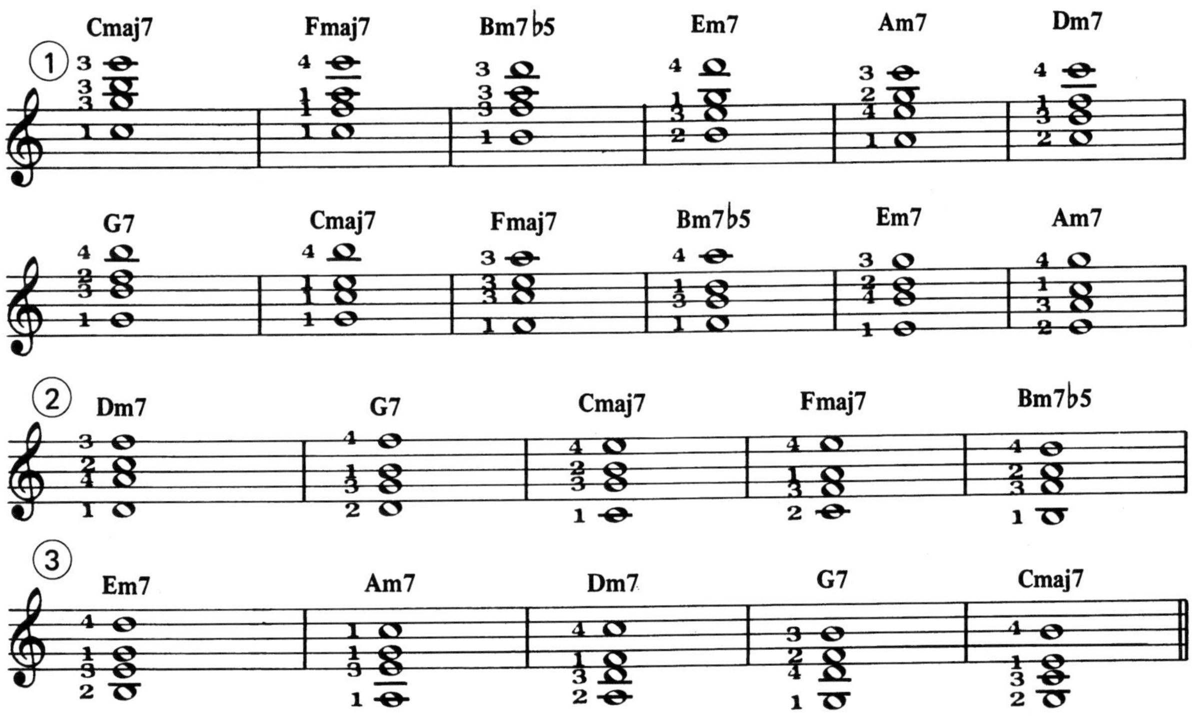

This pattern provides good experience in rapid fingering changes— Finger exactly as marked— Also very good listening experience for harmonies moving diatonically through the circle of fifths— This pattern could be played in key of B (5♯s), starting one fret lower— It can be played up chromatically, as far as fingerboard will allow— Note how well each individual voice moves from chord to chord—

Try in key of "F" starting on high F major 7. Remember, the key signature— One flat (B♭)—

Diatonic chords resolved through C7 (positive) or stronger

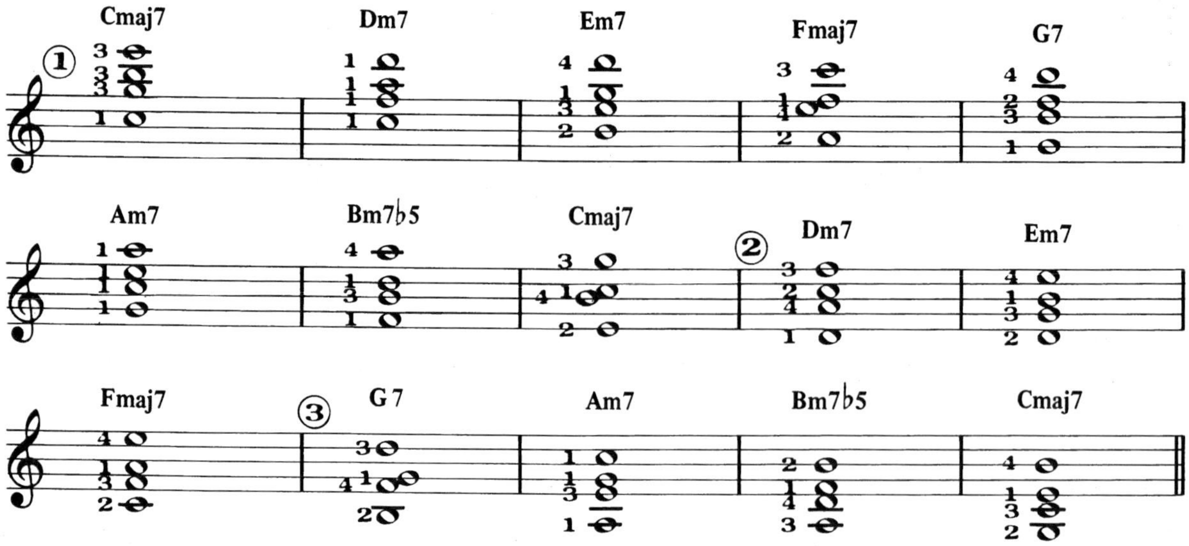

This is an interesting progression through the scale__ Note chords move downward while implied roots move up scalewise__ Try this one with a bass player playing roots for you__ Note unusual Bm7♭5 form immediately before last Cmaj7__

Note smooth resolution of tones from chord to chord__ Try this pattern in other keys__Listen to the chordal movement__

Now try mixing the tonal cycles__

Example

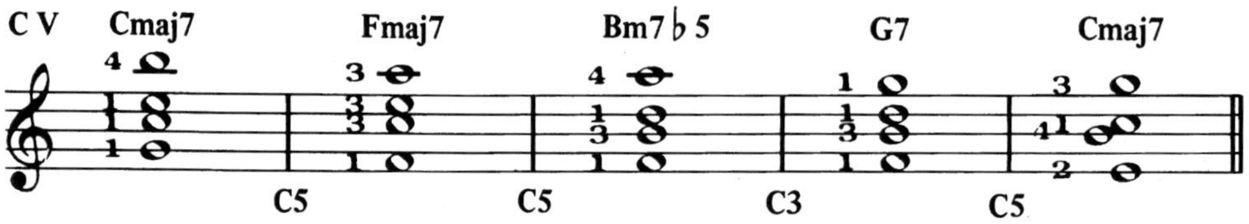

This pattern would be indicated 2 C5 + C3+C5

Another Example

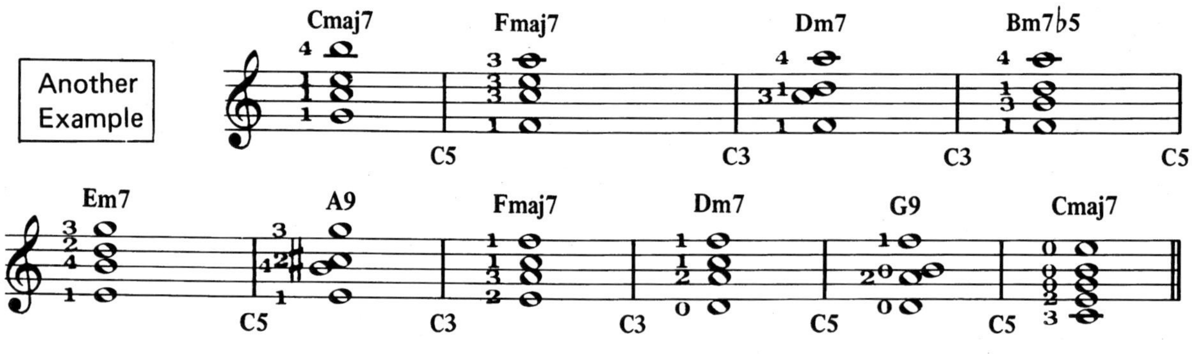

This would be indicated C5 + 2 C3 + 2 C5 + 2 C3 + 2 C5

Another Example

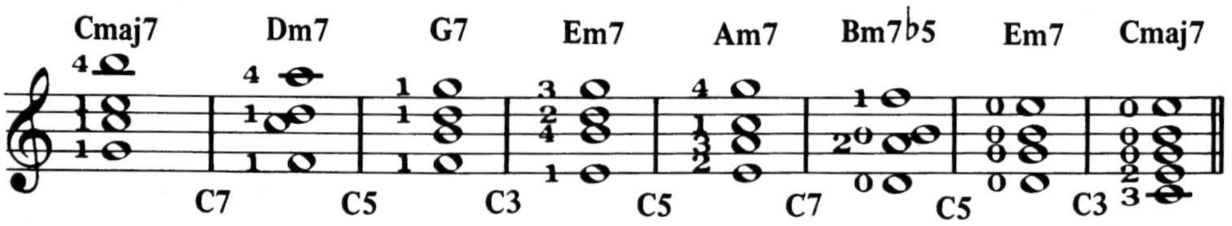

Try making up some in other keys__

Let's try some different divisions of the octave as a basis for chordal material—

divide octave in half

or this way for an ending

divide in three

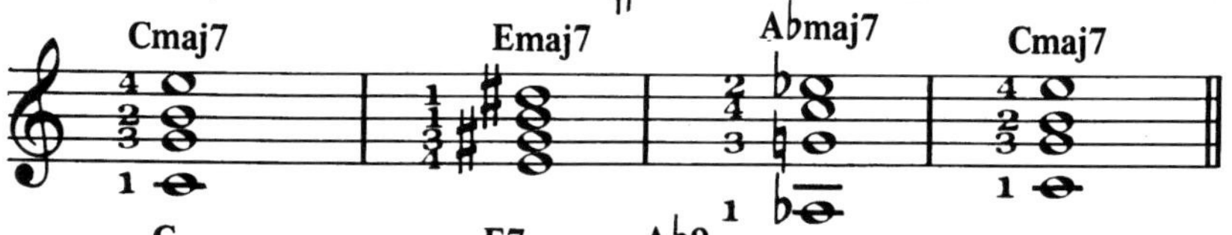

or this way for an ending

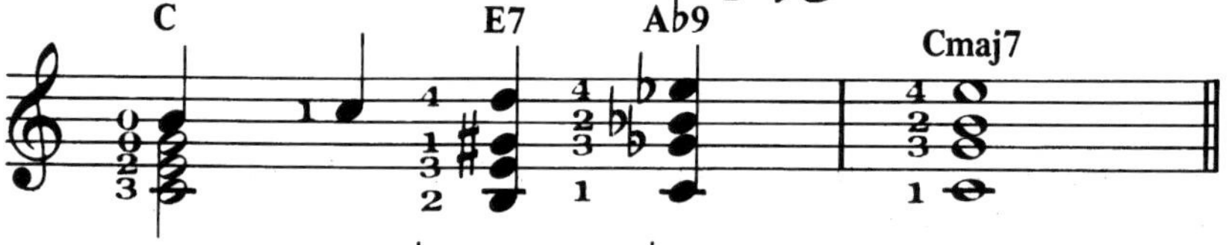

divide in four

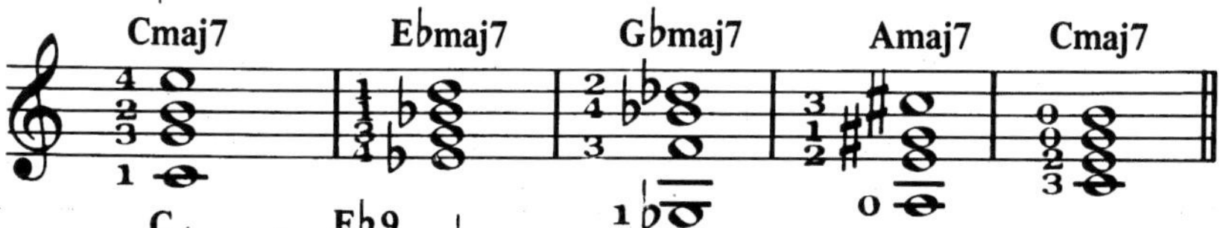

also as an ending

Now you try dividing by 6, then by 12—Make the chords any color – experiment—there's unlimited material available—(What are the tonal cycles?)

Use of Whole Tone Chords on Dom. 7th

First form as sub. for E7 so pedal E strng. can be used—

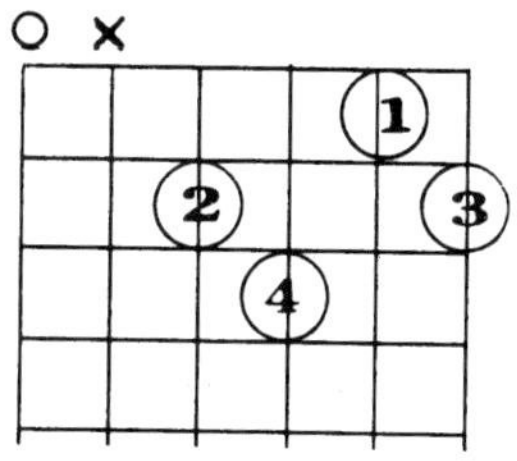

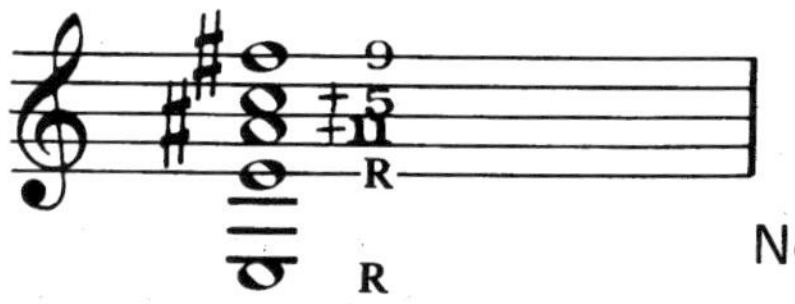

Notice unusual tonal functions in this position.

Now- Using low E string as pedal point move up two frets (A whole step, at a time— And notice unusual inversions.

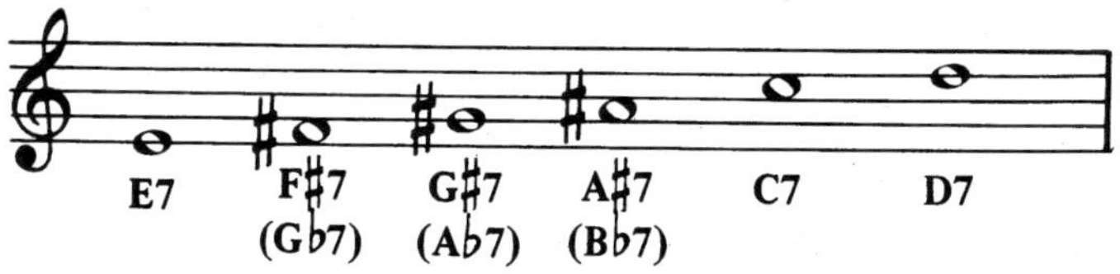

There are only 6 chords, all related to the whole tone scale— This series could be used as dom 7th substitute on any tone in the whole tone scale—

In relation to the given root__ Chords 3 – 5 – 6 Give best sound.
The series make excellent passing chords__

There are only two series, the same as whole tone scales. The second series would start 1/2 higher and use open "A" string as the pedal point. ⟶

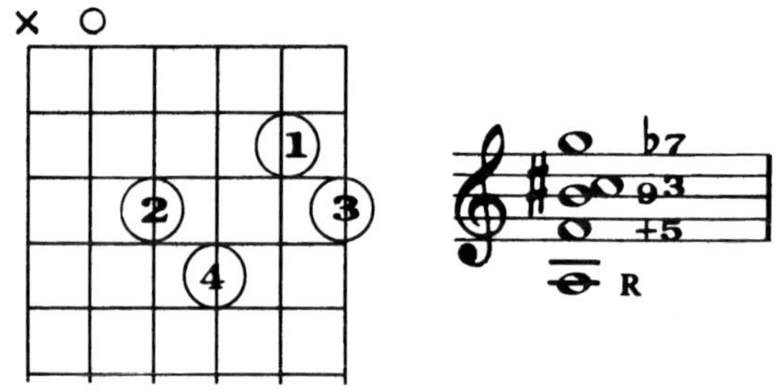

– Same movement and theory applies –

The four note chords may be re-voiced to include other tones from whole tone scale – same movement applies__(same theory)

E7 (orig. C7♭5)

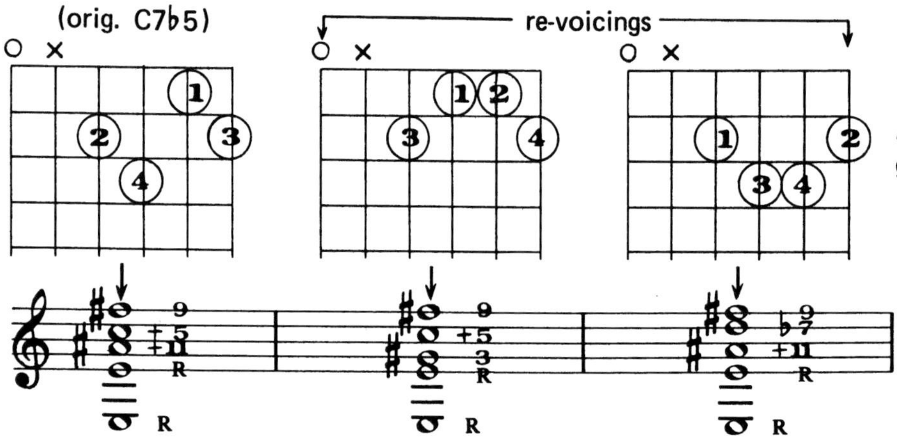

Add "C" root to this form good + 11 voicing –*

*All of this may be used for +11 sub. (Handle with care__)

– Some additional forms of whole tone chords –

C7+5 C9+5

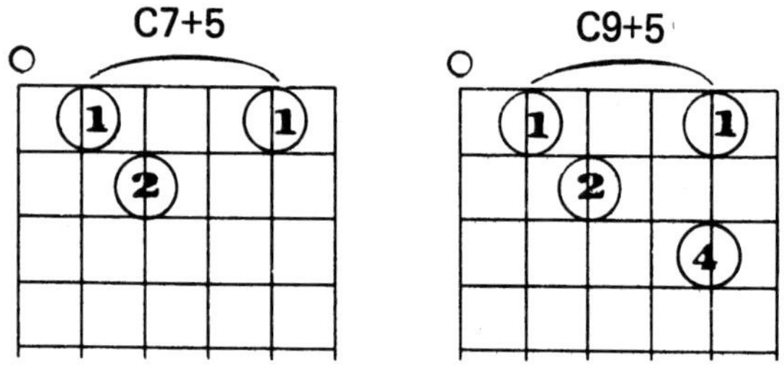

Remember to use all of this material with care. Though all chords here sound good, they'll soon "wear thin" if they are overused.

Also any form of dom. 9th chord with 5th omitted may be treated as whole tone chord__

C9 F9

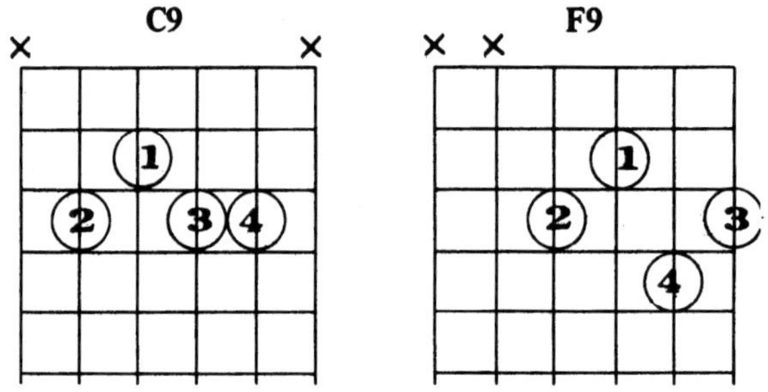

Analyze as ⟶ D7 ——— as G7

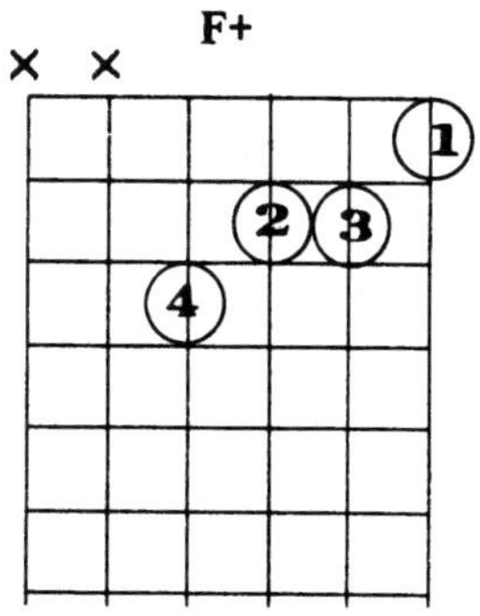

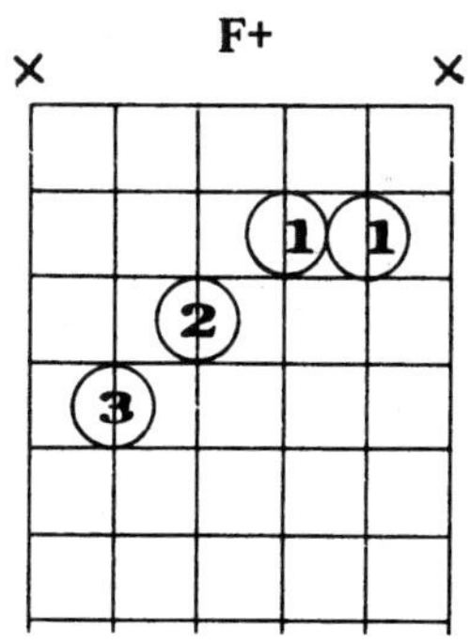

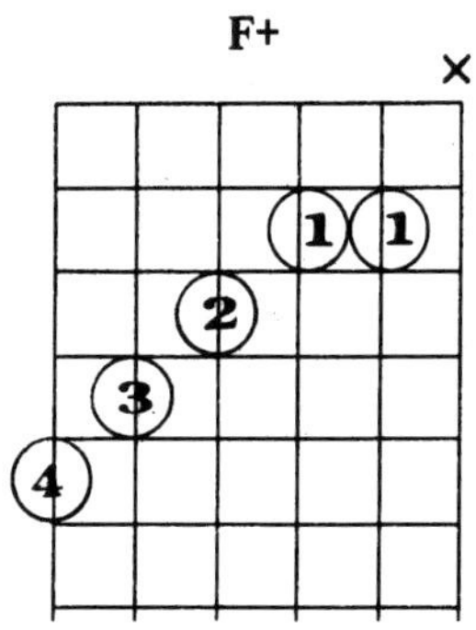

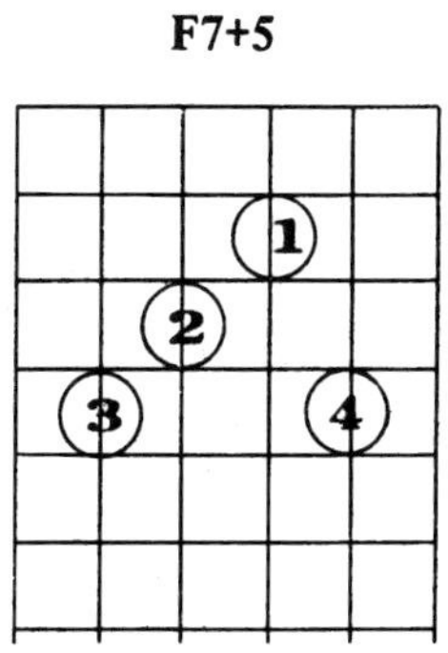

These have been arbitrarily designated as F chords — Remember, they may be named using any tone of the whole-tone scale — Analyze them in relation to other roots (thinking of dominant chords) and resolve them to the appropriate tonic major 7 or major 6 chord.

F ⟶ B♭maj.
G ⟶ C maj.
A ⟶ D maj.
B ⟶ E maj.
D♭ ⟶ G♭maj.
E♭ ⟶ A♭maj.

These three pages have only scratched the surface regarding the possibilities. There are many additional forms — Remember all changes should be made in relation to the whole-tone scale — Voicings should be made with this in mind.

Forms serving several functions—

Any dom. 9th chord (without the root) may also be used as a "min7♭5" or a "min6" form — To remember the different functions — Use the dom. 9 as a starting point. Think of it as the root of a major triad and the other two "uses" become immediately apparent — Remember — The 9th chord is actually minus the root — [it is implied].

For example

is also Bm7♭5 and Dm6
(note that roots form outline of
major triad – G – B – D.)

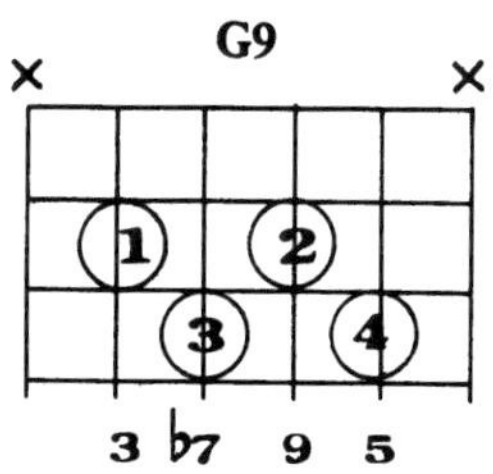

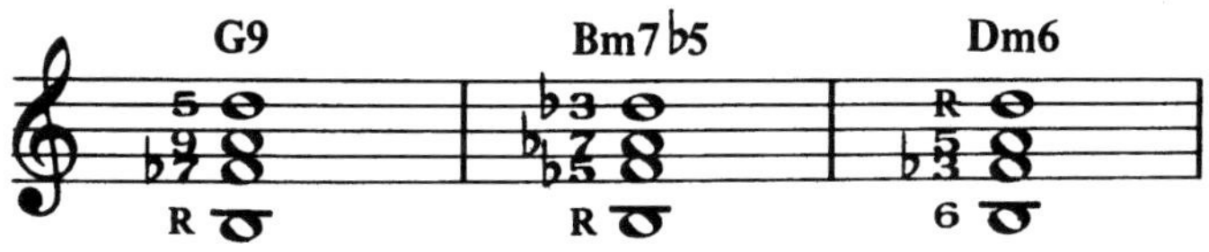

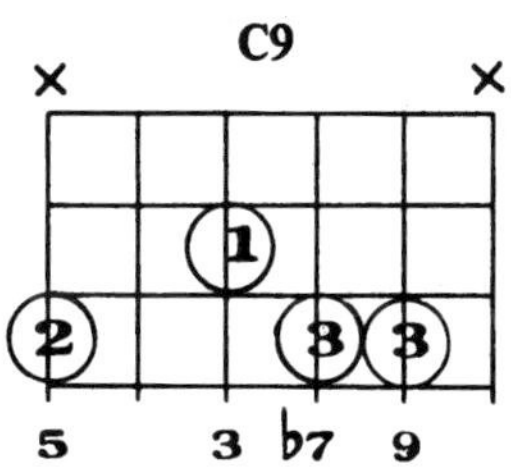

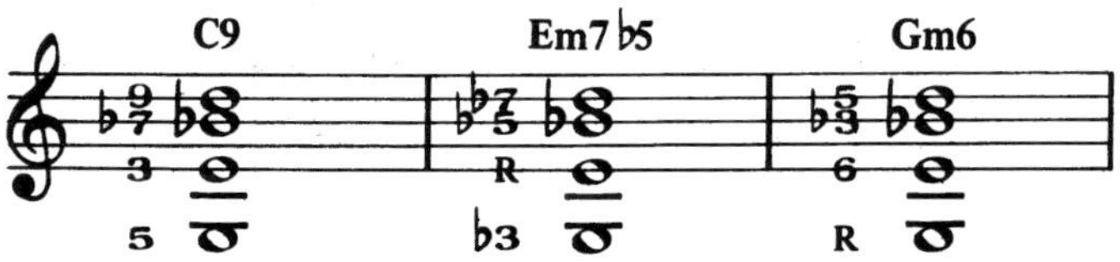

F9

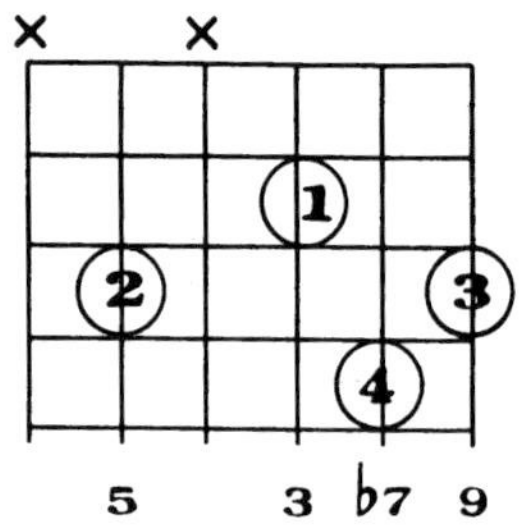

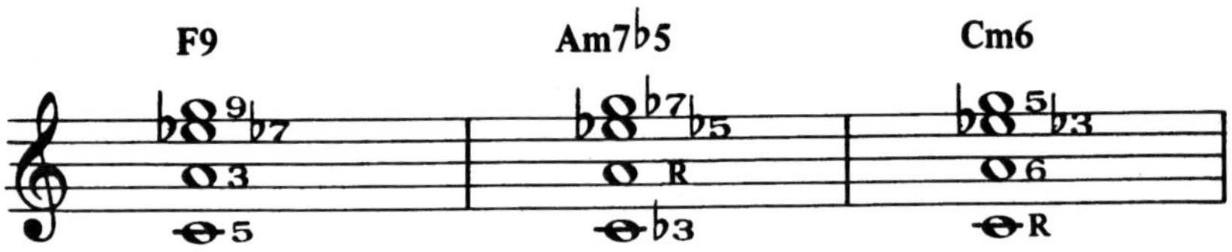

Bb9

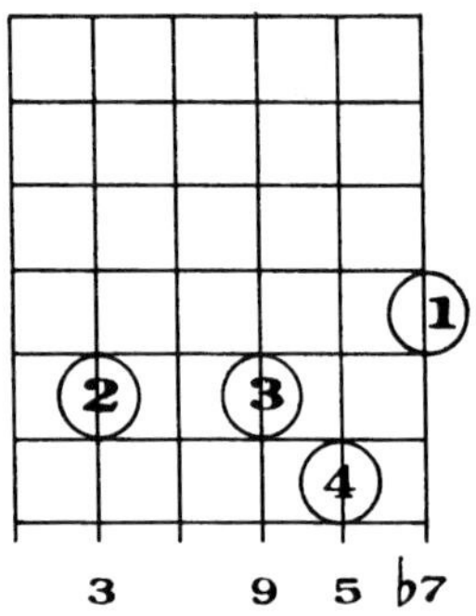

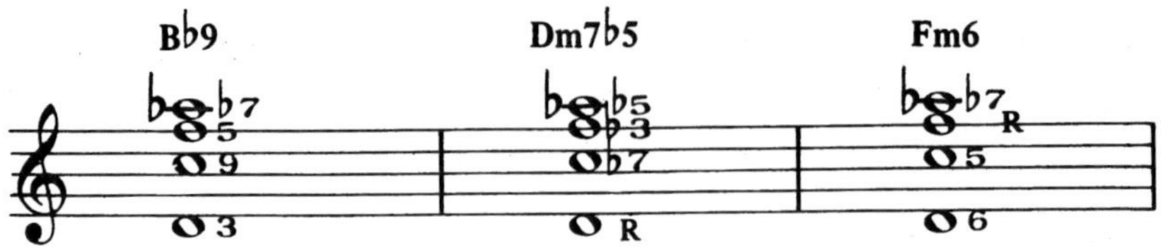

Eb9

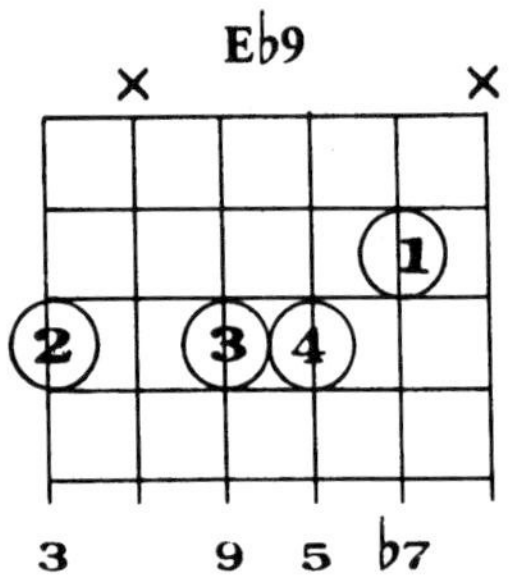

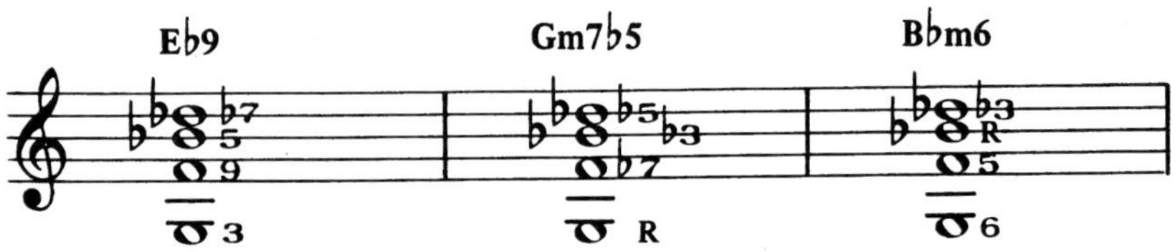

Ab9

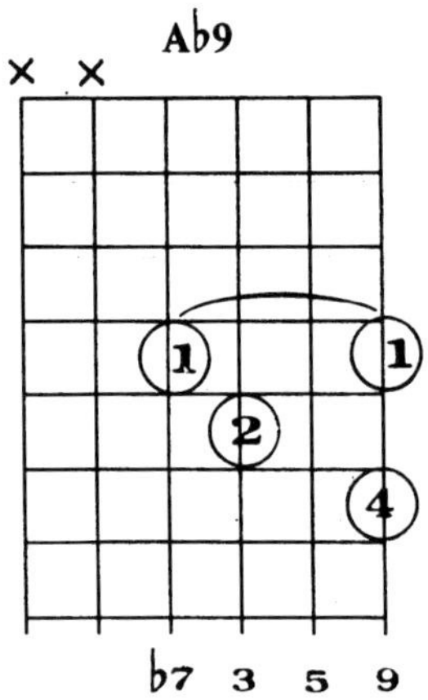

Db9

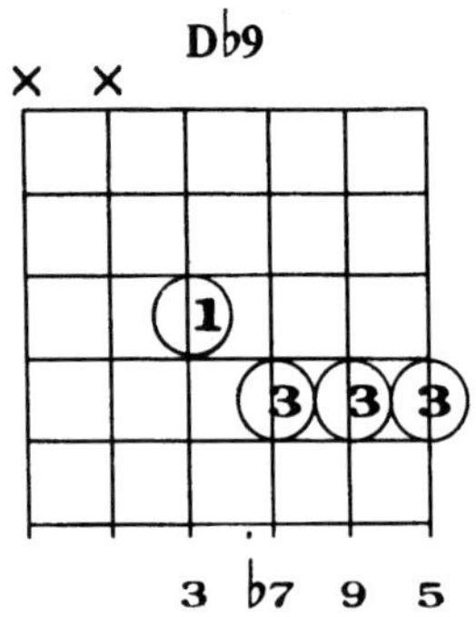

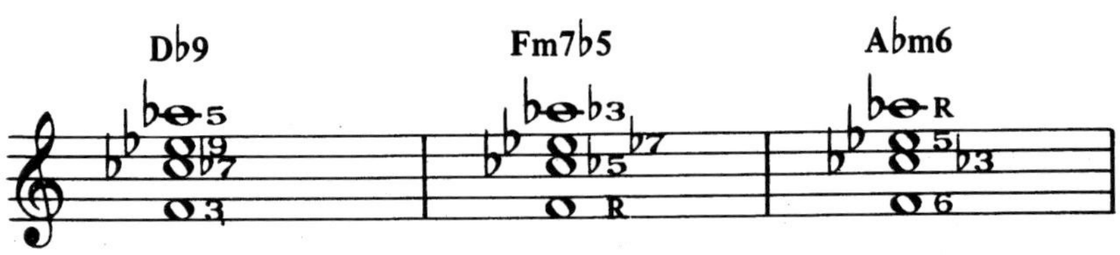

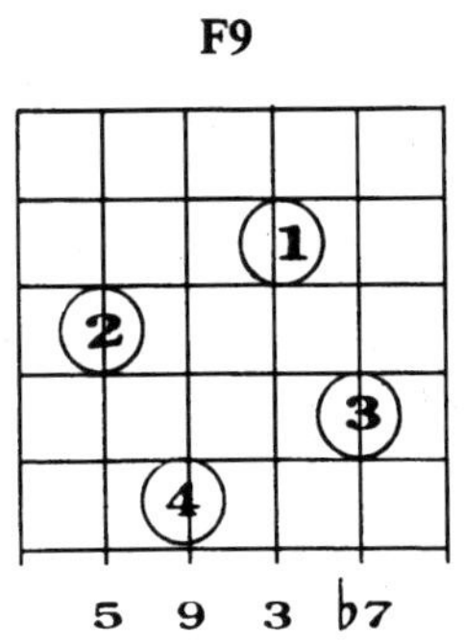

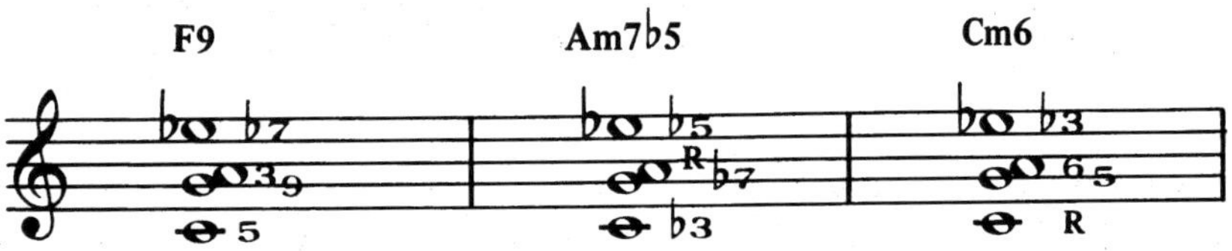

These forms provide 11 different forms for each chord — [This does not exhaust possibilities] .

> These chords are extremely practical and well worth the time spent learning to use them properly. They provide many interesting possibilities when you work out chordal accompaniments to songs. They also provide excellent material for introductions, modulations, and endings. The higher voicings are excellent for jazz "comping".

Following are more examples of forms which may be called by more than one name. Understanding of the tonal functions in these chords opens unlimited areas in your chordal playing. Remember! Just knowing where to put your fingers isn't enough — Know what the tones in the chord are doing — How they're functioning in relation to a given root tone.

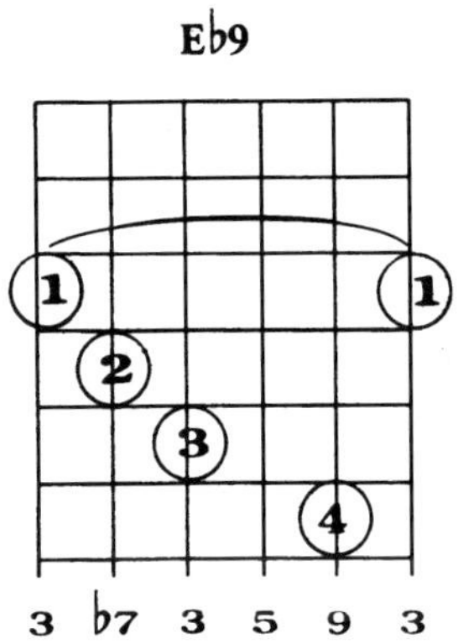

Using all 6 strings. Use as a 9th is shaky due to three 3rds in chord. (Very good m7b5 however).

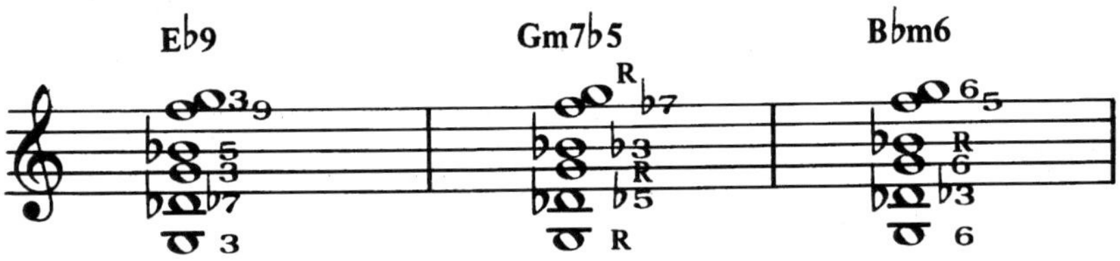

[handle usage with care on this one]

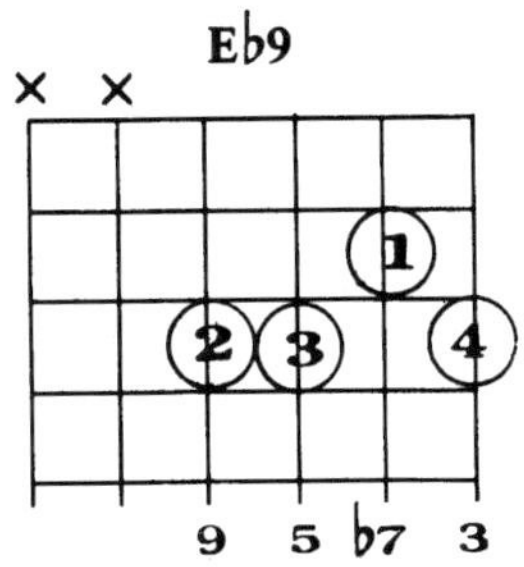

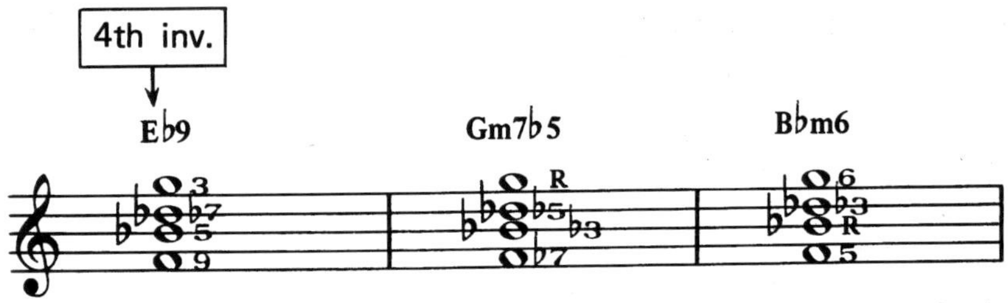

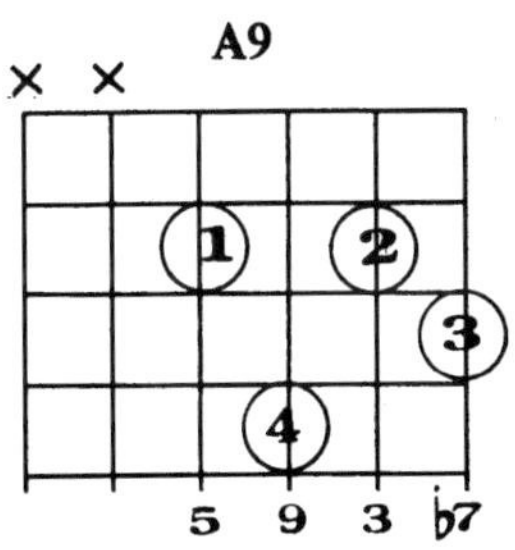

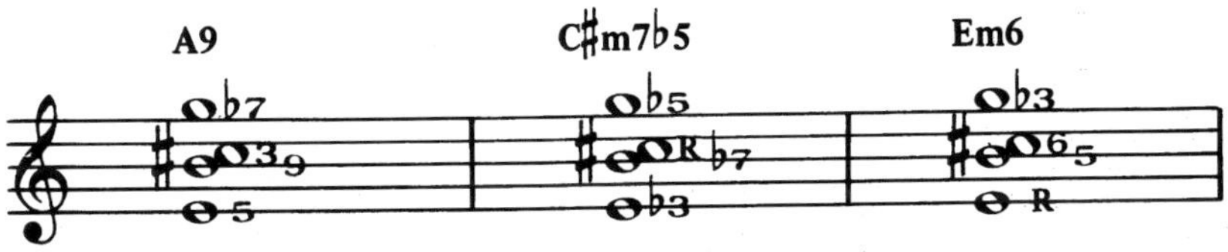

SUGGESTED STUDY FOR PREVIOUS FORMS

Resolve each of the forms according to each of the three functions (1) think of the 9th as a V chord and return it to I (2) think of m7♭5 as ii chord and return it to V, and (3) think of m6 as iv chord and return to i —

For example

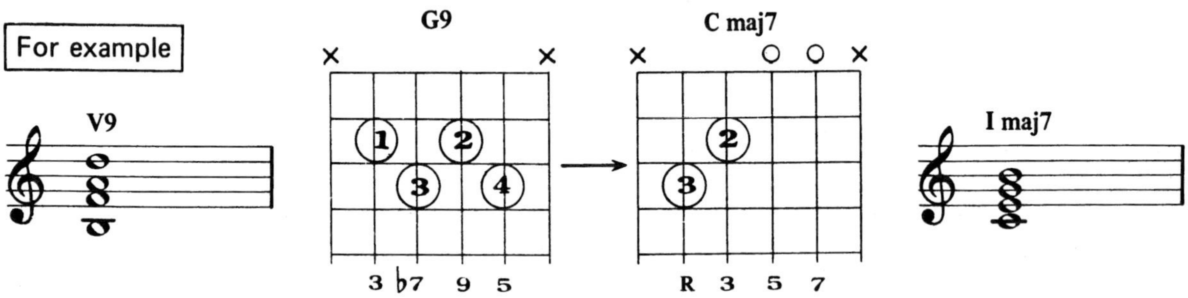

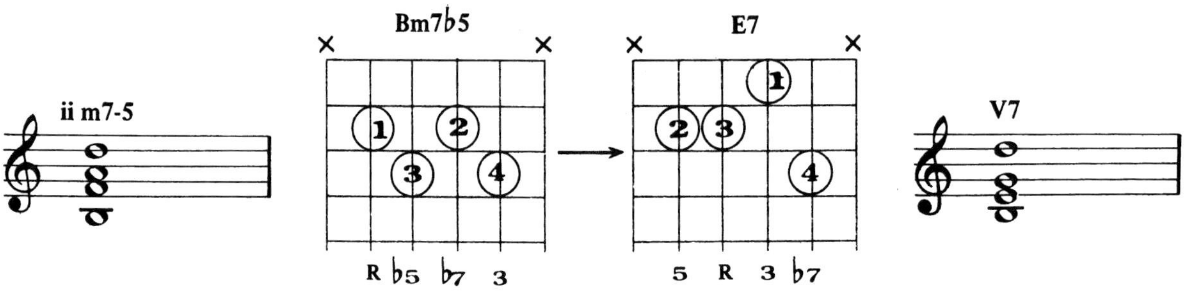

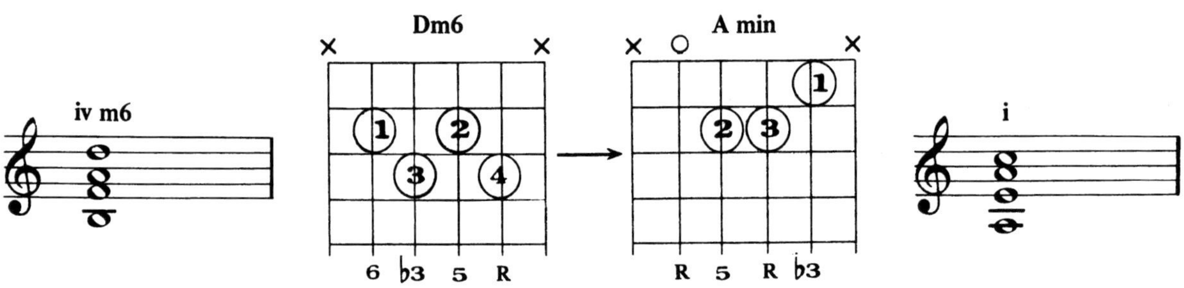

Take each of the remaining 10 forms through each resolution — like above – this will demonstrate the possibilities of unlimited usage of these forms —

I6 may also be used as vi m7

Thinking backwards then — A minor 7th chord could also be called a major 6th (a minor 3rd higher)

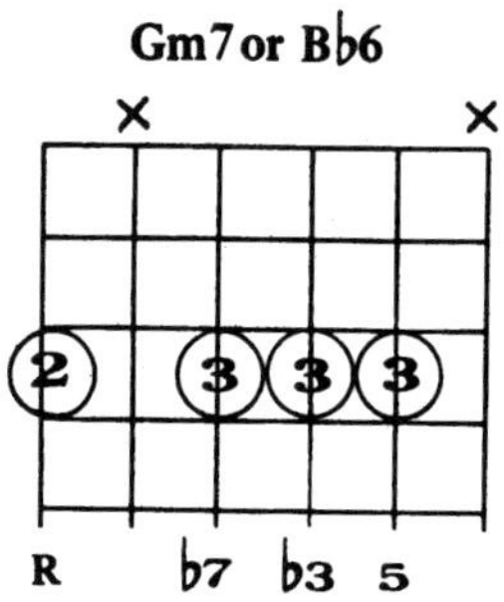

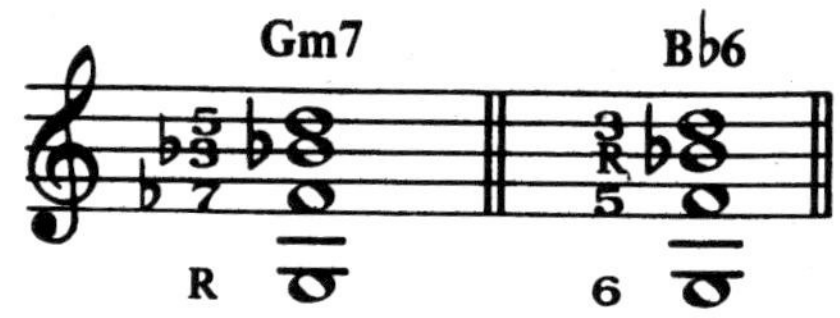

Although theoretically possible, the sound of this substitution does not satisfy the ear. Calling the chord B♭6, and using it this way, puts the 6th tone in a register much too low —

Use this substitution with caution — Think back to the harmonic overtone series —

Two important, and heavily used, chord patterns (or progressions) based on IM7, I6, ii m7, V9 — Using the "G" form and the "C" form — The 2nd chord in each pattern provides better "bass-root-pattern" if analyzed as vi m7 – [I – vi – ii – V] one of the most common patterns in popular music —

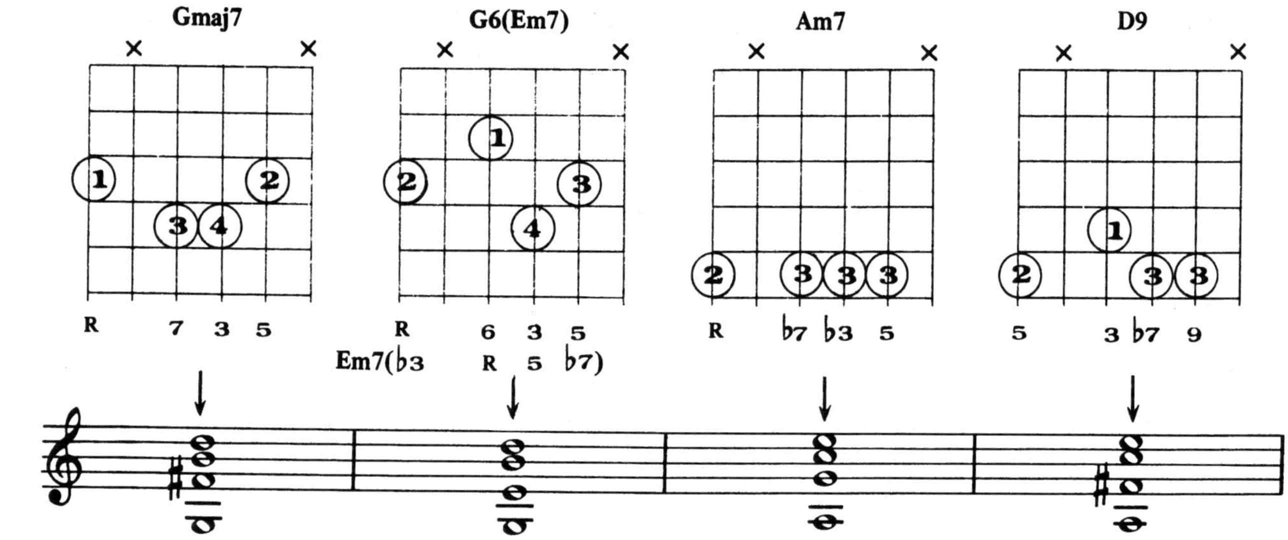

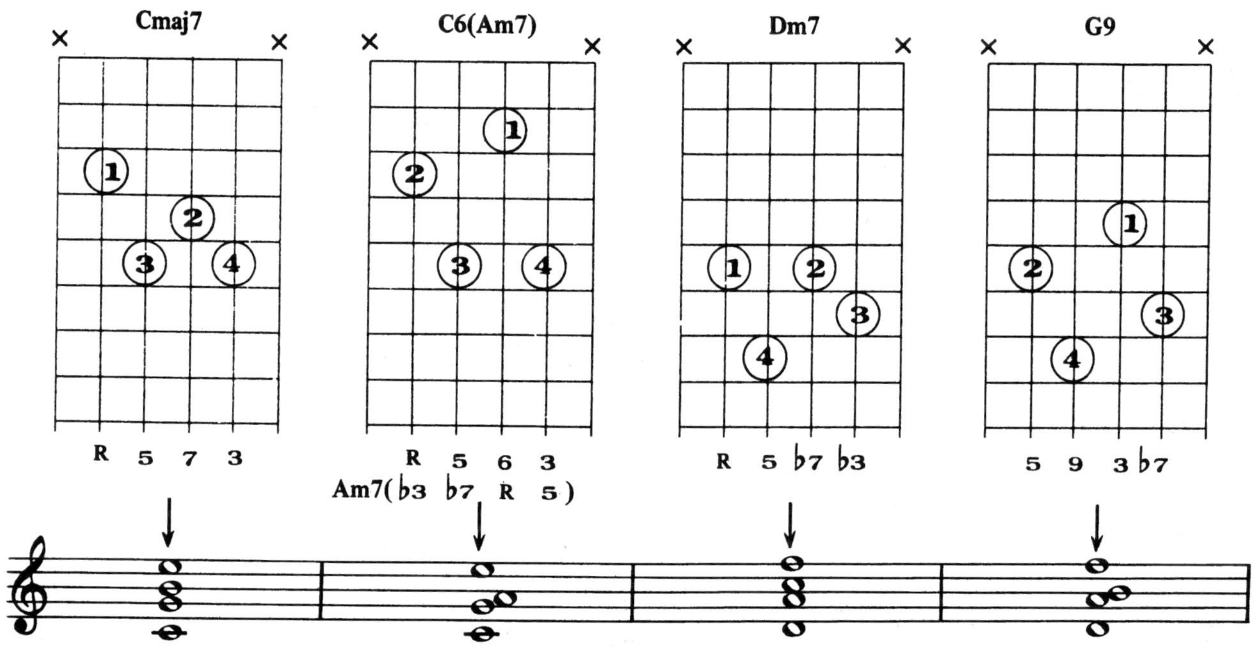

Try the two previous patterns as accompaniment for the following melody. (2nd chord is vi m7)

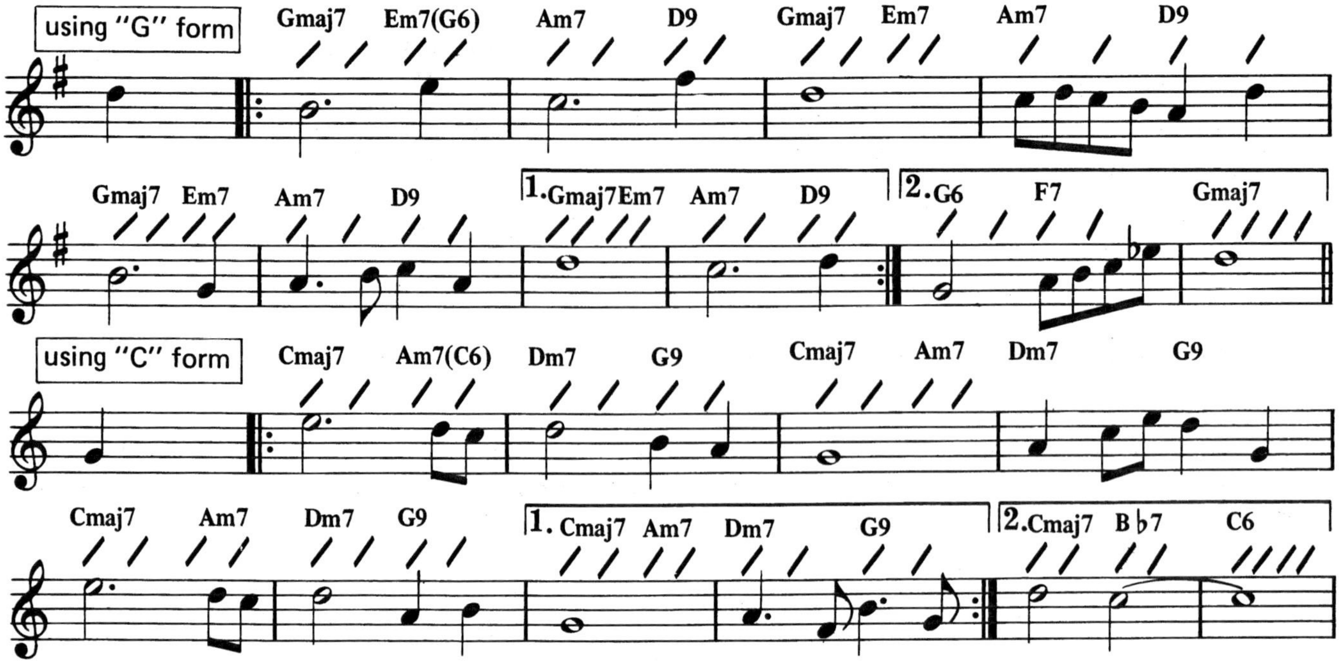

How many popular songs, or standards, can you remember— Which could be played using the above two patterns? There are many—

ANOTHER GOOD EXAMPLE OF I - vi - ii - V

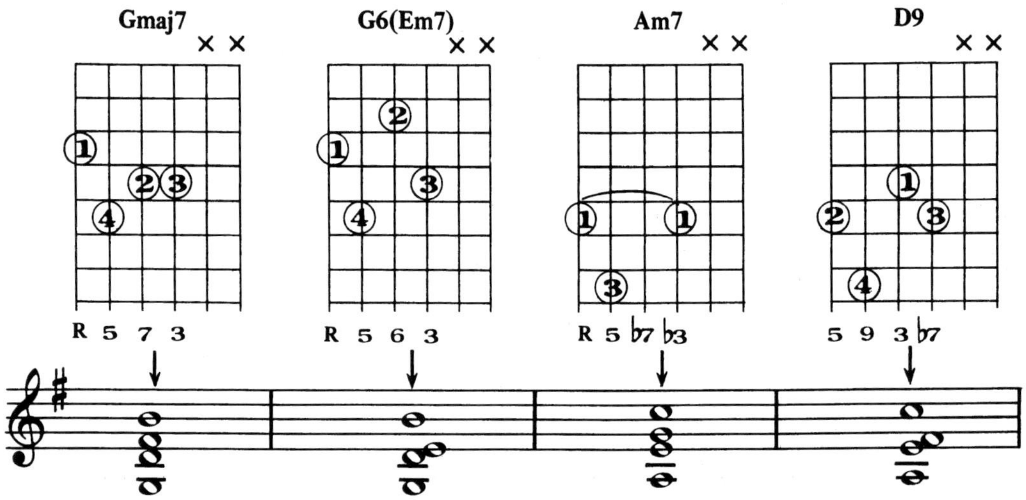

This is good one. Nice, "deep" sound—

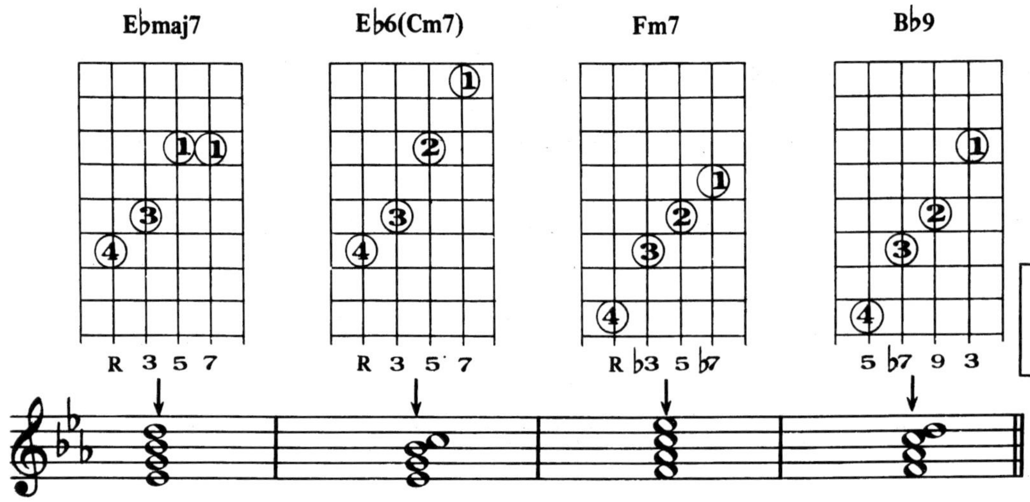

This one isn't too easy. The fingers must really stretch out — This is a good example of "closed harmony"

This is the lowest available position for this progression.

I – vi – ii – V with some harmonic variations

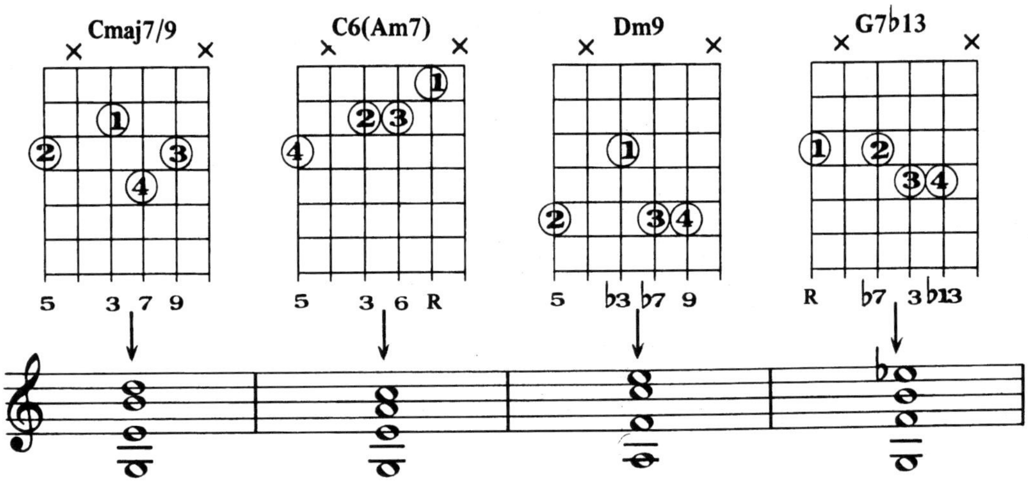

Final chord is G7+5 also – Calling it ♭13 justifies the voice leading back to the C maj7/9 chord –

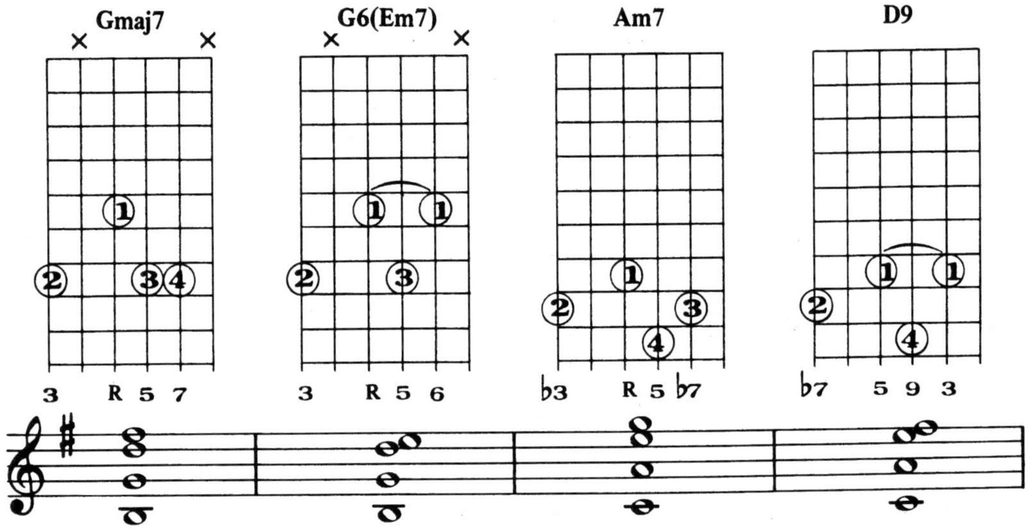

The inversions make this an interesting variation on the basic form.

Get familiar with these patterns in all keys– Look for other ways to play the basic pattern– Give careful consideration to melodic outline formed by top notes of chords.

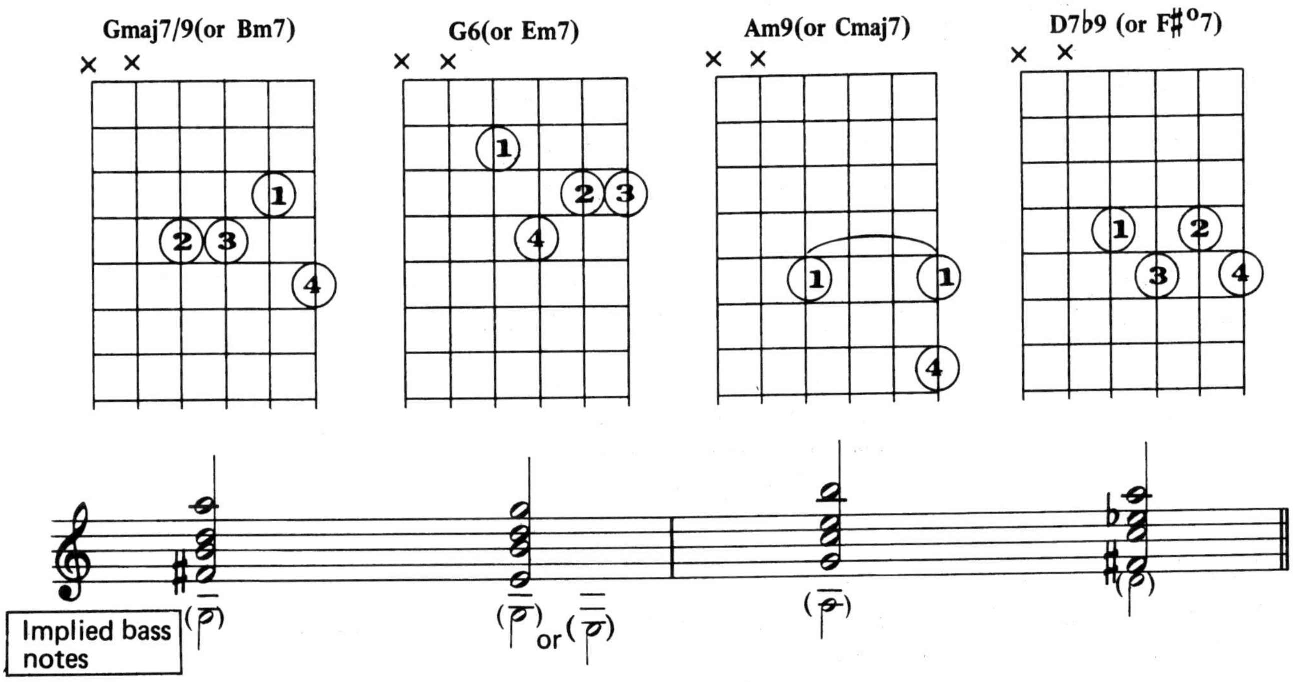

Above example of chord movement uses substitute changes for each chord—

1st chord is called I maj7/9 and is actually iii m7, 2nd inv.

Gmaj7/9 or Bm7

2nd chord is called I6 and is actually vi m7, root pos.

G6 or Em7

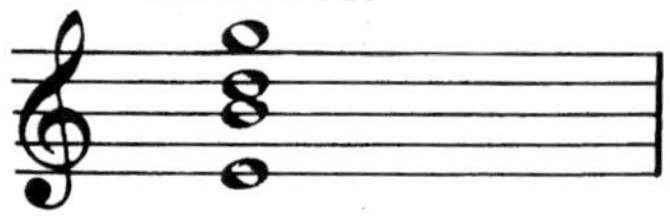

3rd chord is called ii m9 and is actually IV maj7, 2nd inv.

Am9 or Cmaj7

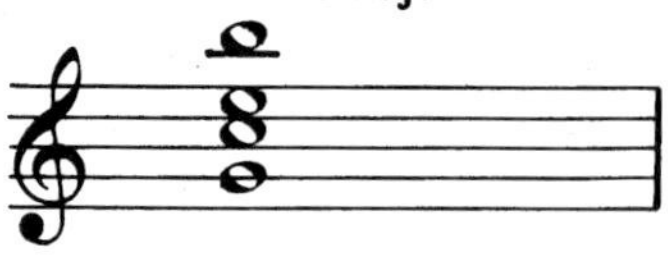

4th chord is called V7♭9 and is actually vii °7.

D7♭9 or F♯°7

These are good substitutions to remember. They will work using other forms— Avoid getting them too low— Remember, they sound an octave lower than written.

Use of vi m9 and iii m7 as substitute changes for I maj7.

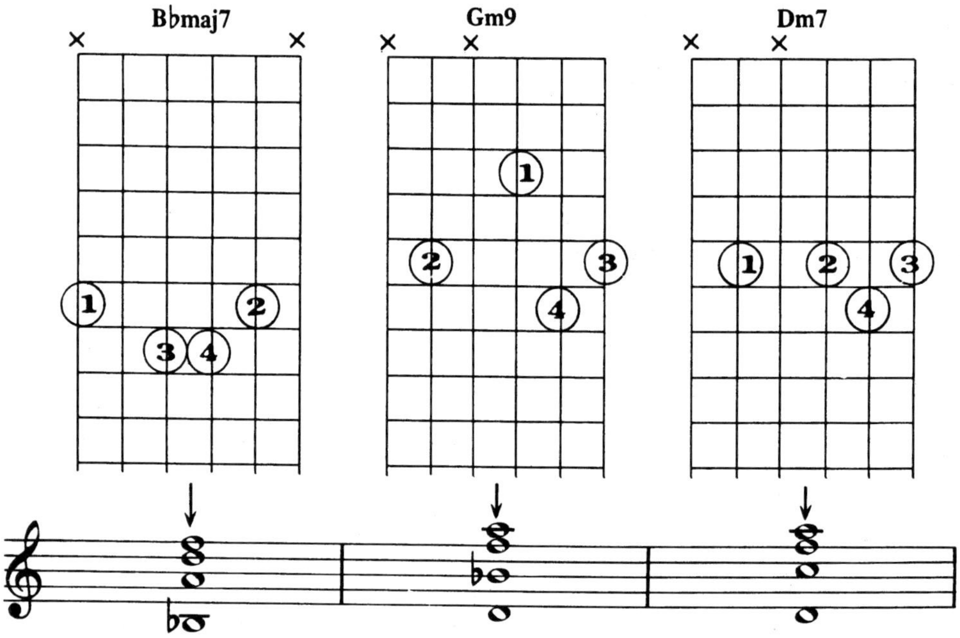

tonic major 7th form

1st inversion of major 7

1st inversion of major 7/9

Analysis in relation to I maj 7th

(Note Gm9 is 5 – ♭3 – ♭7 – 9 No root –)

Dm7 is complete R – ♭7 – ♭3 – 5...thus any form of iii m7 is excellent substutute for I ma7 –(Avoid low positions of chord when using as a substitute.)

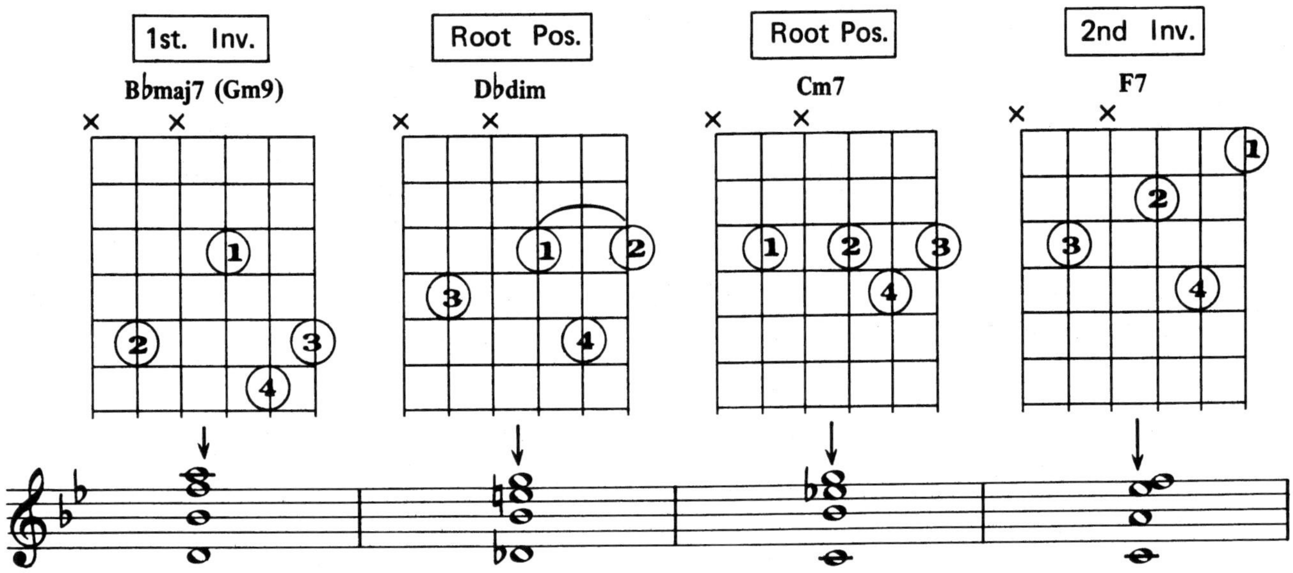

Use of sub. I in Progression. Note excellent leading of voices from chord to chord — Try the same progression using Dm7 as sub. for B♭ maj7

Use suspension on D♭° to add variety to progression.

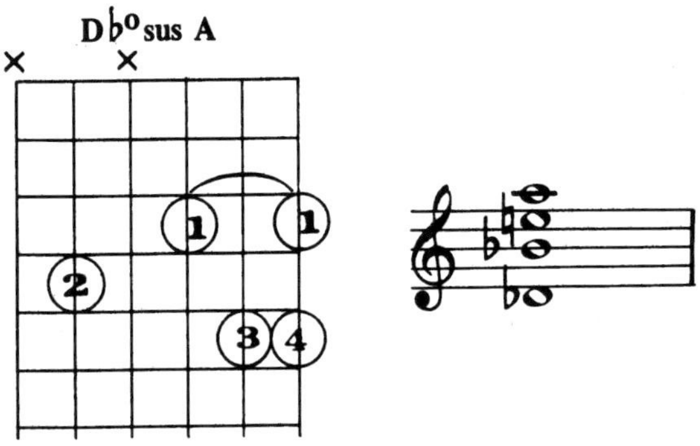

Resolve to F9 or to F7♭9 on final dominant chord.

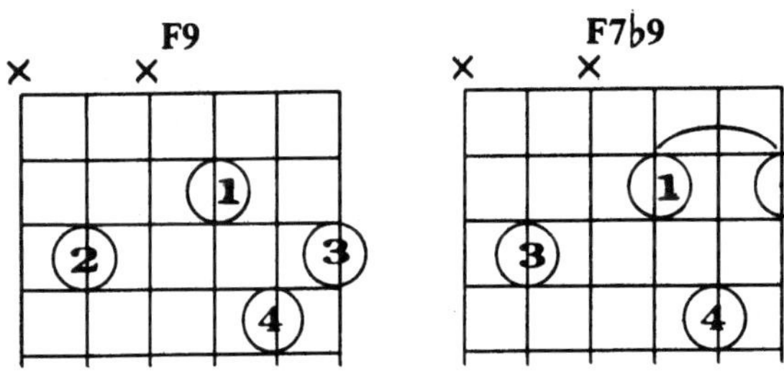

Diminished 7th may be used for 7♭9 chord

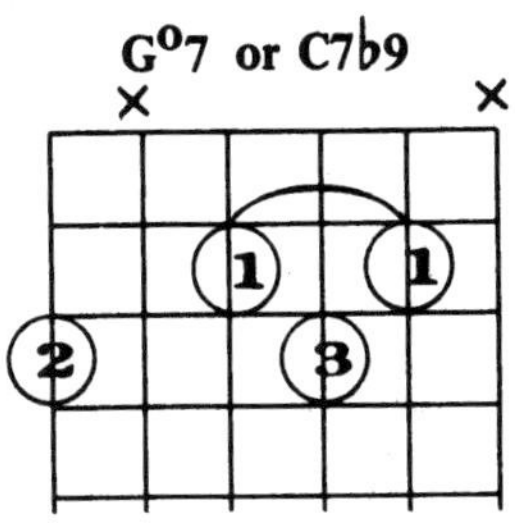

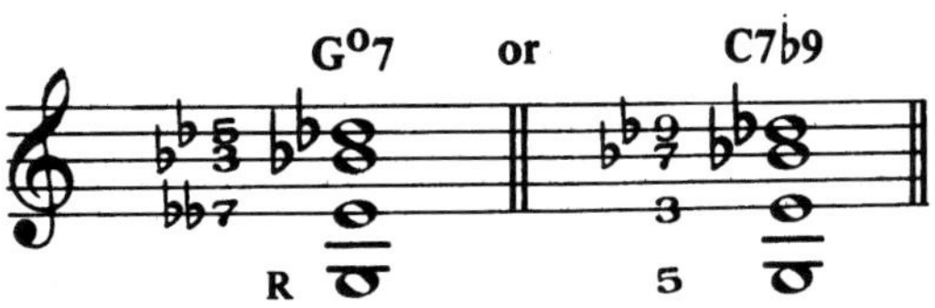

(contains no root) important

Theoretically the ♭♭7 in a G°7 should be spelled F♭.)

This is a very practical substitution — Remember that the diminished 7th may be called by any of the tones which it contains – and repeats itself, in a different tonal arrangement, every 3 frets – due to it's construction – all minor 3rd intervals.

For example

Using enharmonic spelling to show tonal similarities.

correct spelling.

Then, in reality there are only 3 diminished 7 chords. Then, we might add, the same movement principle would also apply to the 7♭9 chord, minus it's root

Let's examine some usages of 7♭9

C7 ♭9 (minus root)

Ⓐ

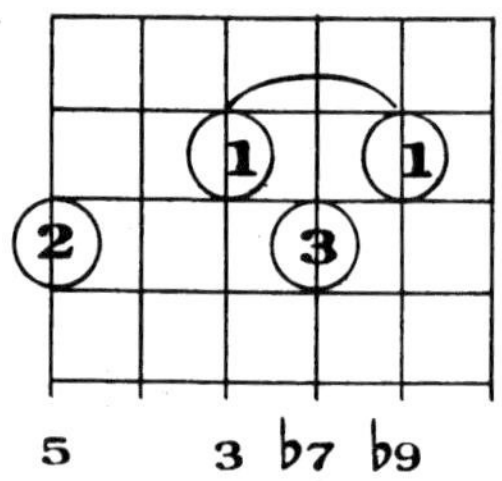

Returns to F maj7 through C5 resolution.

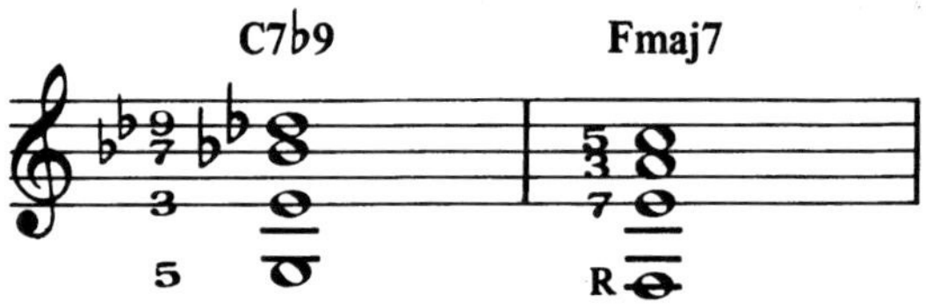

Now, thinking of the Dim. 7 movement, let's think of the other names for this form – (C – E♭ – G♭ – A) dim. 7th spelling.

So, theoretically, it may also be called: E♭7♭9 – G♭7♭9 – A7♭9 (all without roots included).

Let's see if it works through C5 resolution to the appropriate major 7th chord—

Ⓑ

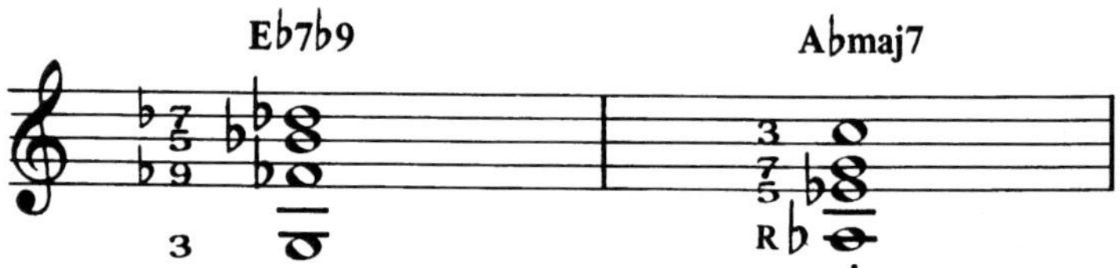

note F♭ instead of E♮ to indicate ♭9 of E♭7♭9.

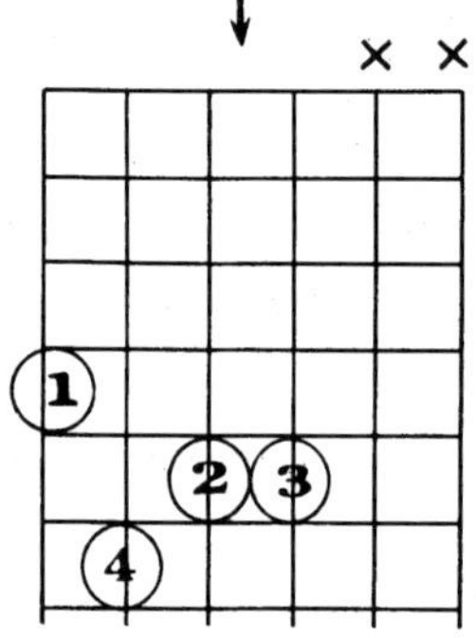

Works well!

Good contrary motion between two outside voices.

G♭7♭9 (Let's call it F♯7♭9 to ease the spelling!)

(C)

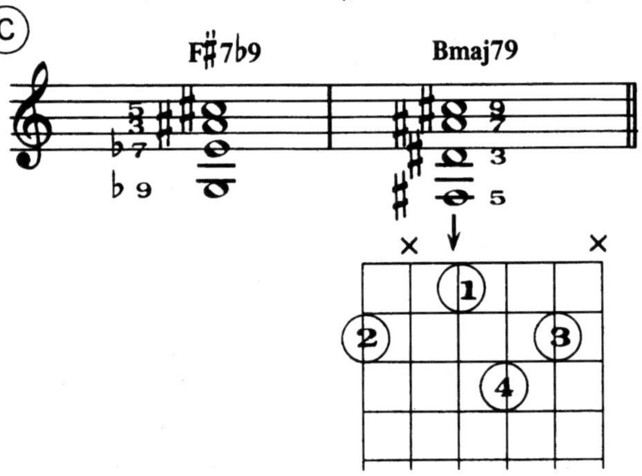

Works well!

(D)

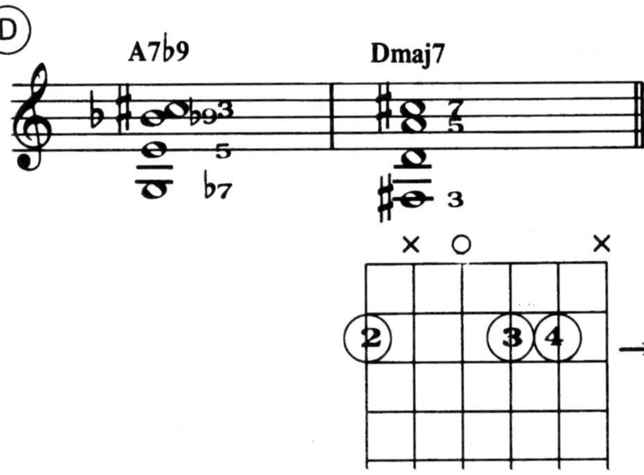

Use this fingering as you move up fingerboard.

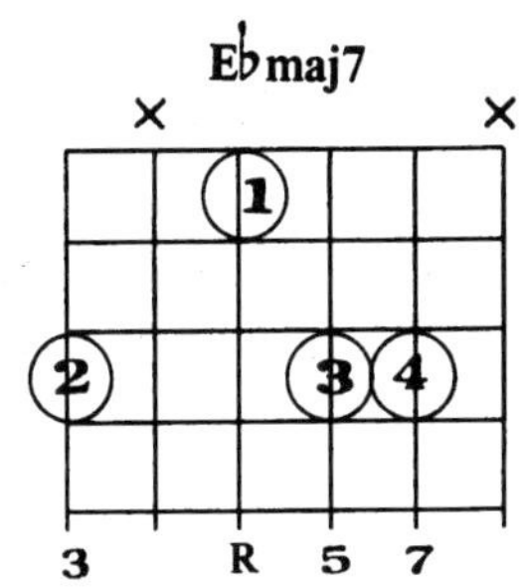

Each of the resolutions works — now think in terms of moving the 7♭9 to another position and resolving it to the same tonic-maj7 — also in another position.

on the third fret

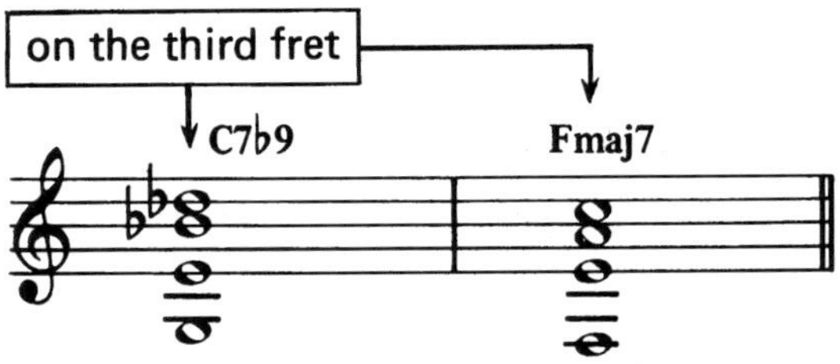

Now move to 6th fret

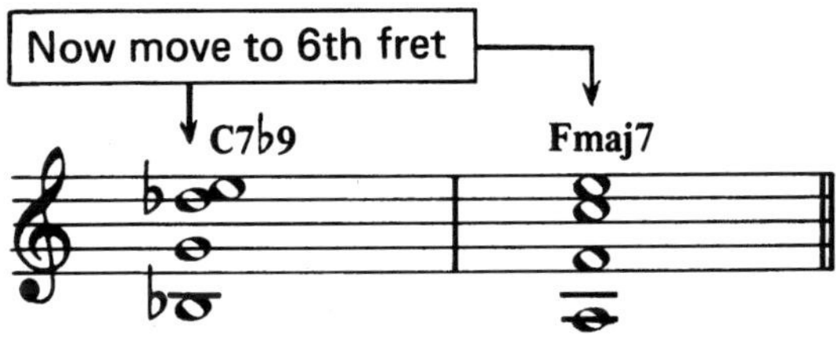

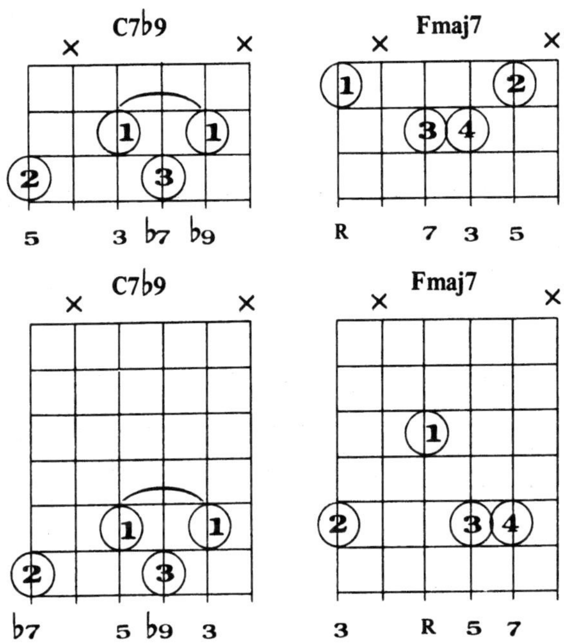

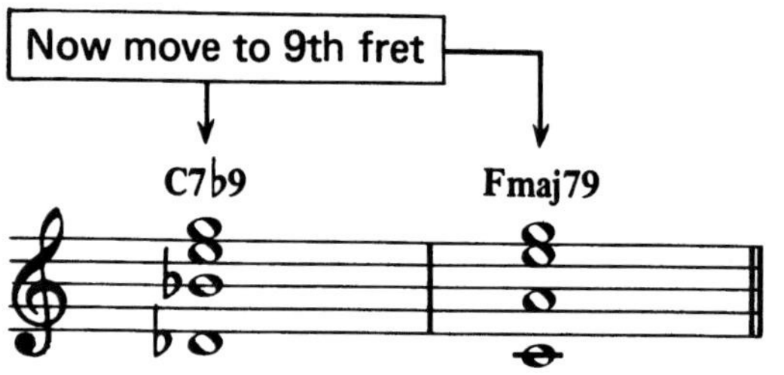

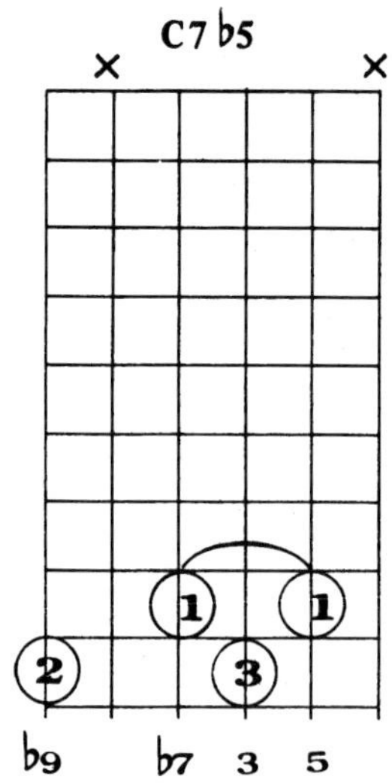

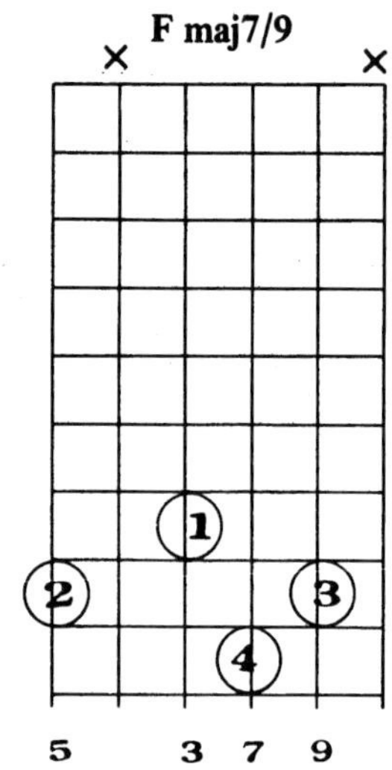

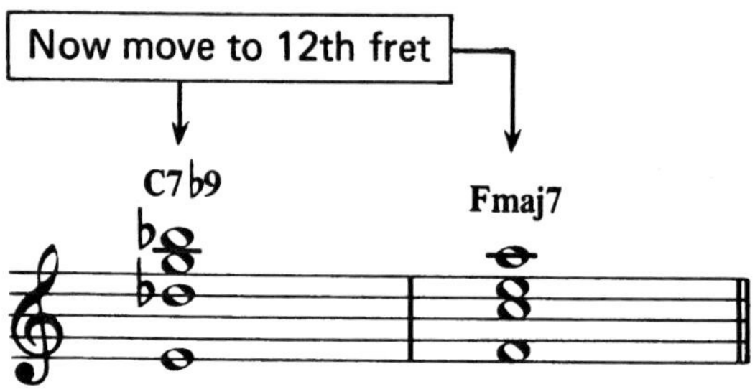

This is tough without cutaway neck. (possible though).

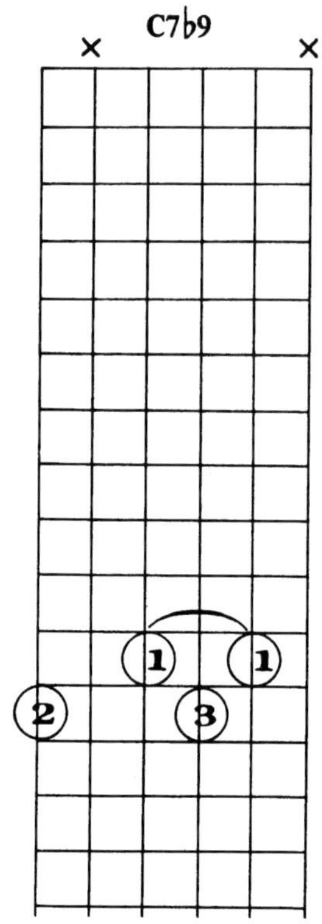

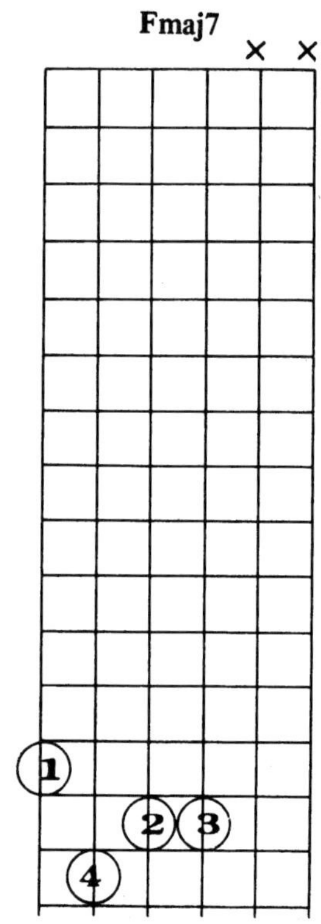

The same voicings are available at other positions on the neck, using higher string combinations. For example the resolution at the 9th fret in the preceding series is possible in a lower position.

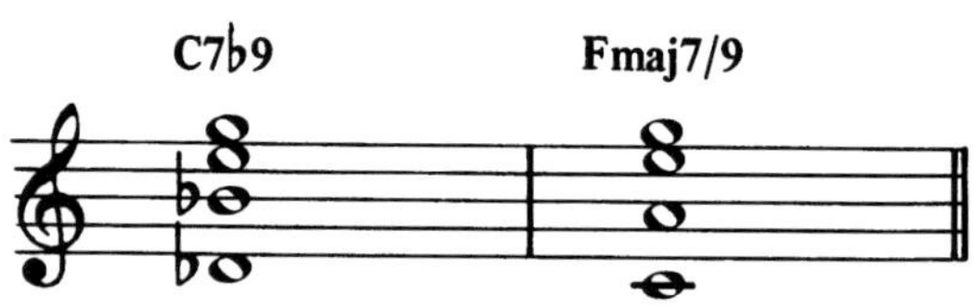

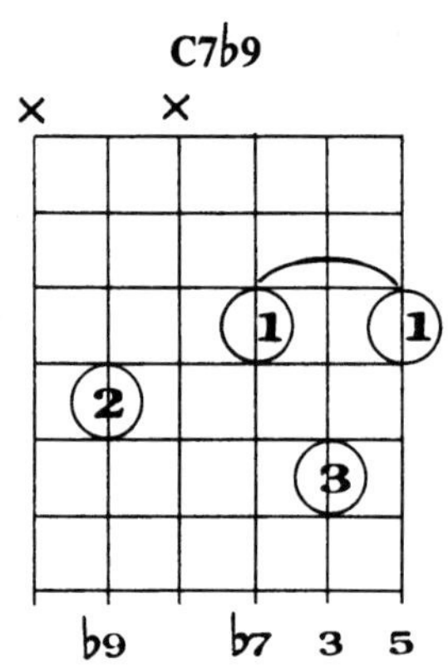

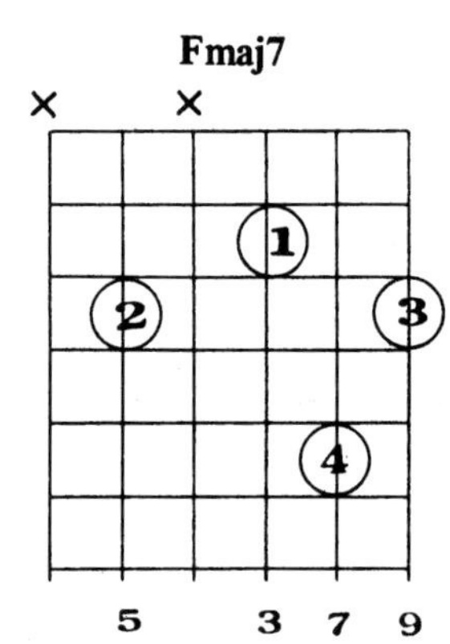

Here's the one we played on the 12th fret before.

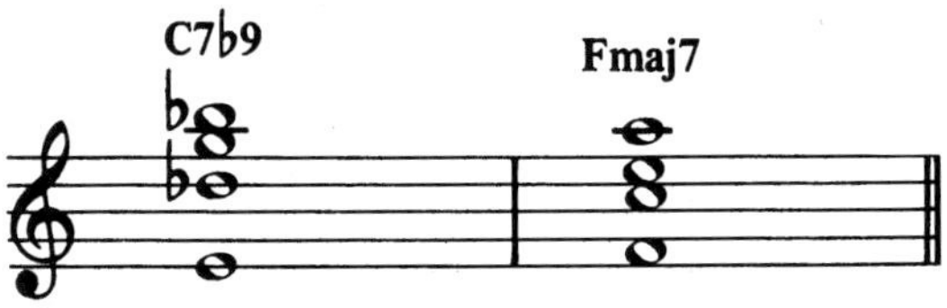

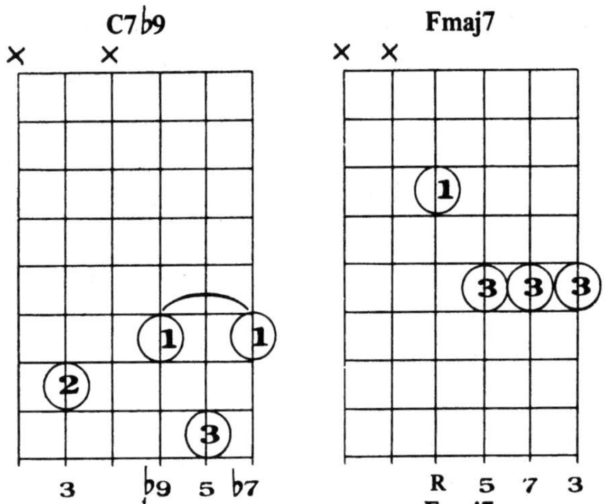

Here's the one we played on the 3rd fret before (An octave higher)

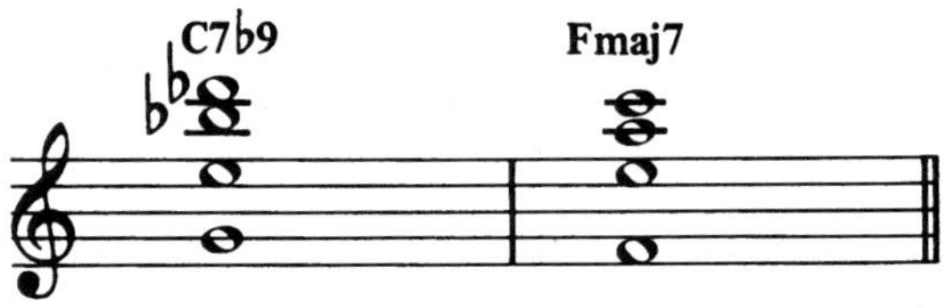

This one would complete the <u>previous cycle.</u>

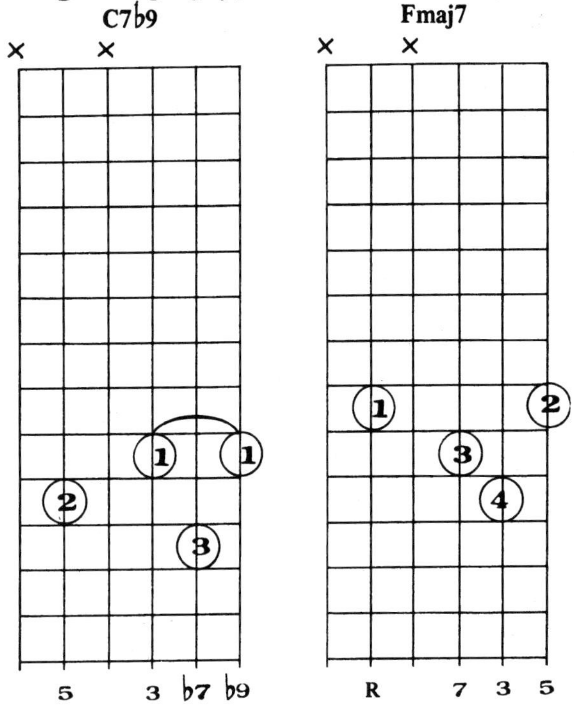

Diminished chords with added tones—

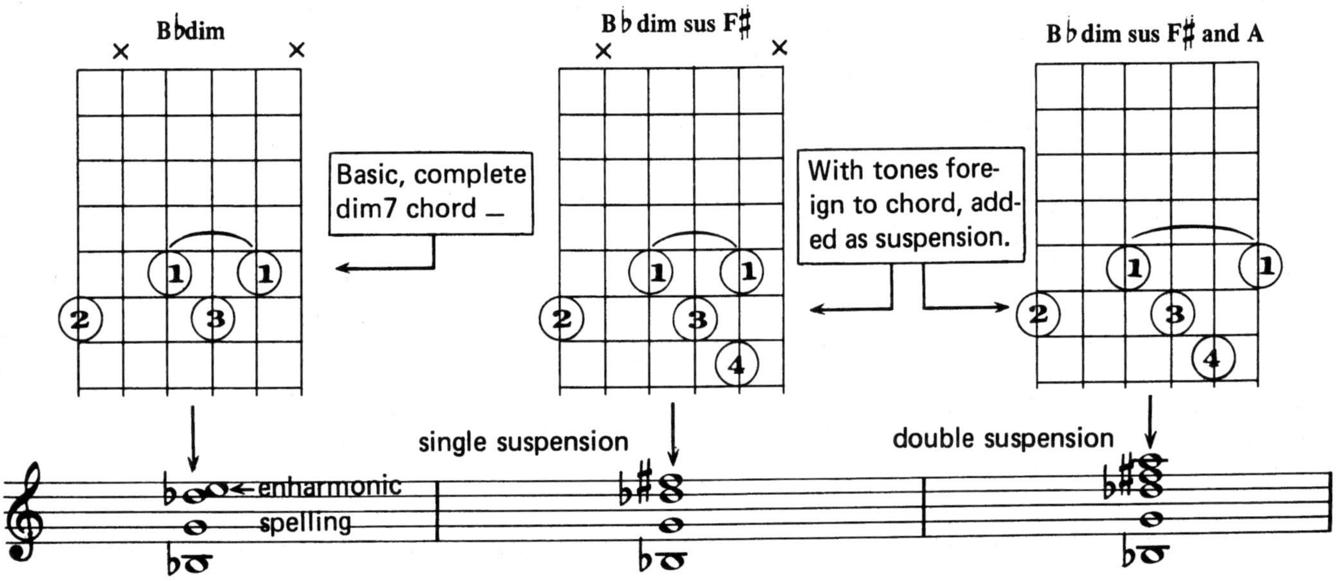

Same principle, only using four tones on the top four strings— Easy to finger—

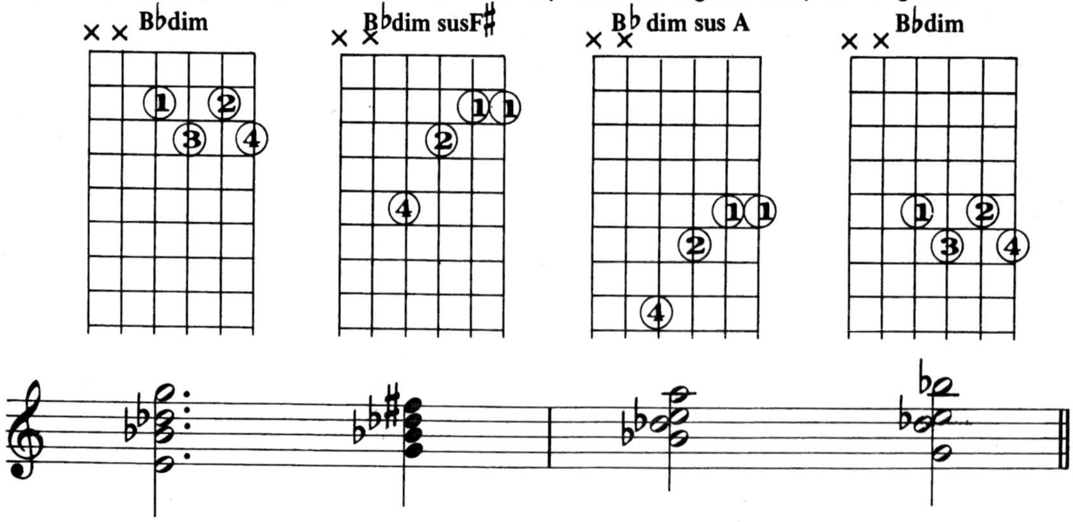

Use is obvious. Use as passing chords where diminished chord is called for, and use for chord melody playing.

A series of diminished chords with suspensions used as passing tones between each chord—

Gbdim

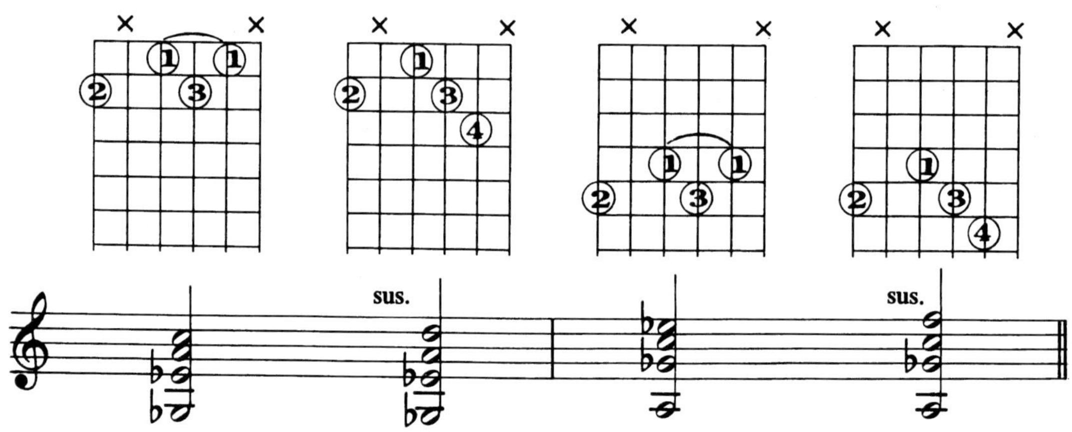

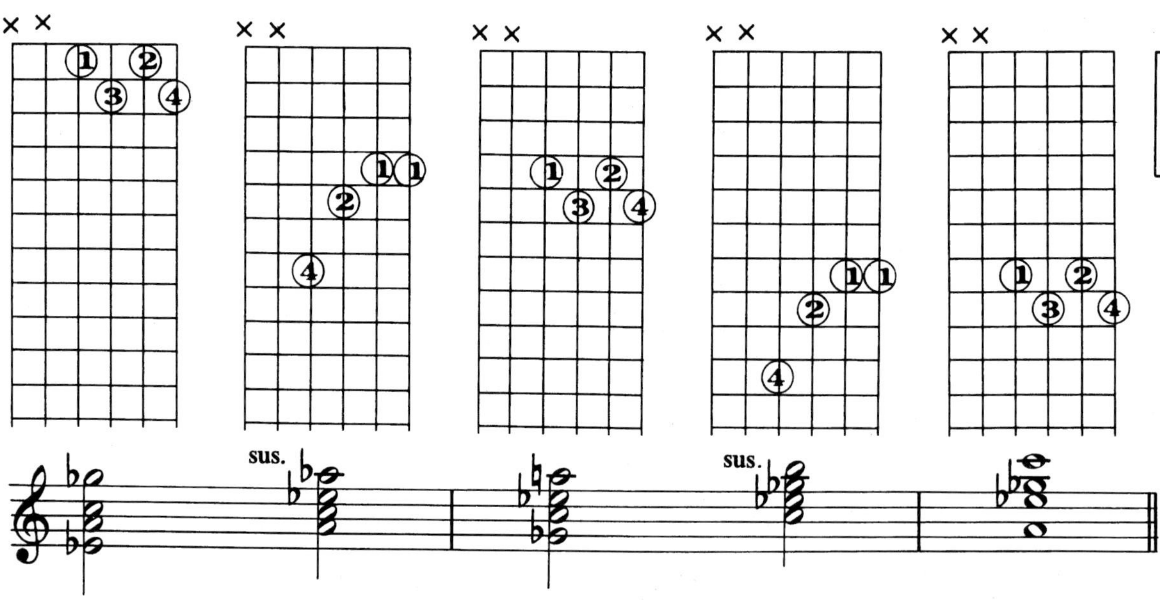

Enharmonic spellings used

Listen to the way this pattern sounds— It is a good intro pattern, plus many other uses—

An interesting form which may be used as a "ii"; a "V"; a "I"—.

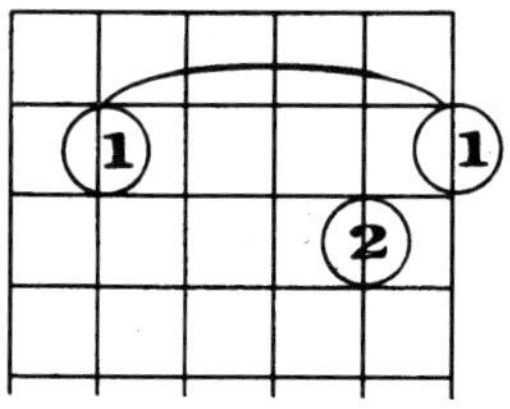

(I)

D6/9

G6/9(maj7) Bm11 E9(sus4)

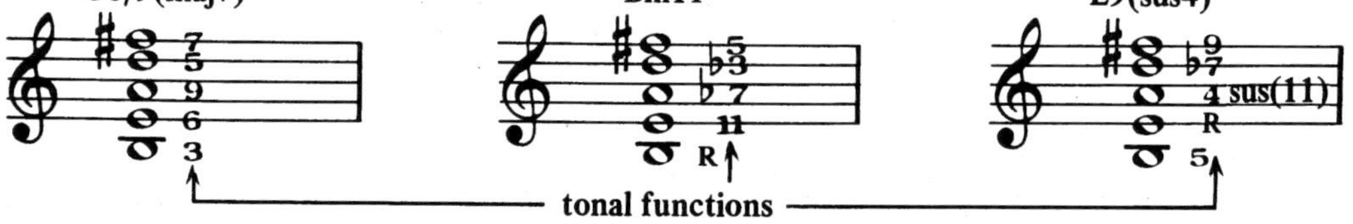

This form has unique possbilities for intros, endings, etc.

Adding auxiliary tone with 4th finger on first string gives additional possibilities.

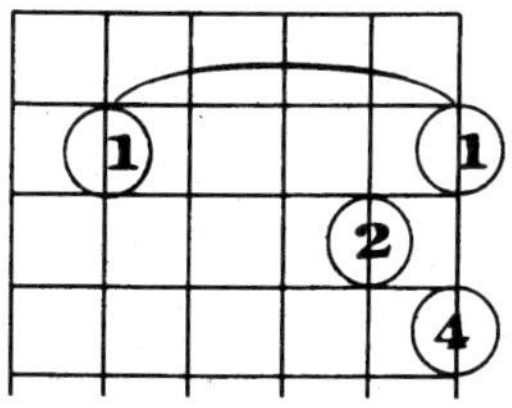

Especially good when used as V7 sus 4

Add (a) tone (or two) for Another good "I"

C6/9+11

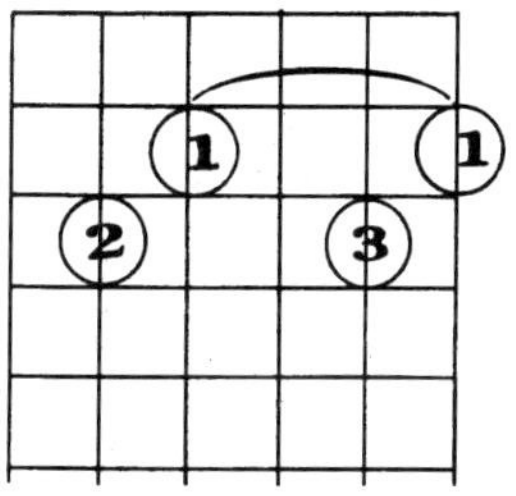

Cmaj7/9+11

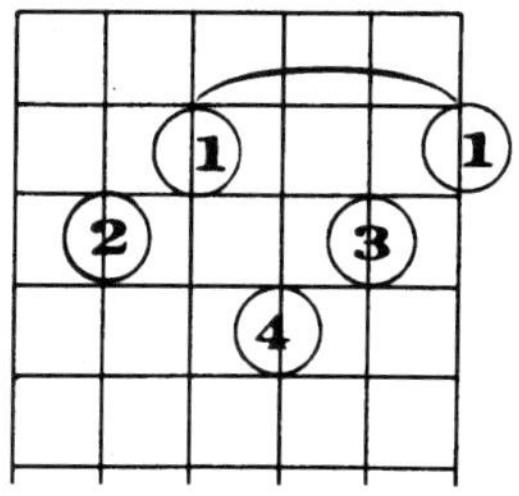

Moving Chords Via Voice Leading.

Many guitarists do not have a large number of chords at their disposal and when moving from one chord to another make long jumps back and forth along the fingerboard. Watch the average rock and roll player do the I – IV – V blues pattern. In key of F he'll leap from 1st to 6th – back to 1st and then to 8th fret – for the F, B♭, & C chord. This is not only indicative of poor musical taste, but represents a great deal of "lost motion" and work—

Example:

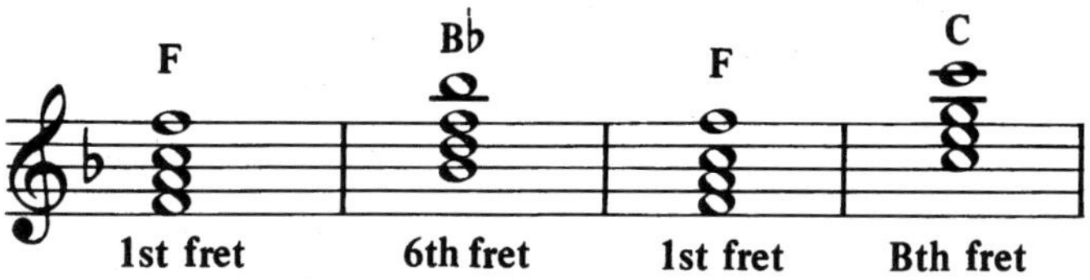

Wouldn't it make more sense like this:

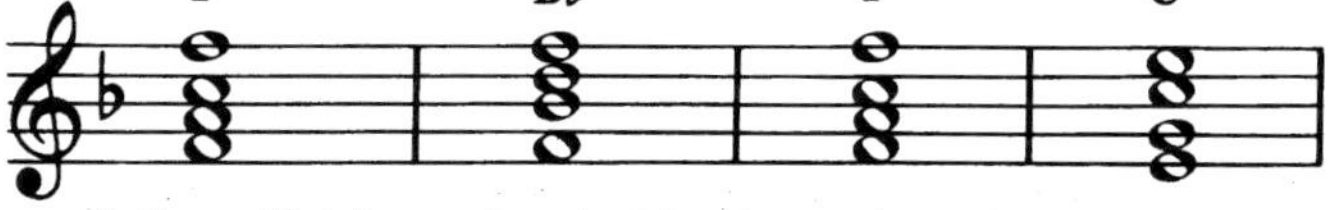

(all available at the 1st fret)

This would be the basic premise in voice leading — "Hold common tones and / or go to nearest tone in the following chord"

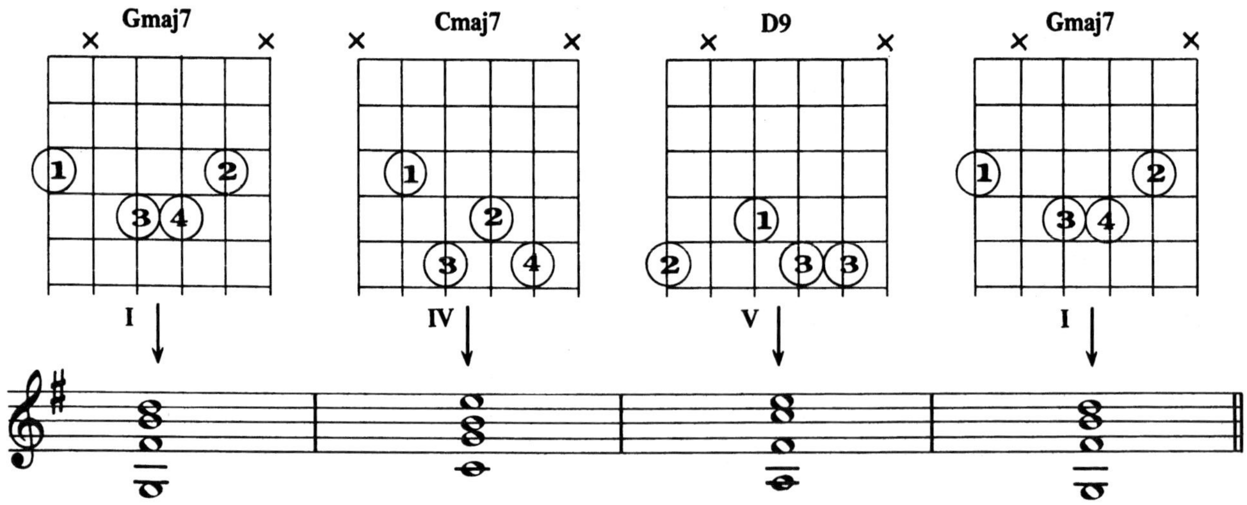

Good voice-leading would infer that the parts would be easily sung — No big leaps, and few awkward intervals. This is really not instrumentally important, but does make for very smooth chordal resolutions — [It would be a most important factor in choral writing, where parts would be sung].

Playing chords on the guitar sounds better if you avoid big leaps. (Unless you're after a special effect) move to the closest next chord, if at all possible.

This :

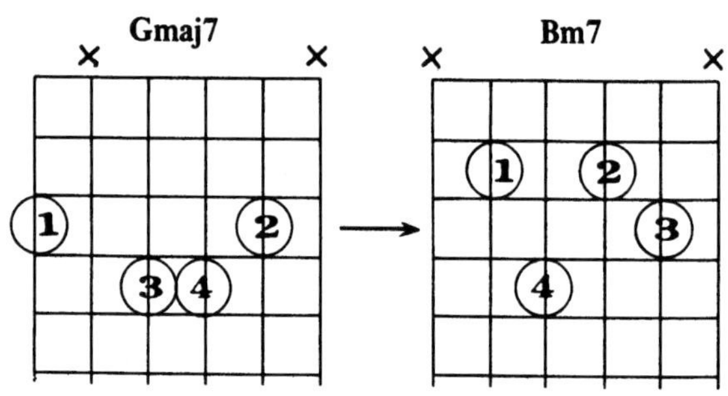

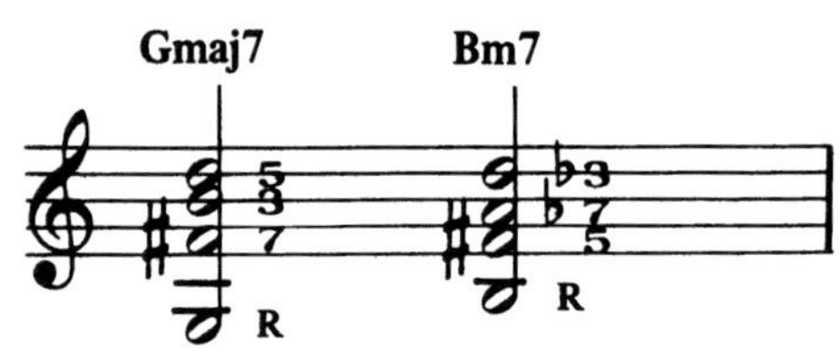

Has two common tones holding — (Actually contains three common tones).

Not this:

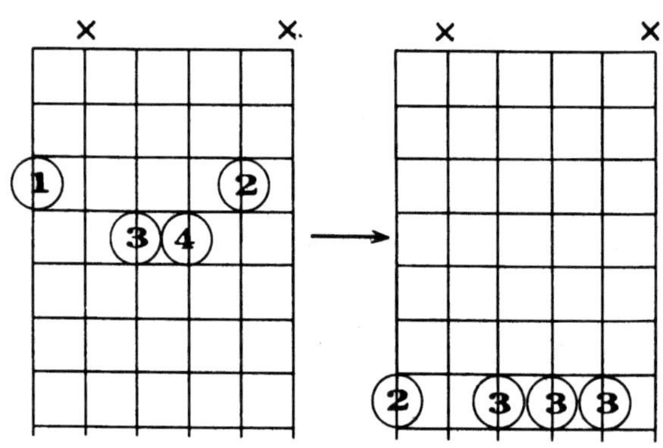

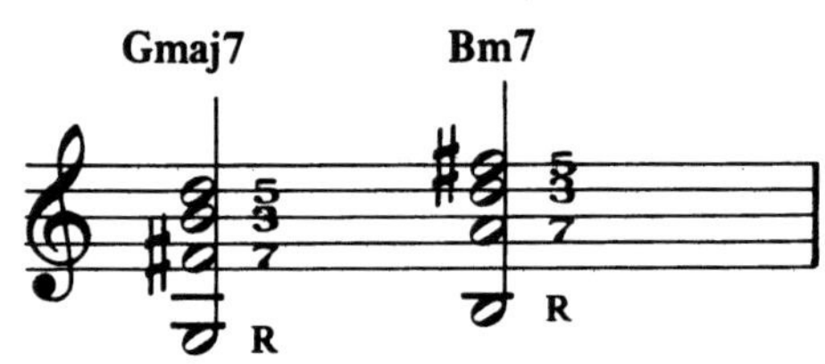

First example is good, close move. Second example has every "voice" leaping — As mentioned before if special effect is what you're after — O.K. — If not, go to the closest next chord —

Chordal resolutions using ii m7 → V9 → I

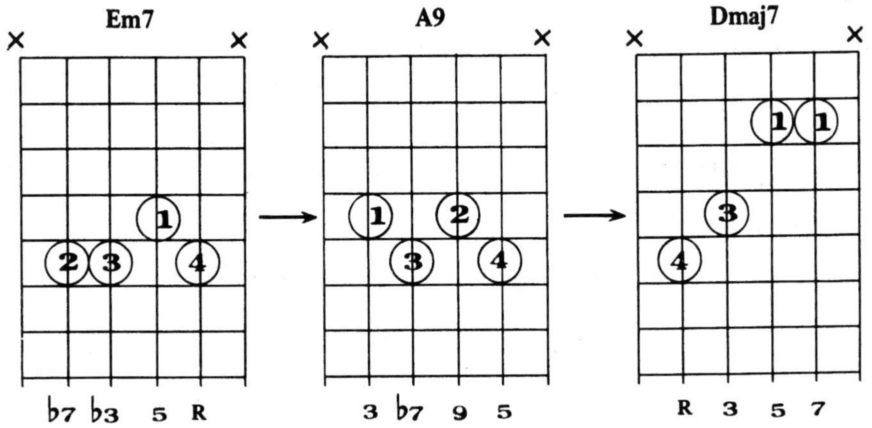

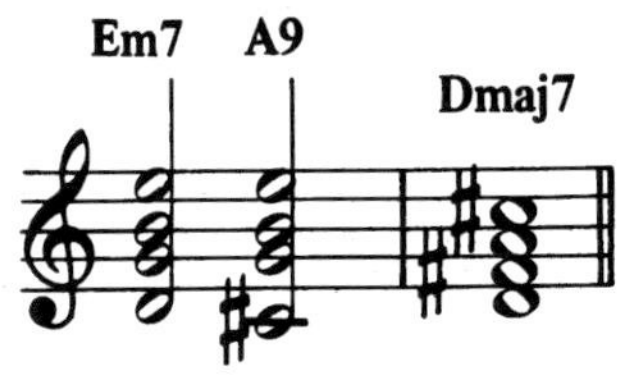

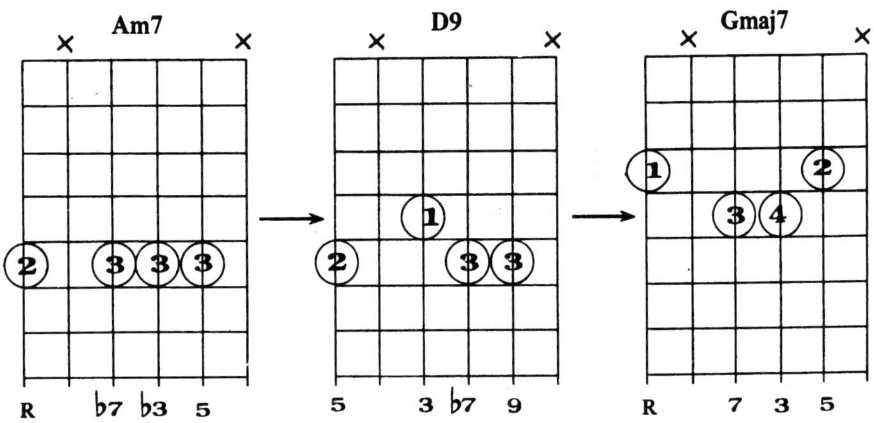

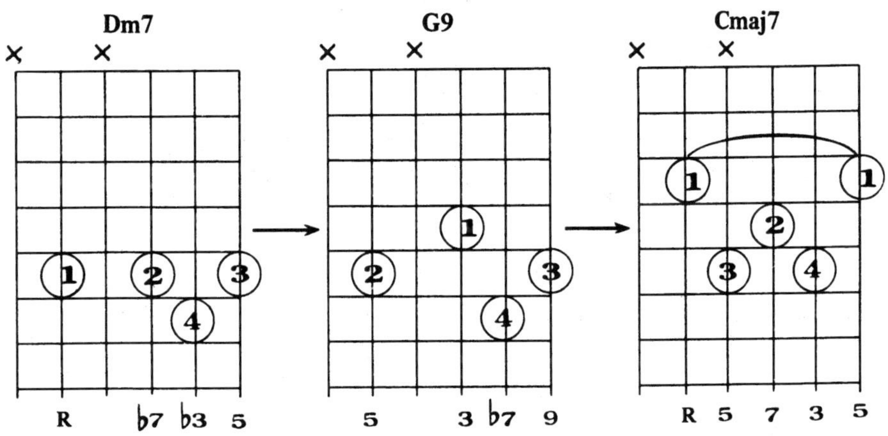

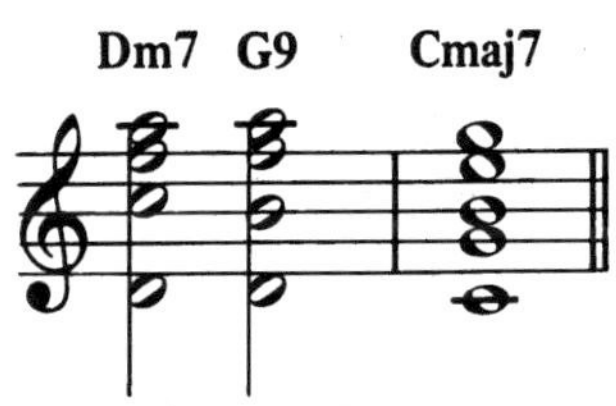

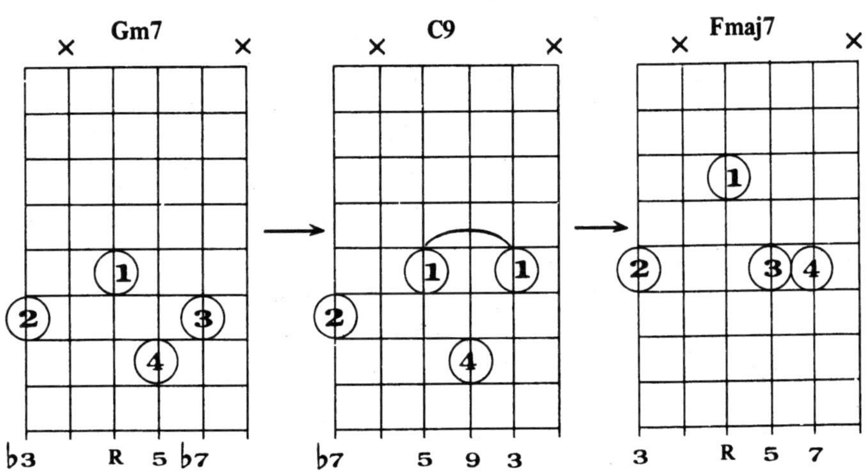

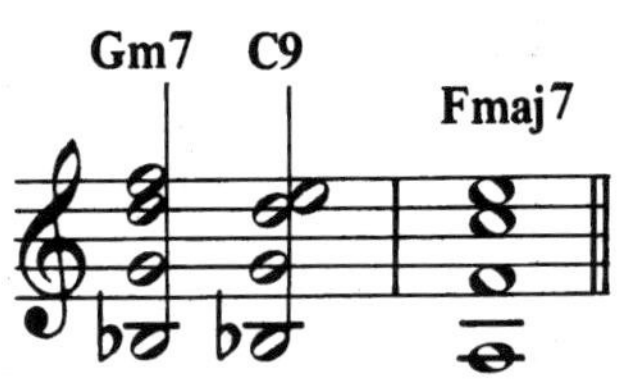

interesting inversions in this one—

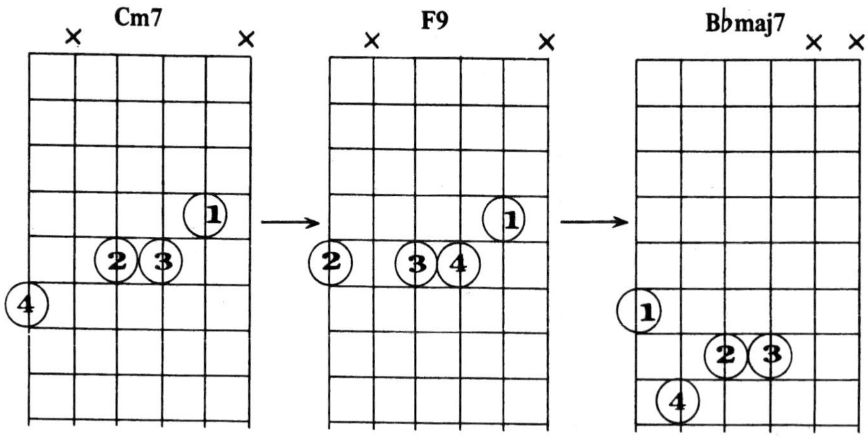

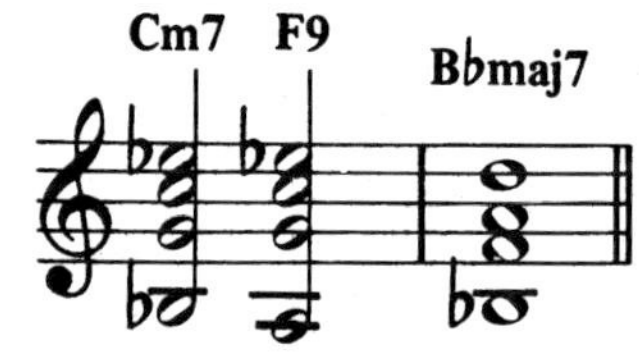

interesting inversions in this one also —

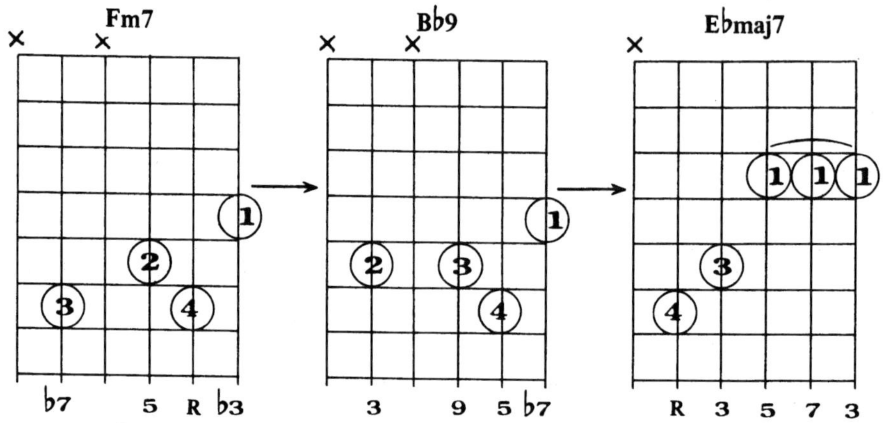

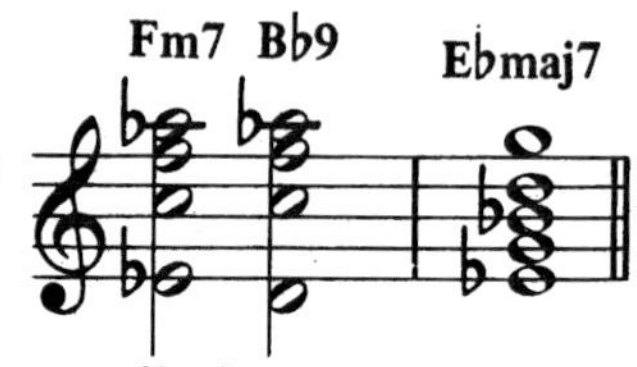

to eliminate double 3 in Eb maj7, play root tone on 4th string, 1st fret.

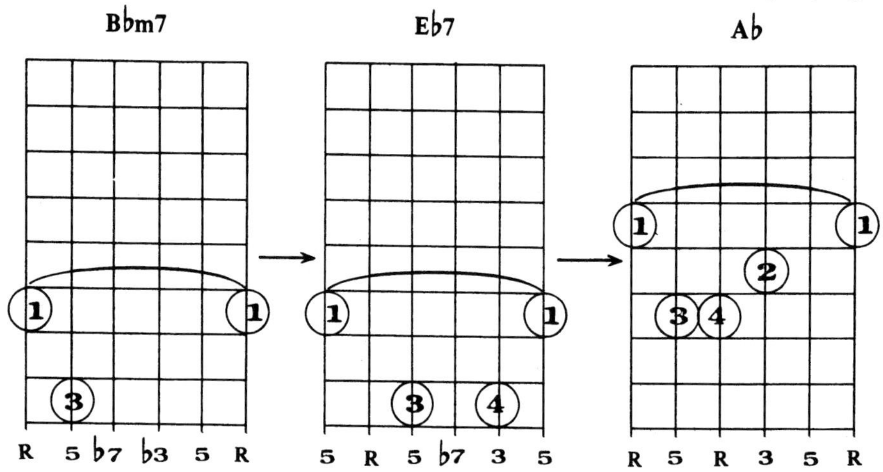

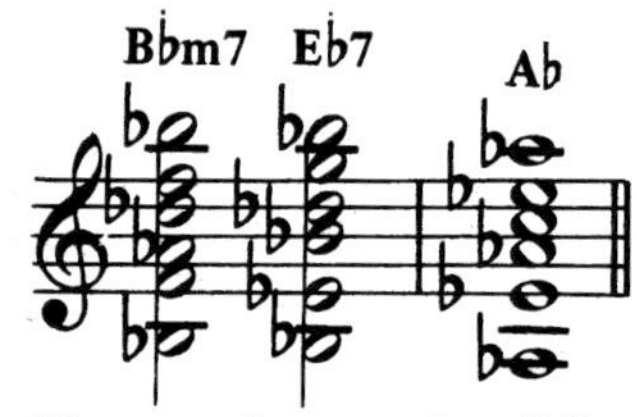

Six string, simplified movement — low tension chords — interesting "return" to 1 maj 7th.

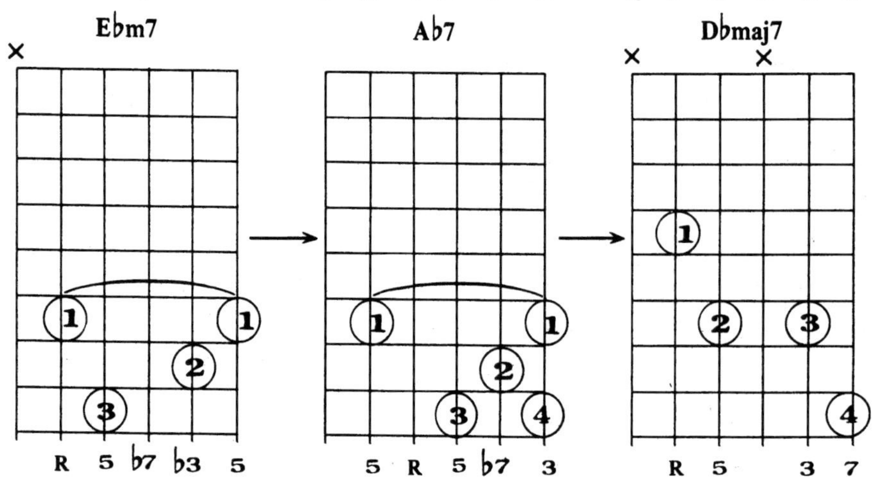

Interesting "return" to I maj 7th.

Deaden (3) string with 2 finger.

The following chordal exercises are presented for three reasons : (1) to train fingers to move swiftly and surely, (2) to develop your ear to hear chords in relation to each other, and (3) to help you become familiar with the fingerboard in all positions.

Each exercise is presented in a low position to start. When you learn the exercise, take it to the highest fingering position possible and play it down the fingerboard towards the nut—

(A)

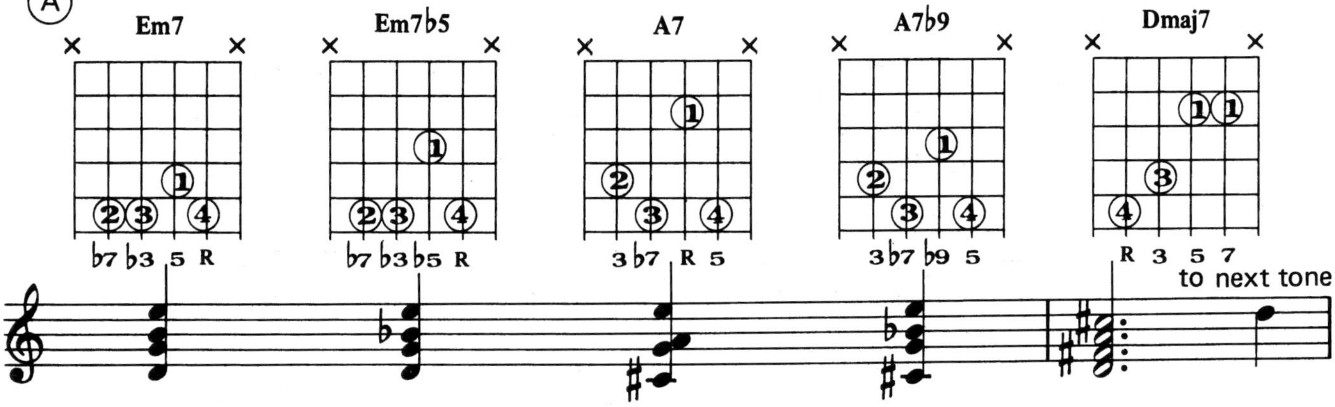

Second finger playing "D" on last beat of final bar will lead into melody note of E♭m7 one fret lower than exercise given. Play through pattern again and move down to Dm7—

Like this :

(B)

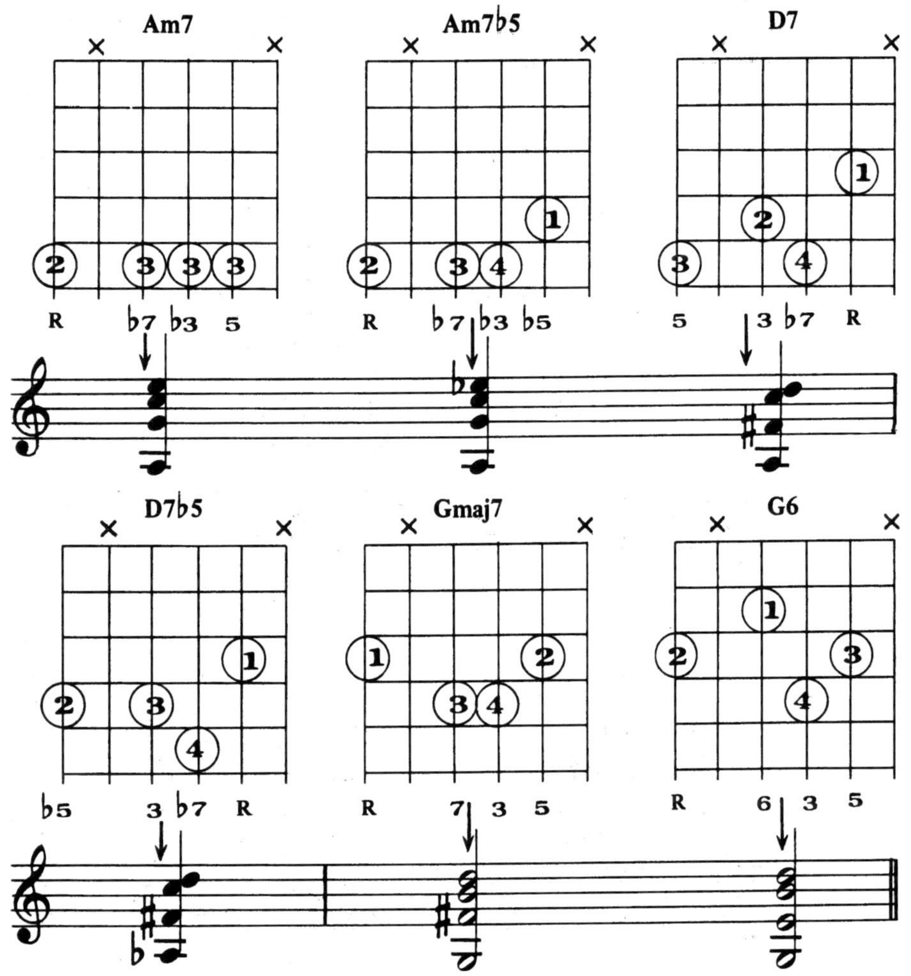

Start as high as possible. When pattern is complete, transform I6 into Im7, which now becomes ii m7 in relation to new key.

(C)

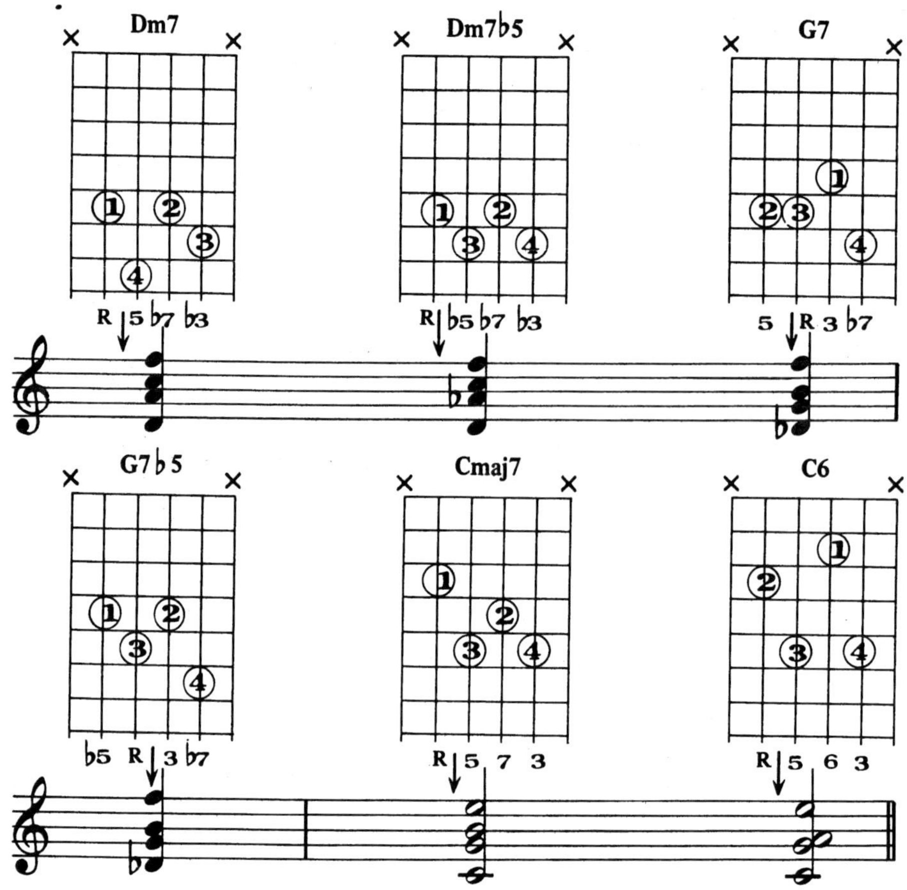

The V7 chord in both (B) and (C) could be transformed into V7♭9 instead of V7♭5__ Try them both ways__

(D)

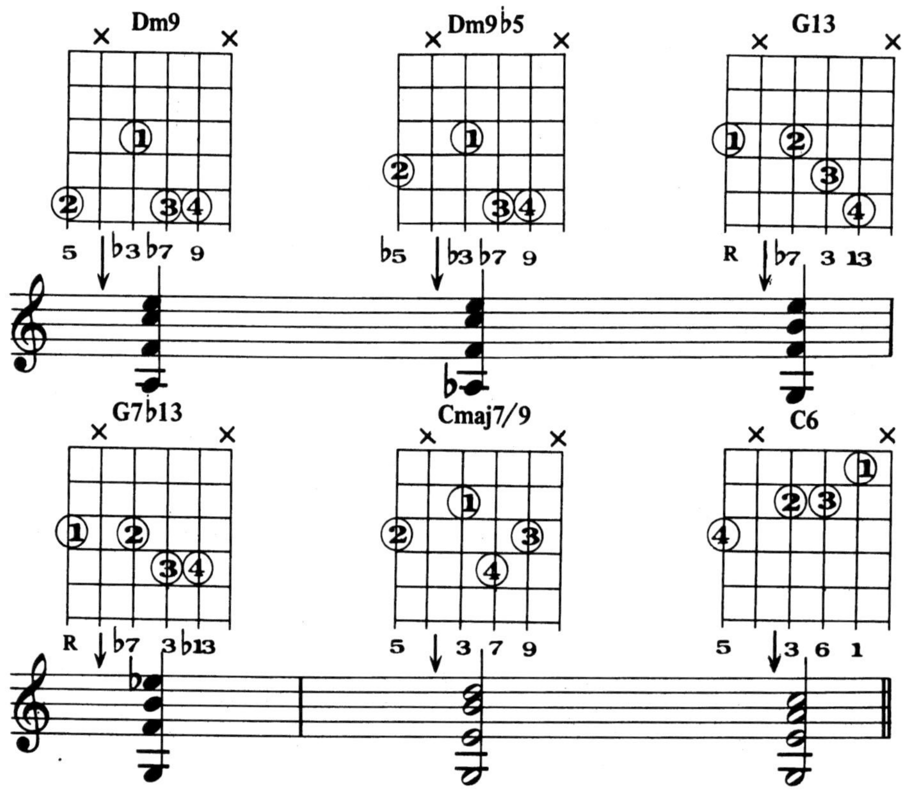

Final I6 chord would transform into m9 and chord pattern would resume. Start as high on the fingerboard as possible. Think of the notes (and their movement)__

(E)

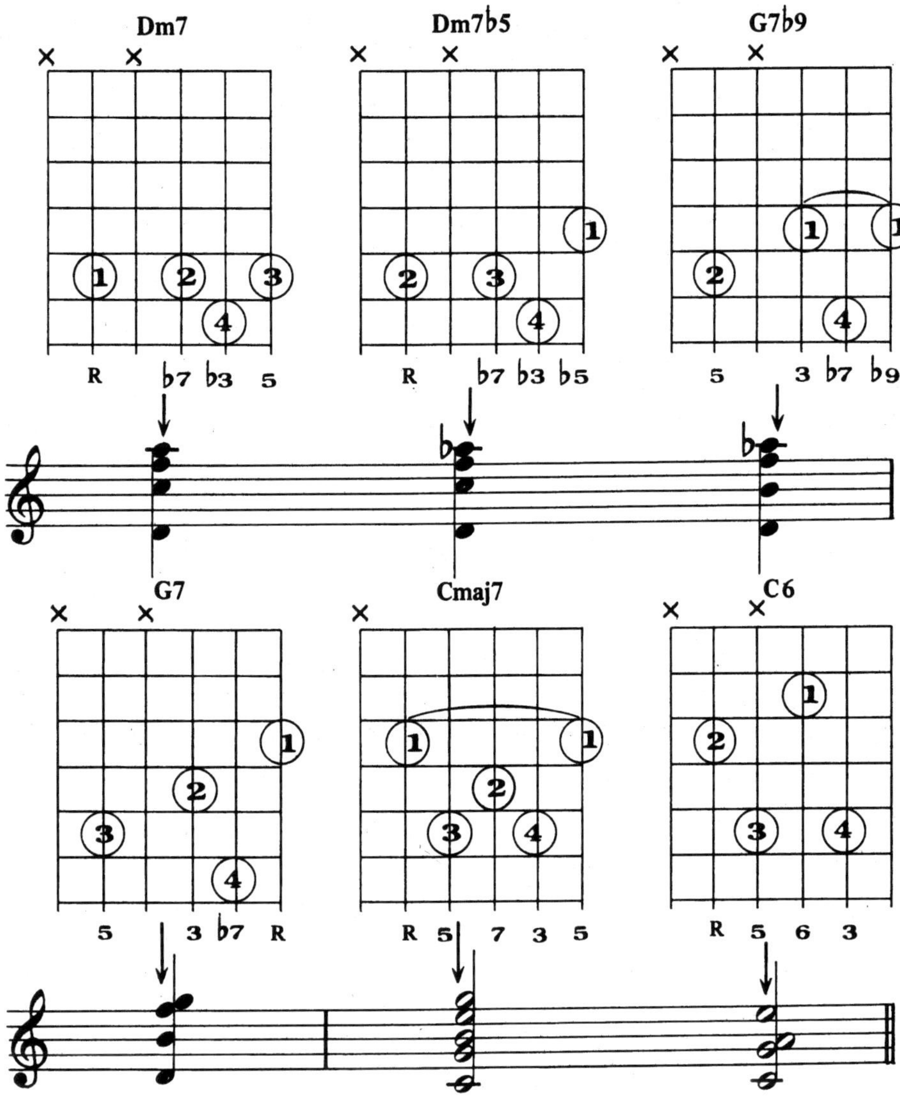

Note 5th tone on top of I maj7 to make voice leading conform – I6 transforms to Im7 which becomes iim7 in new cycle__ Start as high as possible__

(F)

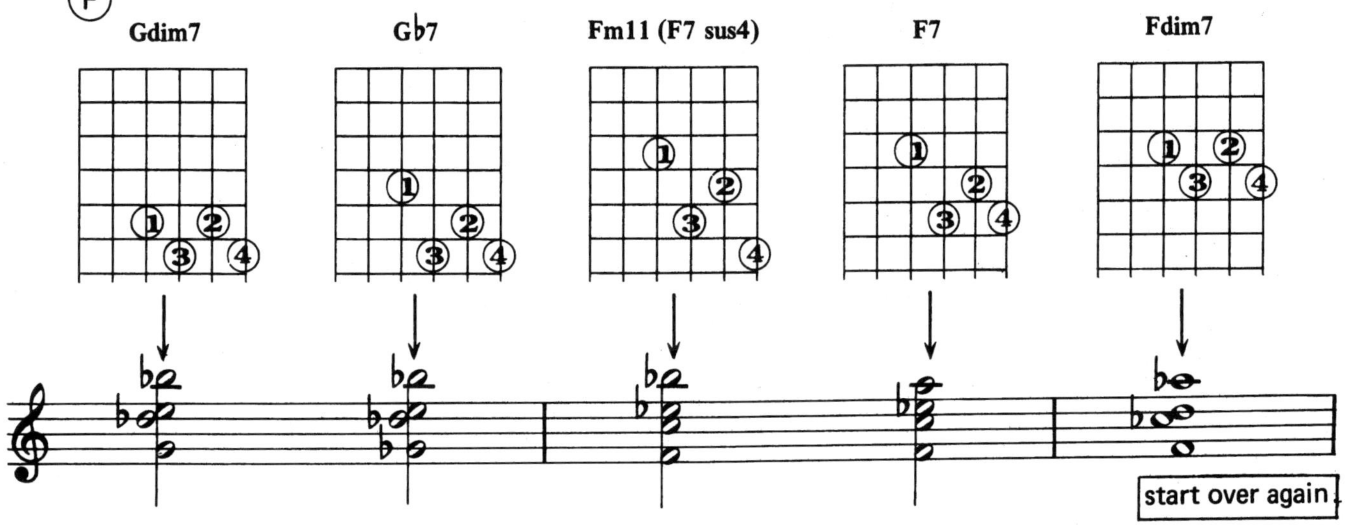

Makes a good arpeggio study— Pick notes singly, while still holding down chord—As fast and accurate as possible.

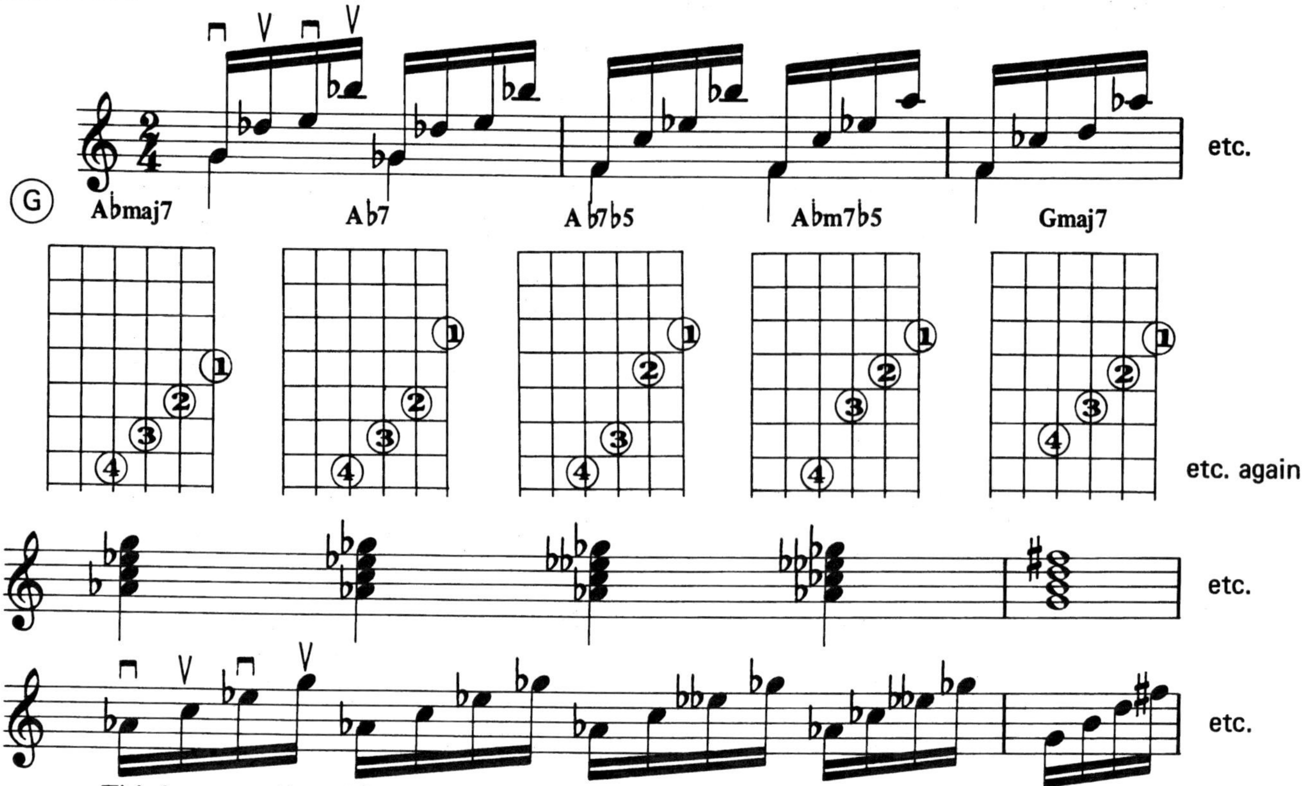

This is an excellent "finger stretcher"—

Passing chordal lines in a progression involving iim7b5 to V7 using two string series—

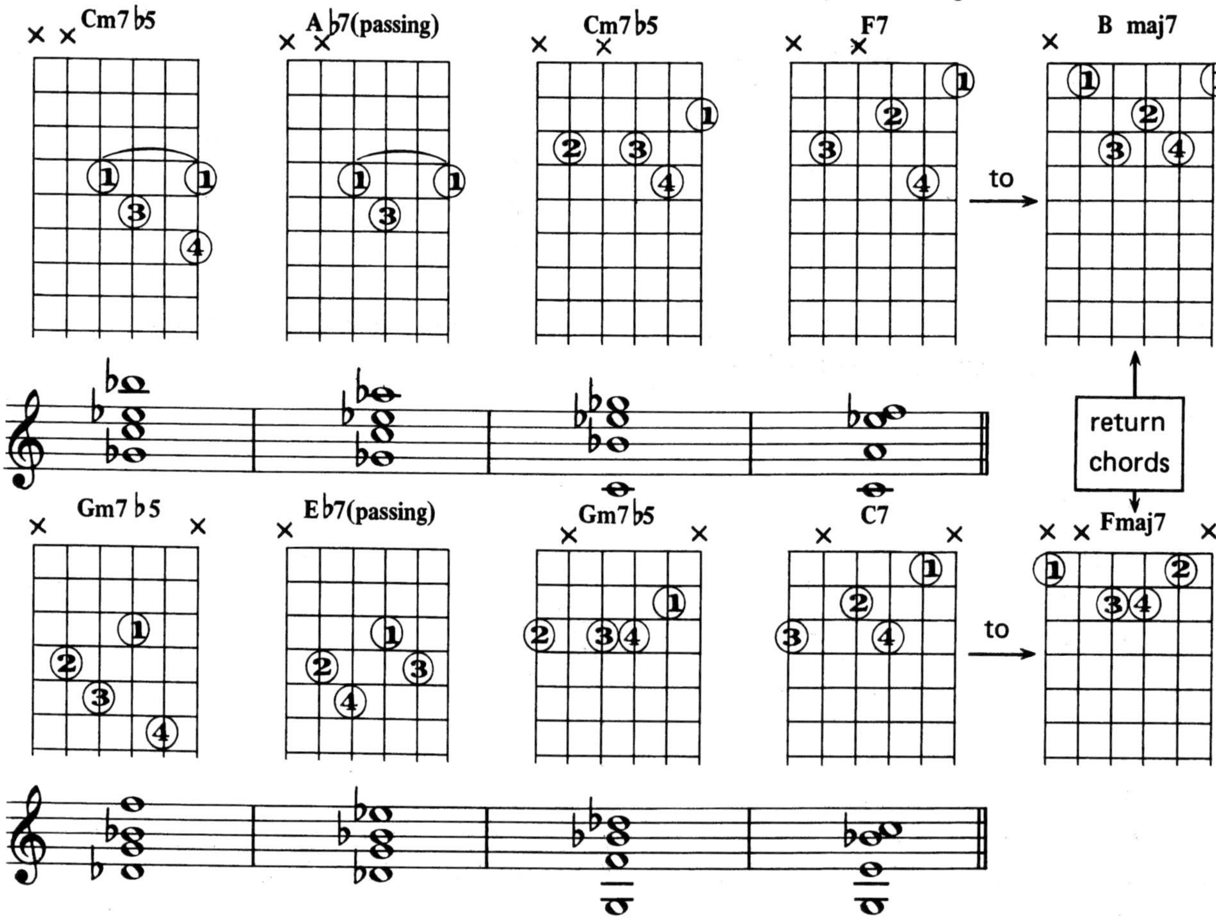

The second chord in each series is a 3rd inv. Dom. 7 chord, but still retains the m7♭5 feeling generated by the chords on either side—

Good device for chord melody playing— The "return chords" may be any "color" depending on the progression – dom7, minor7, tonic 6, etc.

Chord progressions using "voice leading"

Closed voicings for chord type solos is a possibility using three parts instead of four, since the four part closed voicings present some difficult fingering problems—When you "work out" the three note chords, use the closest tones possible to each other – reading down from the top note.

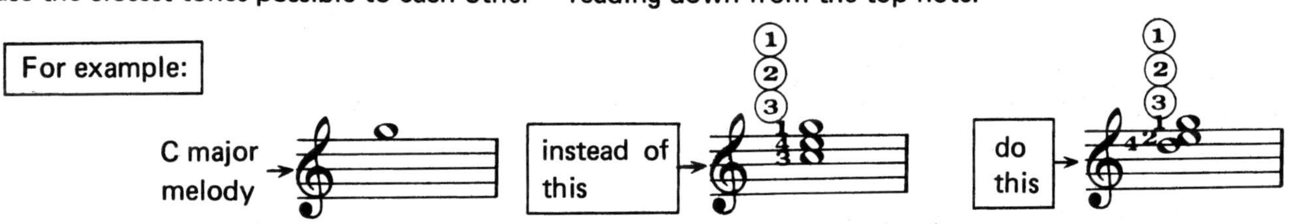

In other words, include high extensions of the harmony whenever possible – 6ths, 7ths, 9ths, etc— gives you a much richer sound – chords Dm7 won't sound like regular guitar voicings—

Example

Notice that we are leaving out important chord tones – they'll be suggested by the bass, or piano, etc —

Here's another example :

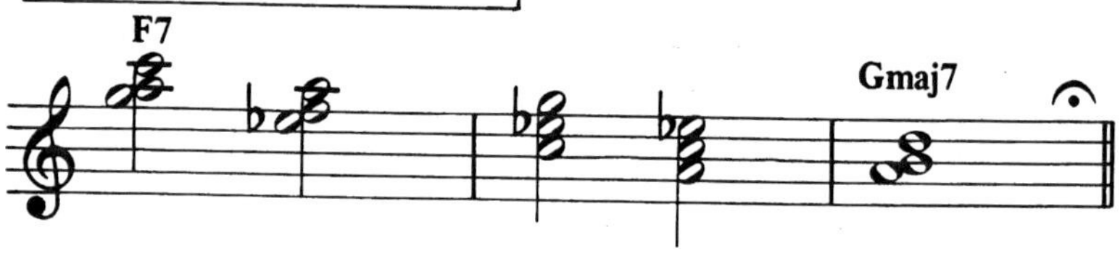

Take a tune you are familiar with, and work out a chord solo using this device—

Try this using the same chord(as a base) and moving up the chord via chordal tones—

Note use of added 6th and 9th tone—

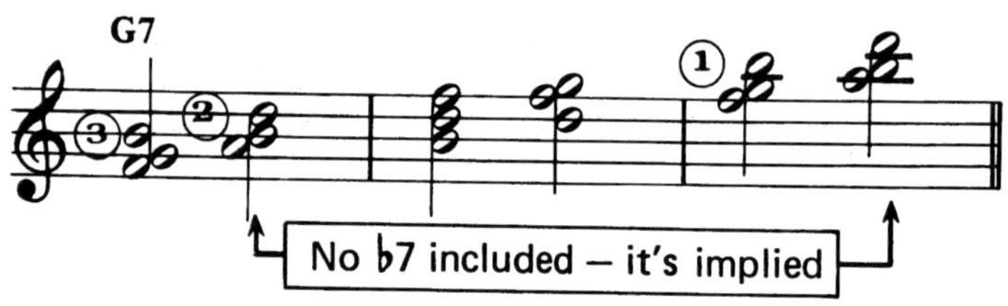

Note use of 9th to maintain "close" sound—

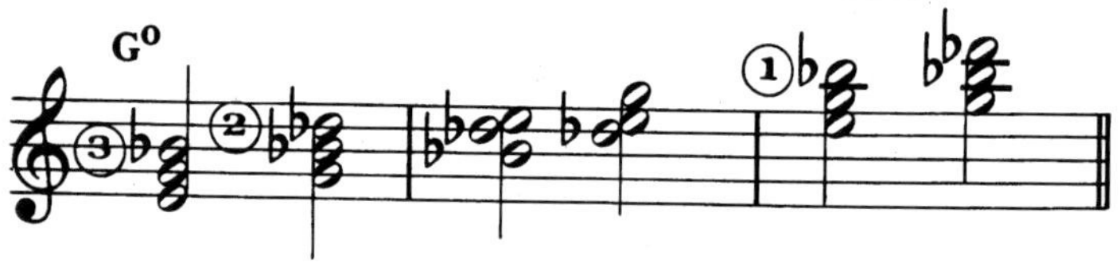

Every chord built the same

A most interesting, and un-guitar-like, sound— With enough practice, you can move these around pretty fast – they're much easier than 4 note forms—

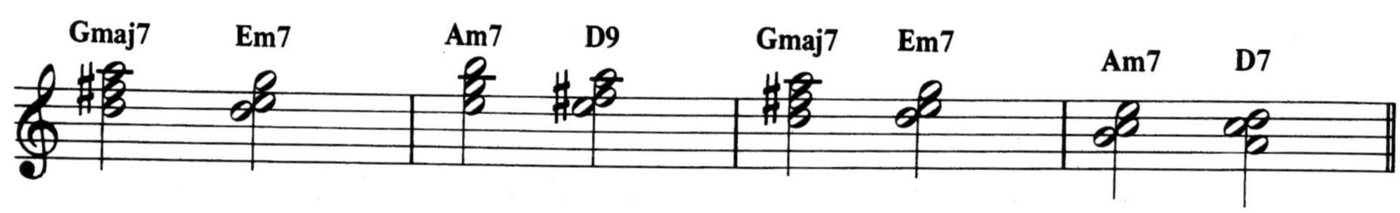

Remember the rule is simple. Play down from the melody note using the next two closest tones in the chord, utilizing 9ths, 7ths, 6ths, etc—Simple, triad harmony will not give you the same kind of sound—

Some interesting chord forms are possible by moving one of the original tones an octave in either direction – closed forms become open forms, and open forms become even wider open—

For example :

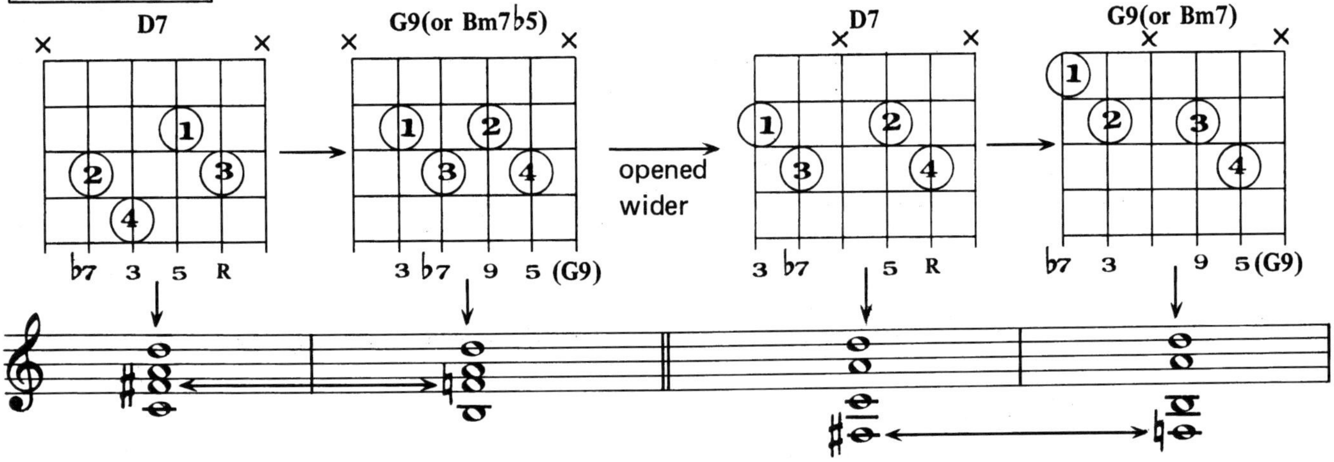

Notice the 2nd voice under the melody note was lowered by an octave in each chord – indicated by the small arrow in each of the two series—

Take a closed pos. Chord and do the same thing.

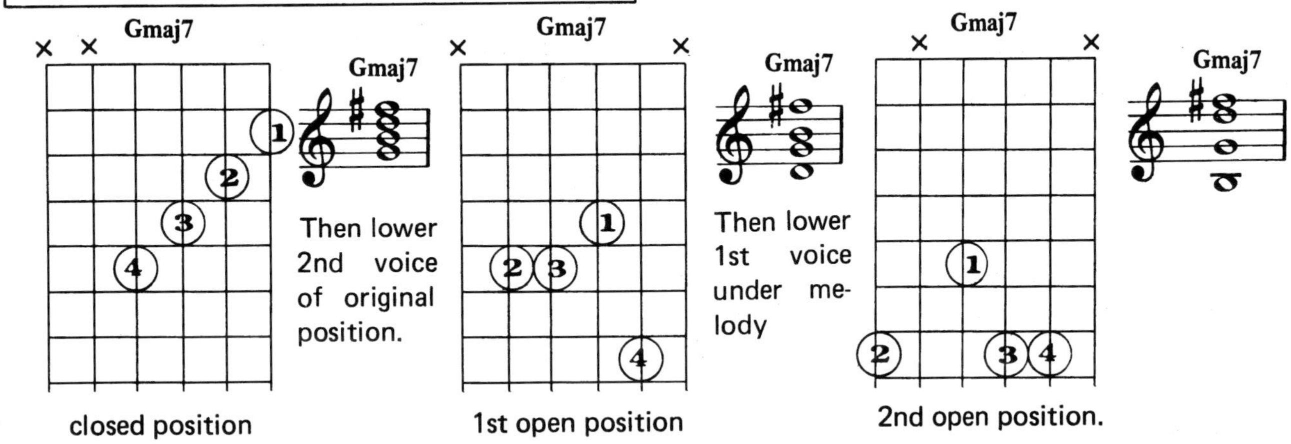

This gives you another way to expand your vocabulary of chords. Experiment with the other forms you know— Try doing this with other 4 note forms on top four strings. Use the following forms to get yourself started—

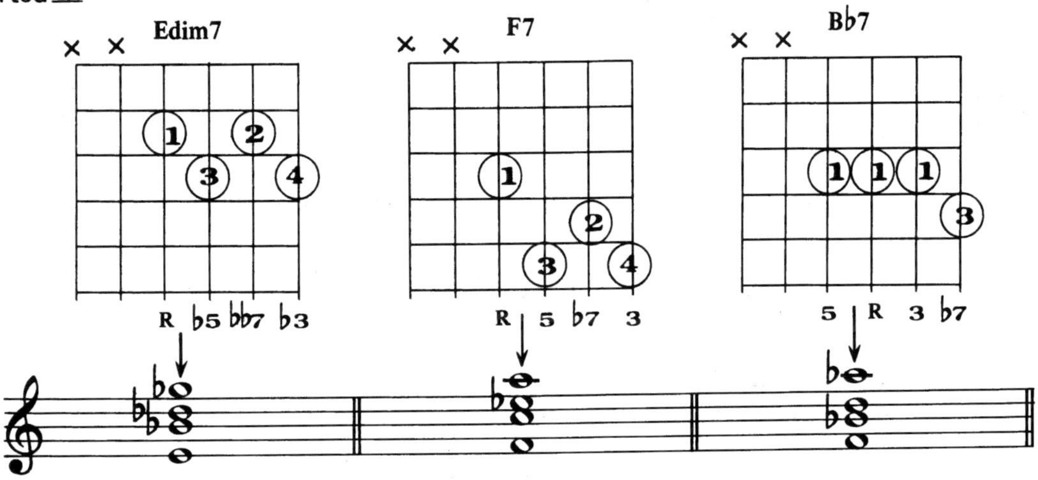

Expanding these three forms will give you some new, interesting voicings – remember, you must "deaden", or "block-out" strings not in use when you move the other tones. Try picking the new chords using right hand fingers__ Note the unusual forms you get__

Notate the results so you get a much better picture of the new chord__ Notice voice leading possibilities into other chords__Use the new forms till they become easy to get__

Chords using open strings for special effects.

At first glance, if you saw the following chord notated, you would probably think it impossible.

Through utilization of open ⑤, ②, ① strings this very difficult voicing becomes a simple matter.

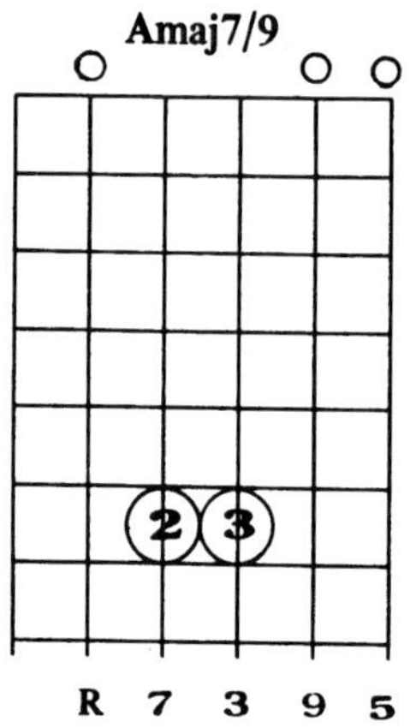

Unusual sound – C♯(chord 3rd) sounds before B♮ (chord 9th), though positions are reversed via notation.

Transforms to →

and to

Try them

Remember our discussion of 13th chords when we mentioned that ♭7 and 13th next to each other in chord was impossible via ordinary fingerings?

Try this

Looks impossible, unless we use ① & ② strings open__

Like this

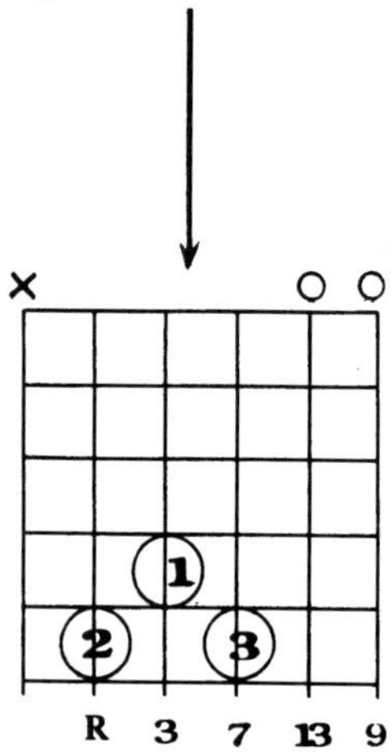

The 9th on top of the chord softens the dissonance generated by the minor 2nd interval (C – B) in the chord__

How about this?

Becomes an easy matter using the open strings.

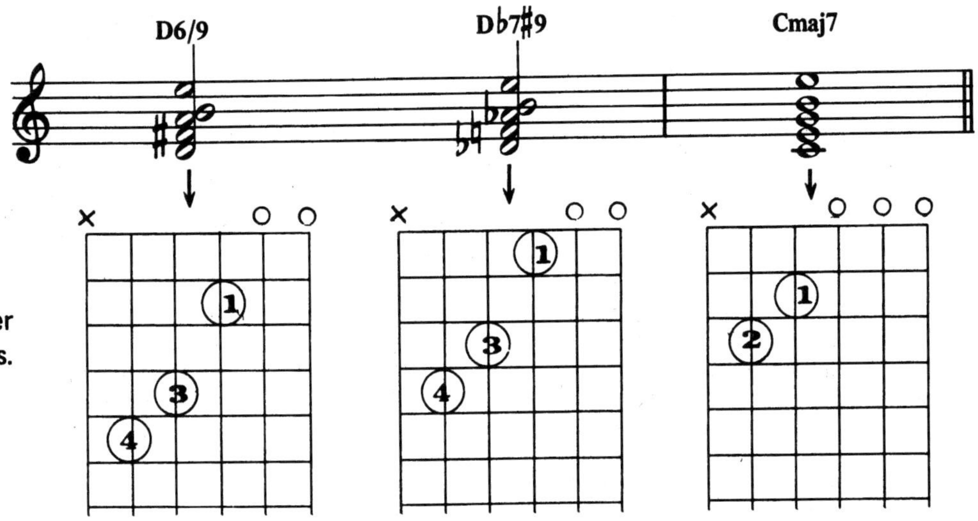

Consider the following melody and chord symbols.

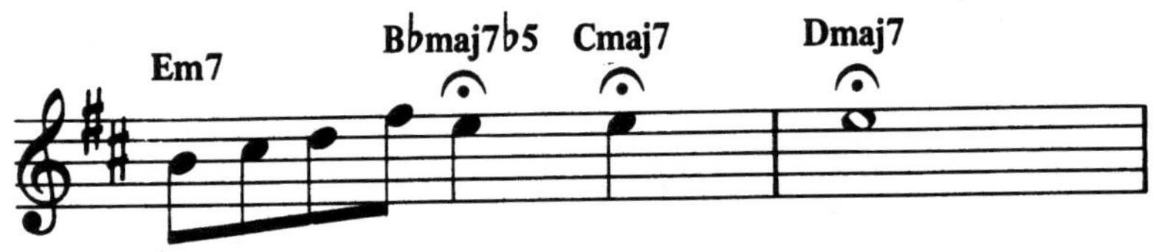

This could involve some fingering problems on the last three "held" chords— Let's approach it using the same maj7 form and utilizing the top string (1) open.

Like this

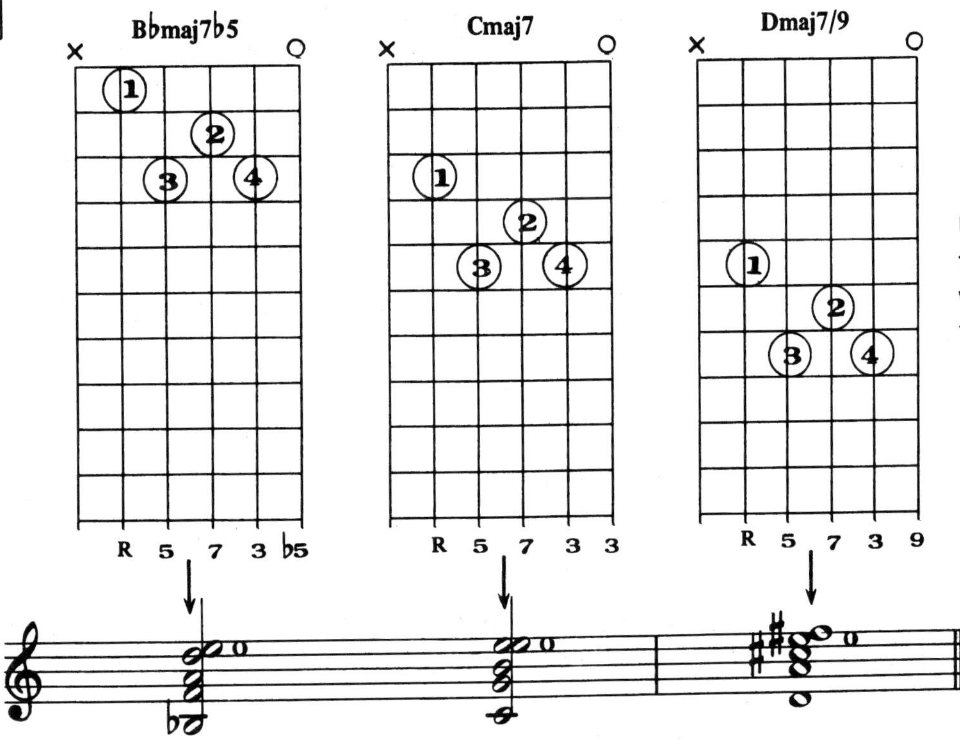

Unusual sound on final chord – but very good, effective device.

This requires some thinking to do correctly— You could do via trial and error method— Just take forms you already know and include the open strings—Your ear will soon tell you what will work and what won't work—

Example

Take the following major 7th form and move it up fingerboard a fret at a time—
[include top two open strings]

Fmaj7

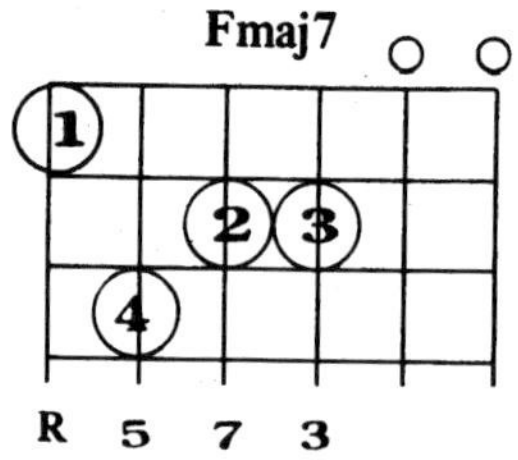

1st Fret	Fmaj7♭5 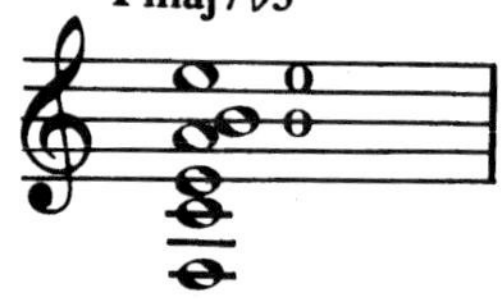	Yes!	2nd Fret →	No!
3rd Fret	Gmaj7(add6) 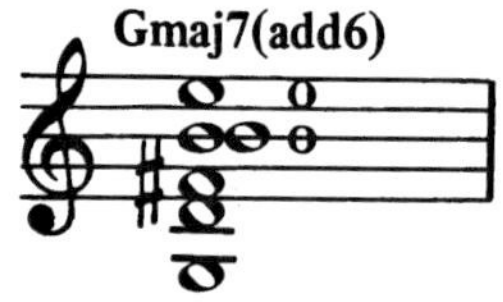	Yes!	4th Fret →	No!
5th Fret	Amaj7/9 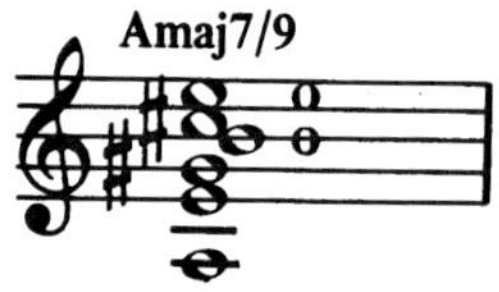	Yes!	6th Fret →	No!
7th Fret →	No!	8th Fret	Cmaj7 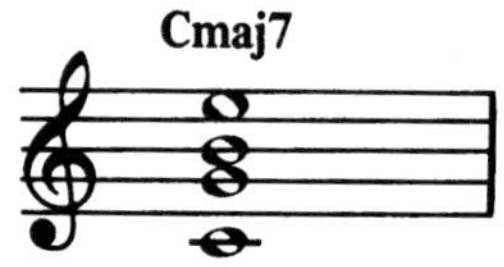	Yes!
9th Fret →	No!	10th Fret	Dmaj7/9(add6) 	Yes!

> 6th and 9th frets you could stretch a point— Both of these positions would sound better with ♭7 in the chord – you may disagree, but as I've said before – "your ear is the final judge"

Try some other forms now. To utilize top three strings open, you have to "finger" chords on the lower three strings, preferably triads—

Lets try a major triad

A♭

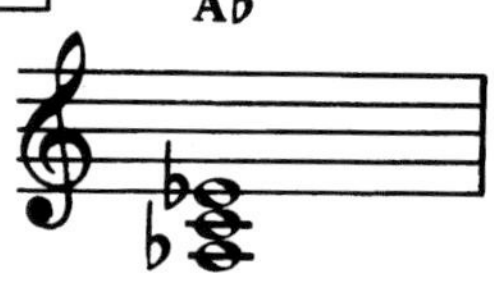

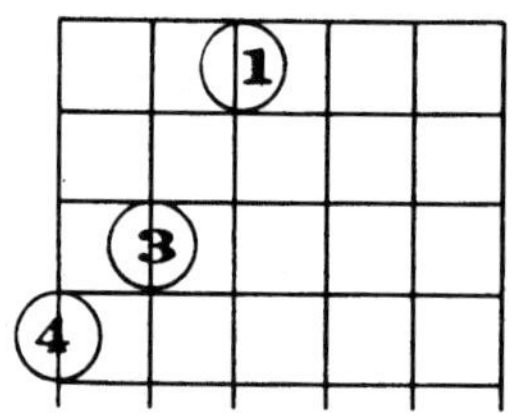

If you add ③ open G you get A♭ maj7— Addition of ② & ① could be stretching a point – you would add ♯9 Ⓑ and +5 Ⓔ —This could become valid for an ending in A♭ if you resolve to an A♭6 chord—

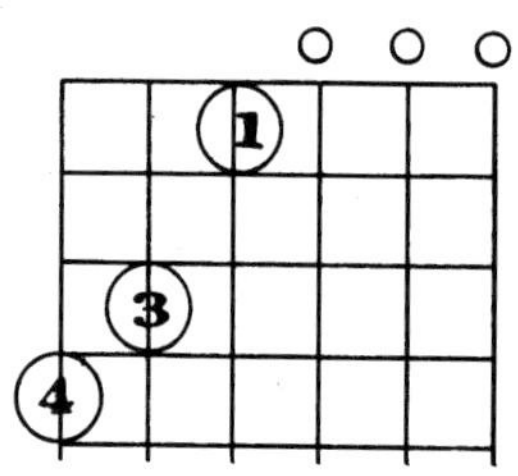

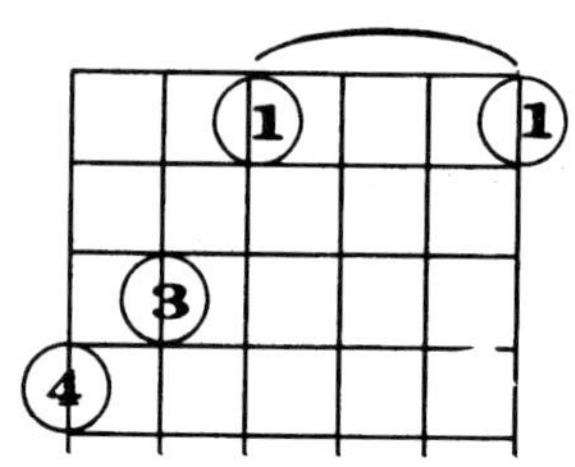

This same triad would work beautifully at the 5th fret and 8th fret

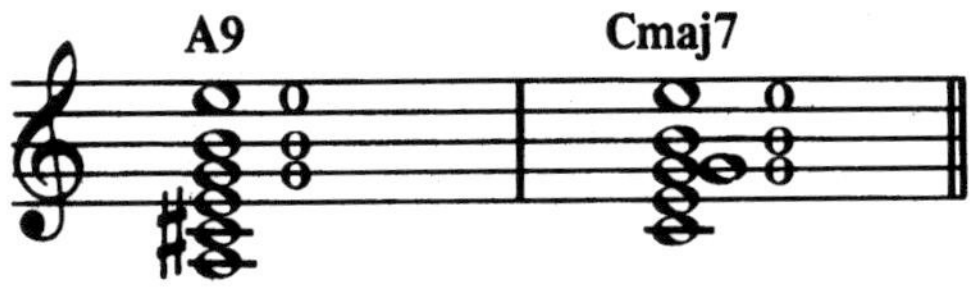

Try it at all positions— Analyze the open strings in relation to the basic triad – the open G ③ will work at 6th fret with B♭ triad— How about the other tones? Experiment with this concept—

Now try with triad on strings ⑤ ④ ③

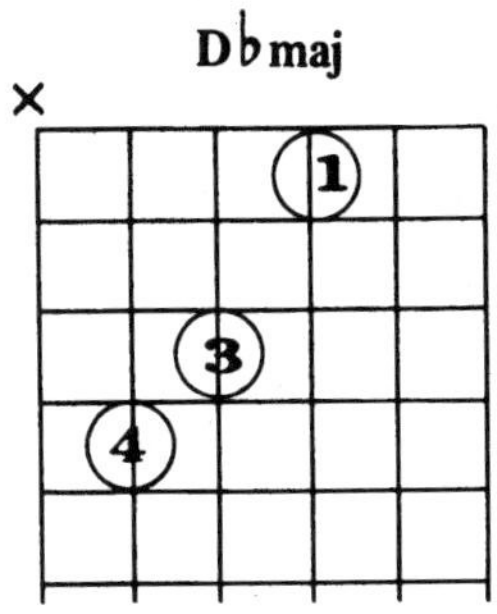

Now, instead of using trial and error method – move it up on paper and see how the top two strings analyze in relation to the basic triad —

2nd and 1st strings work

2nd and 1st strings work

Too dissonant

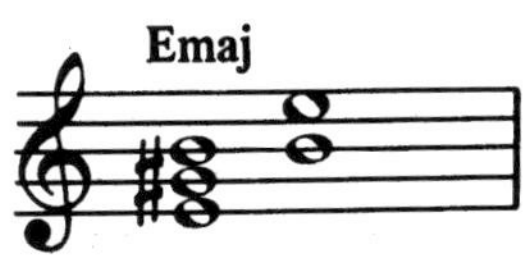

2nd and 1st strings work

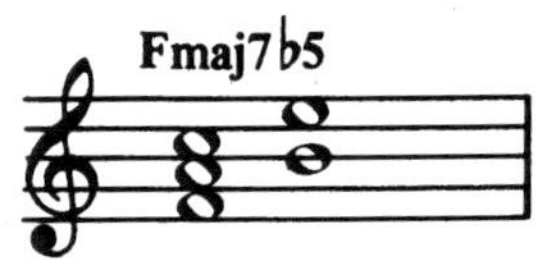

Dissonant, but will work

would work if you stretch a point.

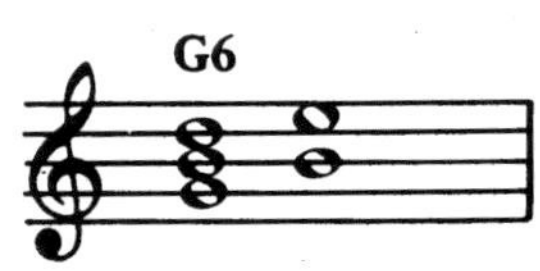

2nd and 1st strings work

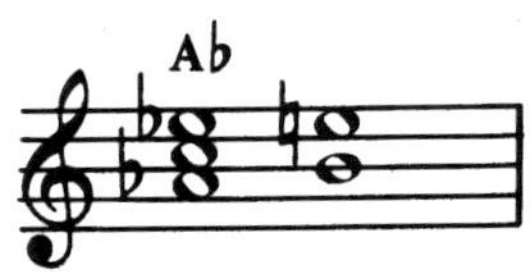

Try this one with low "E" string moving to next chord Ⓐ

Good Cluster works.

Too dissonant

Theoretically, every one would work as part of a chord progression— They are difficult to evaluate as isolated chords—

Here's a good ii – V form using open (2) & (1)

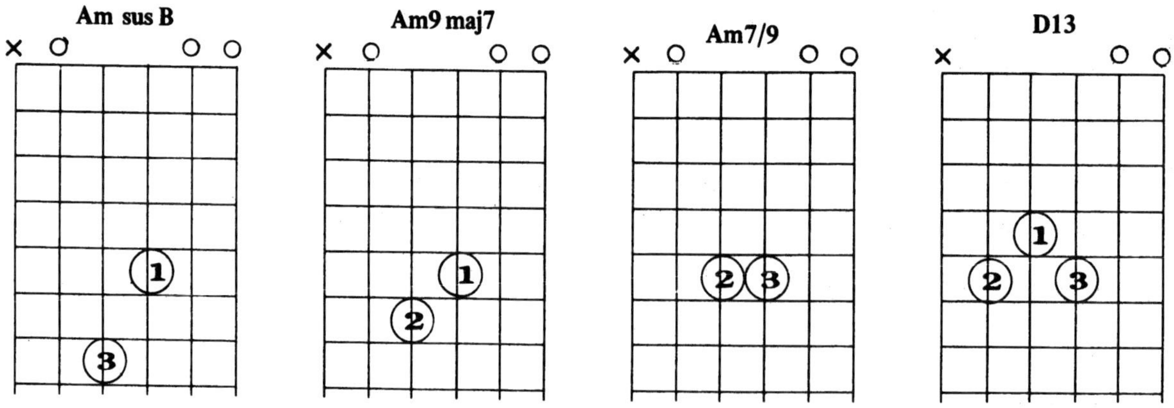

It becomes obvious that you can only do these things at certain places on the neck. If you have time to work out accompaniment patterns, inclusion of the "open string chords" provide an interesting change — They, like all other devices, can be overdone and would soon become tiring and most ineffective.

We have only scratched the surface on the possibilities which are available. Spend some time with this idea and you'll be surprised at the number of voicings available — Practice!

Previous statements regarding chordal movement have indicated some of the standard chord progressions which are familiar to most all players. Actually, chords can move anywhere – from any chord to any chord — Musical experience, taste, and your ability to be creative, will be the criteria which will evaluate these progressions — Unusual chordal progressions have been around, in pop music, a long time — Examine old standards such as "High on a Windy Hill", "How High the Moon", "You Stepped out of a Dream", "All the Things You Are", and many others for examples of modulatory, or "Out of Key" progressions which provide most interesting examples of unusual chordal movement.

Try the following original melody and note the lack of a real "tonal-center" — It becomes more apparent that the key could be A♭ – analyze the melody in relation to the given chord symbols – notice the use of high extensions and altered chordal tones – notice how section (B) moves down chromatically through four keys. This melody is possible as a chord solo in this position. Try it! –.

To be played Bossa Nova style –

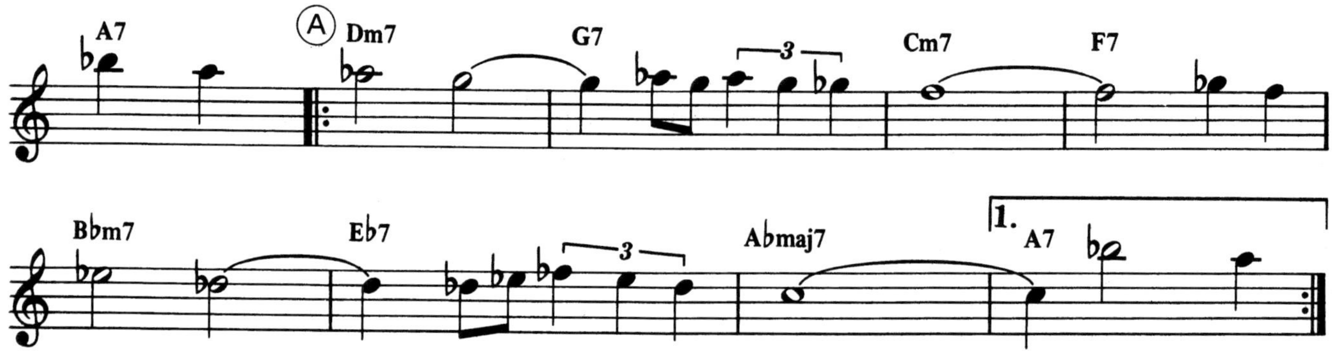

Current exponents of "free-form", in jazz, have completely divorced themselves from chordal lines. This is a difficult concept to understand because of our inability to make a valid judgment based on previous "listening" experiences. It is also a very easy way for a poor performer to "cop-out". Actually "anything goes" and nothing is wrong – so it becomes most difficult to evaluate. There is little we can use to measure it against. We all have a tendency to judge things via comparison with how things have been done before. Truly great performances will stand the test of time. I'm not proposing that we live in the past. However, I do suggest that we offer some consideration to the contributions made by earlier performers. Many current guitarists are doing most interesting things. Close listening to these people will disclose a direct line, historically, to previous performers.

Be adaptable to change, but not just for the sake of change itself. Develop your own critical facilities through listening with an open mind and ear. There are good players in all fields of musical activity, especially in the area of guitar playing. Don't limit yourself! Copying someone else is fine as a learning experience. Your own playing should reflect you, as a person.

Remember, that like a great public speaker, you need an adequate vocabulary to express yourself. This means complete command of the guitar in all areas; chords, scales, arpeggios, picking, etc., etc., etc. People will never know your great ideas if you are unable to express them due to technical limitations.

If your aim is communication remember that simplicity is usually the best avenue of approach.